Indian Army

Agniveer General Duty

Latest Edition
Practice Kit

14 Tests
04 Previous Year Paper
10 Mock Test

Based On Real Exam Pattern

✓ Thoroughly Revised and Updated

✓ Detailed Analysis of all MCQs

Title	: Indian Army Agniveer General Duty
Author Name	: Mr. Rohit Manglik
Published By	: EduGorilla Community Pvt. Ltd.
Publishers Address	: 12/651, First Floor Opp. Arvindo Park, Near Jama Masjid, Indira Nagar, Lucknow, Uttar Pradesh-226016, India

Copyright EduGorilla

ISBN : 978-93-55564-05-4

First Edition

Disclaimer EduGorilla

Compiled and created by EduGorilla Community Pvt. Ltd

Printed By EduGorilla Community Pvt. Ltd.

ROHIT MANGLIK
CEO, EduGorilla

Dear Applicants,

People say *"Success comes to those who work hard."* But I've seen people working hard for their exams day in and day out for marginal success. While others succeed in their examinations by putting in just half the work. So are they God Gifted? No! I believe that it's because they work *smart* and not just *hard*. Similarly, for your exams, you should strategize your preparation so as to increase the likelihood of success. Well with EduGorilla get ready to increase your *chances of selection* in your exam by *16x*.

EduGorilla helps you in not only working *hard* but also working in a *smart and strategic* manner. With EduGorilla's preparation package, you get a chance to make your exam preparation easy, and a fun learning path towards selection. Finding the right path to your preparations can be difficult if you don't know in which direction to head. Don't worry, we have you covered! EduGorilla will be your guide to success in your journey. With our Preparation Package, you can prepare strategically and beat the exam in just one attempt.

EduGorilla's Preparation Package includes-

• **Test Series**   • **Books**

Our preparation package is handcrafted as per the latest changes, expert opinions, and students' discretion. Thus, enabling you to get through each stage of the selection process for your exam.

Our Books are designed by the teachers and experts of the respective exam with a combined 150+ years of experience; to provide you with easy, efficient, and effective learning. Our books are smart, in the sense that not only do they give you the answers to the questions but also provide similar questions for practice.

EduGorilla's competent Test Series gives you real-time experience and confidence through which you can clear your offline or online exam in just one attempt. We currently host 83,000+ mock tests for 1,440+ competitive and academic exams.

Thus, EduGorilla misses no chance to assist you in your preparation and covers all stages of the exam, so that you don't have to look anywhere else.

We provide complete preparation packages for defense, banking, teaching, and other National & State-Level exams. Hence, it doesn't matter which exam you aspire to because you will reach your success.

ALL THE BEST !
Let EduGorilla be your Guide to Success.

Rohit Manglik,
Founder and CEO, EduGorilla

INTRODUCTION

EduGorilla focuses on guiding students to succeed in their examinations. With that in mind, our book, titled "Indian Army : Agniveer General Duty", has been drafted through the collective efforts of our distinguished experts with 150+ years of combined experience. This book consists of questions that are created following the latest changes in the syllabus and exam pattern. We compiled the book on the basis of questions that are most likely to appear in the Indian Army Soldier GD Exam. Through EduGorilla's "Indian Army : Agniveer General Duty" your chances of success will increase 16x.

EduGorilla does this through our Complete Preparation Package. This package consists of well-conceptualized and structured content in the form of questions that are tailor-made according to your needs and will help you practice for exams in a smart way by pinpointing all the necessary information. It also provides hints and solutions, along with a smart answer sheet for your self-evaluation. You can assess your shortcomings and work accordingly on areas that may require more of your attention.

EduGorilla promises to help you succeed in your examination and accomplish your dream goals. We believe in our aspirants and see them at the top of the merit list. And the first step towards the top is to start preparing with us. EduGorilla's "Indian Army : Agniveer General Duty" includes the following attributes.

➤ Well-Researched Content

➤ Top-Notch Quality

➤ Detailed Answers and Analysis

➤ Smart Answer Sheet

➤ Exam Relevant Questions

Therefore, EduGorilla fortifies your preparation and makes it durable enough to help you stand tall and beat the examination.

Indian Army Soldier GD Exam
Scan QR code for Eligibility, Exam Pattern, Syllabus and more.

Book ID: 0492

TABLE OF CONTENTS

General Knowledge

Q.1 During the 19th century, who among the following wrote Satapatra Series?

[Officers Training Academy (OTA), 2020], [Indian Military Academy (IMA), 2020]

A. M. G. Ranade
B. B. G. Tilak
C. Bankim Chandra Chatterjee
D. G. H. Deshmukh

Q.2 Which was the first country to host the Asian Games?
A. China　　**B.** Japan　　**C.** India　　**D.** Korea

Q.3 Which of the following is a non-Indian religion?

[Allahabad High Court ARO, 2020]

A. Buddhism
B. Jainism
C. Judaism
D. Hinduism

Q.4 Which of the following is the incorrect pair of country and capital?
A. Azerbaijan - Baku
B. Belgium - Brussels
C. Bolivia - La Paz
D. Austria - Canberra

Q.5 When is the International Workers' Day?
A. 15 April
B. 12 December
C. 1 May
D. 1 August

Q.6 The tomb of Ibrahim Lodi is situated at:
A. Panipat
B. Gurugram
C. Mahendragarh
D. Rohtak

Q.7 Who has been authorized to constitute Finance Commission to review financial position of Panchayat?
A. The Chief Minister of a State
B. The Speaker of a legislative assemb
C. The President of India
D. The Governor of a State

Q.8 Which of the following hill station is referred to as the "Kashmir of South India"?
A. Ranni
B. Munnar
C. Panchalimedu
D. Soordelu

Q.9 Alps mountains are of which type?
A. Volcanic　　**B.** Fold　　**C.** Residual　　**D.** Block

Q.10 Warli folk Painting is indigenous to which state?
A. Maharashtra
B. Rajasthan
C. Gujarat
D. Himachal pradesh

Q.11 Where is the headquarter of the Road Infrastructure Development Company (RIDCOR) of Rajasthan located?
A. Ajmer　　**B.** Jodhpur　　**C.** Jaipur　　**D.** Kota

Q.12 Dr. Anil Avchat died on 27 January 2022. He was related to which field?
A. Mathematician
B. Film director
C. Singer
D. Writer

Q.13 Who has been crowned Miss Universe 2021?
A. Roshanara Ebrahim
B. Noa Kochba
C. Harnaaz Sandhu
D. Nandita Banna

Q.14 Which of the following has started the revolt of 1857?
A. Zamindars
B. Sepoys
C. Peasants
D. Plantation workers

Q.15 Which state governor released the book titled 'Making of a General-A Himalayan Echo'?
A. Tripura
B. Meghalaya
C. Manipur
D. West Bengal

General Science

Q.16 Electron has equivalent mass to that of:
A. Proton　　**B.** Neutron　　**C.** Positron　　**D.** Neutrino

Q.17 The Knot is a measure of:
A. Solar radiation
B. The curvature of spherical objects
C. The speed of the ship
D. The intensity of earthquake shock

Q.18 Bi-focal lens are required to correct:
A. Astigmatism
B. Coma
C. Myopia
D. Presbyopia

Q.19 For a real object, which of the following can produce a real image?
A. Plane mirror
B. Concave mirror
C. Concave lens
D. Convex mirror

Q.20 Which is not used as a nuclear fuel?
A. Uranium
B. Thorium
C. Plutonium
D. lead

Q.21 The major components in LPG are:
A. Methane
B. Butane
C. Propane
D. Both (B) and (C)

Q.22 Which one of the following is not an example of colloids?
A. Milk
B. Jelly
C. Tincture of iodine
D. Fog

Q.23 What is diluted acetic acid commonly known as?

[SSC Constable (GD), 2019]

A. Oleum
B. Blue vitriol
C. Vinegar
D. Alum

Q.24 'Bauxite' is an ore of which of the following metal?

A. Calcium **B.** Aluminium
C. Magnesium **D.** Sodium

Q.25 Which of the following gases is heavier than oxygen?
A. Carbon dioxide **B.** Ammonia
C. Methane **D.** Helium

Q.26 At rest, a well-trained athlete will have a heart rate _____ a normal person.
A. Higher than **B.** Lower than
C. Same as **D.** Incomparable to

Q.27 Auxin inhibits the growth of:
A. Apical buds
B. Lateral axillary buds
C. Roots on stem cuttings
D. Parthenocarpic development of fruits

Q.28 Systematics involves:
A. Identification of organisms
B. Nomenclature of organisms
C. Relationship and classification of organisms
D. All of the above

Q.29 The kingdom Protista forms a link with kingdom _____.
A. Plantae **B.** Fungi
C. Animalia **D.** All of these

Q.30 Most resistant stage in the life cycle of angiosperms is its:
A. Embryo stage **B.** Seed stage
C. Flowering stage **D.** Fruiting stage

Maths

Q.31 The difference between compound interest and simple interest at the same rate on $Rs.\,25000$ for 2 years is $Rs.\,250$. Evaluate the rate of interest.
A. 6% **B.** 8% **C.** 10% **D.** 12%

Q.32 The number of rectangles that you can find on a chess board is:

[UPSESSB TGT Mathematics, 2016]

A. 144 **B.** 1296
C. 256 **D.** None of these

Q.33 A triangle ABC is circumscribed on a circle such that it touches the triangle at PQR as shown in the figure. It is given that BP = AC = 7 cm and BC = 10 cm. Find the length of AB.

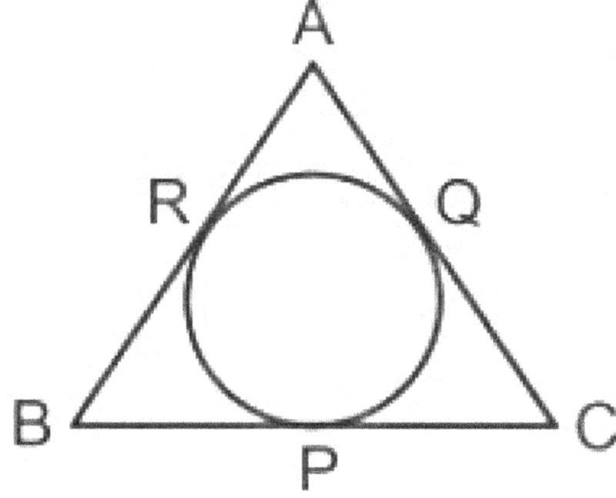

A. 10 cm **B.** 7 cm **C.** 11 cm **D.** 12 cm

Q.34 If 17^{2020} is divided by 18, then what is the remainder?

[Indian Military Academy (IMA), 2020]

A. 1 **B.** 2 **C.** 16 **D.** 17

Q.35 Simplify $18 + 5 - 2 \times 50 \div 5$.
A. 3 **B.** 7 **C.** 8 **D.** 9

Q.36 A discount of 8% on the marked price of a bat enables a man to get a ball worth Rs. 256 for free. how much did the man pay for the bat?
A. Rs. 3200 **B.** Rs. 2856 **C.** Rs. 2944 **D.** Rs. 3000

Q.37 Sayma reaches bus stand at $9:35$ am and is told by Zeenat that the previous bus has left at $9:25$ am as per her watch. If Zeenat's watch is 5 minutes fast and the frequency of bus is every 20 minutes, for how long Sayma has to wait to catch the next bus?

[CTET Paper - I, 2021]

A. 20 minutes **B.** 15 minutes
C. 10 minutes **D.** 5 minutes

Q.38 What number should be subtracted from each of 50, 61, 92, 117 so that the numbers, so obtained in this order, are in proportion?

[CTET Paper-II (Science & Mathematics), 2019]

A. 14 **B.** 17 **C.** 19 **D.** 23

Q.39 Direction: Choose the correct alternative from given ones that will complete the series.
1, 8, 7, 14, 15, 21, 25, ?
A. 28 **B.** 32 **C.** 30 **D.** 29

Q.40 What will be the highest three digit number which when divided by $3, 7$ and 21 leaves the remainder 2?
A. 978 **B.** 982 **C.** 983 **D.** 989

Q.41 The average weight of students in a class is 43 kg. Four new students are admitted to the class whose weights are 42 kg, 36·5 kg, 39 kg, and 42·5 kg respectively. Now the average weight, of the students of the class is 42·5 kg. The number of students in the beginning was?

A. 10   **B.** 15   **C.** 20   **D.** 25

Q.42 An unbiased die is thrown once. The probability of getting a prime number is:

A. $\frac{1}{4}$ **B.** $\frac{1}{2}$ **C.** $\frac{1}{5}$ **D.** $\frac{1}{3}$

Q.43 Pipe A can fill the cistern in 3 hours and pipe B can fill the cistern in 4 hours. If they are opened alternatively with pipe A opened first then how much time will it take to fill up the cistern?

A. $\frac{10}{3}$ hours   **B.** $\frac{7}{2}$ hours

C. $\frac{5}{2}$ hours   **D.** 4.5 hours

Q.44 A cuboidal solid gold bar of dimensions 16 cm $\times 11$ cm $\times 8$ cm is melted to form a certain number of solid hemispheres of radius 2 cm each. Find the number of such hemispheres?

A. 84   **B.** 64   **C.** 72   **D.** 96

Q.45 Gaurav earns Rs. 800 per day. After some weeks, he earns Rs. 960 per day. What is the percentage increase in his daily earnings?

A. 16%   **B.** 20%   **C.** 18%   **D.** 14%

Logical Reasoning

Q.46 Four friends live in a locality. A's house is to the west of B. B 's house is to the south of C and C's house is to the east of D. In which direction is B's house as to D?

[UP Police Constable, 2019]

A. North -East   **B.** South-East

C. North-West   **D.** South-West

Q.47 Direction: Select the odd letters from the given alternatives.

A. AZ   **B.** DW   **C.** GT   **D.** VR

Q.48 Rohan is the father of Mohan who is the brother of Ramesh who is the grandson of Rishi and there is no female member in the family then how is Rishi related to Rohan?

A. Father   **B.** Son

C. Grandson   **D.** Grandfather

Q.49 Direction: Select the letter-cluster that can replace the question mark (?) in the given letter-cluster series.

$AE, KQ, EI, LR, IO, ?, OU, NT$

[SSC Sub Inspector (CPO), 2020]

A. MR **B.** NR **C.** MS **D.** NS

Q.50 If TOUR is written as 1234, CLEAR is written as 56784 and SPARE is written as 90847, find the code for CARE.

[Intelligence Bureau Security Assistant, 2017]

A. 1247   **B.** 4847   **C.** 5247   **D.** 5847

// Smart Answer Sheet //

Correct — Indicates percentage of students who answered questions correctly.

Skipped — Indicates percentage of students who skipped questions.

Q.	Ans.	Correct / Skipped	Q.	Ans.	Correct / Skipped	Q.	Ans.	Correct / Skipped	Q.	Ans.	Correct / Skipped	Q.	Ans.	Correct / Skipped
1	D	15.41 % / 6.25 %	11	C	32.33 % / 5.41 %	21	D	51.81 % / 11.51 %	31	C	22.33 % / 15.86 %	41	C	13.01 % / 16.36 %
2	C	44.0 % / 4.35 %	12	D	25.29 % / 2.46 %	22	C	25.85 % / 11.95 %	32	B	13.79 % / 17.09 %	42	B	26.8 % / 14.96 %
3	C	72.08 % / 4.41 %	13	C	53.04 % / 5.08 %	23	C	31.1 % / 9.77 %	33	C	9.49 % / 15.13 %	43	A	12.56 % / 16.59 %
4	D	26.3 % / 3.91 %	14	B	40.03 % / 5.53 %	24	B	50.31 % / 11.55 %	34	A	16.36 % / 17.53 %	44	A	9.55 % / 17.08 %
5	C	56.39 % / 4.36 %	15	C	18.15 % / 5.41 %	25	A	38.25 % / 11.61 %	35	A	39.64 % / 15.8 %	45	B	25.52 % / 17.98 %
6	A	49.08 % / 6.7 %	16	C	14.01 % / 9.44 %	26	B	18.65 % / 9.49 %	36	C	11.33 % / 17.76 %	46	B	26.07 % / 13.8 %
7	D	20.38 % / 6.53 %	17	C	46.79 % / 11.67 %	27	B	15.63 % / 9.22 %	37	D	9.77 % / 17.09 %	47	D	32.66 % / 13.79 %
8	B	33.45 % / 5.36 %	18	D	14.29 % / 11.23 %	28	D	33.45 % / 11.89 %	38	B	15.24 % / 17.2 %	48	A	16.25 % / 13.9 %
9	B	25.01 % / 5.25 %	19	B	29.09 % / 11.11 %	29	D	26.63 % / 9.16 %	39	D	19.6 % / 13.9 %	49	C	22.39 % / 14.29 %
10	A	24.57 % / 6.36 %	20	D	37.07 % / 11.62 %	30	B	21.66 % / 11.62 %	40	D	16.97 % / 17.48 %	50	D	40.59 % / 14.63 %

Performance Analysis

Avg. Score (%)	18.0%
Toppers Score (%)	100.0%
Your Score	

//Hints and Solutions//

1. During the 19th century, the 'Satapatra Series' was written by G.H. Deshmukh.

- Gopal Hari Deshmukh was an Indian activist, thinker, social reformer, and writer from Maharashtra.

- His original surname was Shidhaye. Because of 'Vatan' (the right of Tax collection) that the family had received, the family was later called Deshmukh.

- Deshmukh is regarded as a prominent figure of the Social Reform Movement in Maharashtra. At age 25, G.H. Deshmukh started writing articles aimed at social reform in Maharashtra in the weekly Prabhakar under the pen name Lokhitawadi.

- In the initial two years, he penned 108 articles on social reform. All those groups of articles have come to be known in the Marathi literature as Lokhitawadinchi Shatapatre.

Hence, the correct option is (D).

2. India is a founder member of Asian Games and also the host of the first Asian Games. 1982 Asian Games were also held in New Delhi. India is one of the seven countries to have participated in all the editions of the Asian Games.

Hence, the correct option is (C).

3. Judaism is a non-Indian religion.

Judaism Religion:

- Judaism is an Abrahamic, monotheistic, and ethnic religion comprising the collective religious, cultural, and legal tradition and civilization of the Jewish people, also sometimes called Israelites.

- Judaism is considered by religious Jews to be the expression of the covenant that God expression with the Children of Israel.

- It encompasses a wide body of texts, practices, theological positions, and forms of organization.

- Judaism is the tenth-largest religion in the world.

Hence, the correct option is (C).

4. Austria - Canberra' is the incorrect pair of country and capital.

Vienna is the national capital, largest city, and one of nine states of Austria. Vienna is Austria's most populous city, with about two million inhabitants (2.9 million within the metropolitan area, nearly one third of the country's population), and its cultural, economic, and political center. It is the 6th-largest city proper by population in the European Union and the largest of all cities on Danube river.

Canberra is the capital city of Australia. Founded following the federation of the colonies of Australia as the seat of government for the new nation, it is Australia's largest inland city and the eighth-largest city overall. Unusual among Australian cities, it is an entirely planned city.

Hence, the correct option is (D).

5. 1 May is the International Workers' Day.

International Workers' Day, also known as labour day in most countries and often referred to as May Day, is a celebration of labourers and the working classes that is promoted by the international labour movement and occurs every year on 1 May.

Hence, the correct option is (C).

6. The tomb of Ibrahim Lodi is situated at Panipat.

Ibrahim Khan Lodi was an 'Afghan Sultan' of the 'Delhi Sultanate' who became Sultan in 1517 after the death of his father Sikandar Lodi. He was the last ruler of the Lodi dynasty. He was defeated and killed at the Battle of Panipat by Babur's invading army. He died on 21 April 1526.

Hence, the correct option is (A).

7. Article 243I of the Indian Constitution prescribes that the Governor of a State shall constitute a Finance Commission to review the financial position of the Panchayats.

The commission is required to make recommendations regarding:

- The distribution between the State and the Panchayats of the net proceeds of the taxes, duties, tolls and fees leviable by the State, which may be divided between them under this Part and the allocation between the Panchayats at all levels of their respective shares of such proceeds.

- The determination of the taxes, duties, tolls and fees which may be assigned as, or appropriated by, the Panchayats.

- The grants-in-aid to the Panchayats from the Consolidated Fund of the State.

The governor of a state ensures the laying of a State Finance Commission's recommendations to the table of the state legislature.

It also includes a memorandum of action taken by the government on the Commission's report.

Hence, the correct option is (D).

8. Munnar is also called the "Kashmir of South India" and is a popular honeymoon destination.

Munnar is a town and hill station located in the Idukki district of the southwestern Indian state of Kerala. Munnar is situated at around 1,600 meters (5,200 ft) above mean sea level, in the Western Ghats mountain range.

Hence, the correct option is (B).

9. Alps mountains are of Fold type.

Fold Mountains formed due to the compressive forces generated by endogenetic forces (earthquake, landslide, etc.). Examples of fold mountains are the Himalayas, Alps, Andes, Rockies, Atlas, etc.

Alps mountains range is located in Europe. Mont Blanc is its highest peak.

Hence, the correct option is (B).

10. Maharashtra is known for its Warli folk paintings. Warli is the name of the largest tribe found on the northern outskirts of Mumbai, in Western India. Warli is the vivid expression of daily and social events of the Warli tribe of Maharashtra, used by them to embellish the walls of village houses. It is a style of tribal art mostly created by the tribal people from the North Sahyadri Range in India.

Hence, the correct option is (A).

11. Jaipur is the headquarter of the Road Infrastructure Development Company (RIDCOR) of Rajasthan located.

Road Infrastructure Development Company Of Rajasthan Limited is a Public incorporated on 29 October 2004. It is classified as Non-govt company and is registered at Registrar of Companies, Jaipur. Its authorized share capital is Rs. 10,000,000,000 and its paid up capital is Rs. 3,249,999,870.

Hence, the correct option is (C).

12. Dr. Anil Avchat died on 27 January 2022. He was an eminent Marathi writer. Anil Avchat was also an Indian doctor, social worker.

He was born in 1944 in Pune district. He completed his education from Fergusson College and later obtained his medical degree from BJ Medical College, Pune in 1968. Along with his wife Dr. Anita Avchat, he started "Muktangan", a de-addiction center, in Pune.

Hence, the correct option is (D).

13. Harnaaz Sandhu has been crowned Miss Universe 2021.

- India's Harnaaz Sandhu, hailing from Chandigarh, has been crowned Miss Universe 2021, two decades after Lara Dutta won the title in 2000.
- She beat contestants from Paraguay and South Africa.
- She was crowned at the contest held in Eilat, Israel on 13 December 2021.
- India had earlier won the coveted crown twice with Sushmita Sen bagging the title in 1994 and Lara Dutta in 2000.

Hence, the correct option is (C).

14. The revolt of 1857 was the conscious beginning of the Independence struggle against the colonial tyranny of the British. The revolt began on May 10, 1857, at Meerut as a sepoy mutiny. It was initiated by sepoys in the Bengal Presidency against the British officers.

Hence, the correct option is (B).

15. Manipur Governor, Dr. Najma Heptulla released the book 'Making of a General-A Himalayan Echo'.

- It is written by retired Lt General Konsam Himalayan Singh.
- In this book, he has written about his journey from a small village in Manipur to be the first person from North East India to reach the rank of three-star General of the Indian Army.
- It also highlights the features of Manipur which is also called as 'Land of Emeralds'.

Hence, the correct option is (C).

16. Electron has a similar mass to that of positron i.e., 9.10×10^{-31} kg.

Mass of proton and neutron is 1.67×10^{-27} kg and 1.67×10^{-27} kg respectively.

Hence, the correct option is (C).

17. A knot is one nautical mile per hour

1 knot = 1.15 miles per hour

The term knot dates from the 17th century when sailors measured the speed of their ship by using a device called a "common log."

Hence, the correct option is (C).

18. Bi-focal lens are required to correct the presbyopia. Upper point of bifocal lens consists of concave lens used for distant vision while lower point consists of convex lens facilitate near vision.

Hence, the correct option is (D).

19. Only a concave mirror can produce a real image for any position of object between its focus and infinity.

A concave mirror is a type of spherical mirror that has a reflective surface. This reflective surface remains raised from the inside in the mirror. Therefore, the mirror whose reflecting surface is bulging inwards is called a concave mirror.

Hence, the correct option is (B).

20. Lead is not used as a nuclear fuel. The most common nuclear fuels are uranium – 235 (235U) and plutonium -239(239Pu). Thorium is more abundant in nature than uranium. Thorium can be used as a nuclear fuel through breeding to uranium-233 (U-233).

Hence, the correct option is (D).

21. The major components of LPG gas (liquefied petroleum gas) are propane, butane and ethane. This gas is the main gas used in cooking as a domestic fuel.

LPG is prepared by refining petroleum or "wet" natural gas, and is derived almost entirely from fossil fuel sources, produced during the refining of petroleum (crude oil), or petroleum or natural gas streams. because they emerge from the ground.

Hence, the correct option is (D).

22. Tincture of iodine is not an example of colloids.

The classification of colloids is done on the basis of their constituents which are dispersed phase and dispersing medium. Colloids cannot be discredited by filtration but can be separated by centrifugation. Fat is separated from milk by centrifugation.

Hence, the correct option is (C).

23. A dilute (approximately 5 percent by volume) solution of acetic acid produced by fermentation and oxidation of natural carbohydrates is called vinegar.

Acetic acid (CH_3COOH), also called ethanoic acid, the most important of the carboxylic acids. Vinegar is commonly used in food preparation, in particular pickling liquids, vinaigrettes, and other salad dressings. It is an ingredient in sauces, such as hot sauce, mustard, ketchup, and mayonnaise.

Hence, the correct option is (C).

24. 'Bauxite' is an ore of aluminium.

Bauxite is an ore of aluminium with chemical formula $Al_2O_3.2H_2O$. It is the primary ore of aluminium.

Ore is a naturally occurring mineral or rock from which metal can be extracted.

Hence, the correct option is (B).

25. Carbon dioxide has one carbon atom and two oxygen atoms and a molecular weight of 44. The oxygen in the air is actually two atoms of O with a molecular weight of 32. So, carbon dioxide has a higher density and is heavier than oxygen.

Hence, the correct option is (A).

26. In an adult, at rest, the resting heart rate ranges from 60-100 beats/minute. The vigorous regular exercises which an athlete does helps the heart to function better and pump more blood at a lower rate as compared to the normal sedentary person. The aerobic exercises done by the athletes helps to strengthen the heart muscle and thus reducing the heart rate at rest which otherwise would be higher in a normal adult.

Hence, the correct option is (B).

27. The first discovered plant growth hormone is auxin that plays an important role in the growth and development of plants. The bud which is present on the apex of the stem and root is called apical bud that produces a hormone i.e. auxin that helps in the growth of the shoot tip and root tip but inhibits the growth of the lateral bud. But if the plant is cut then auxin concentration in the plants gets decreased that lead to the development of lateral axillary bud.

Hence, the correct option is (B).

28. The study of the historical relationship of groups of biological organisms is called systematics or it is a branch of science that deals with classification or nomenclature. is a Latin word in which organisms are arranged in a systematic manner. It deals with the population, species, and higher taxa.

Hence, the correct option is (D).

29. The kingdom Protista forms a link with all three kingdoms Plantae, Fungi and Animalia.

Protista is a kingdom in which single-celled eukaryotic organisms are present. Protists don't have well-defined cell boundaries due to the presence of the nucleus. They form a link in different categories. The cell body of Protista contains a well-defined nucleus and membrane-bound organelles. Along with that some have cilia and some have flagella are also present that help in movement. Protist reproduces asexually as well as sexually depending on the external environment. So they show similarity with Plantae, fungi, and Animalia because they all are also eukaryotes.

Hence, the correct option is (D).

30. A basic structure of plant, the seed develops from the ovules after fertilization. Seed contains the embryo which is enclosed by the seed coat. In angiosperms, the seed is found inside the fruit. One of the ability of angiospermic seeds is they can induce seed dormancy which prevents seed germination and protects seed from harsh environment. Seed coat contains flavonoids that prevent damage from UV rays. Seeds are very resilient to harsh environments.

Hence, the correct option is (B).

31. Given-

The difference between compound interest and simple interest at the same rate on $Rs.\,25000$ for 2 years is $Rs.\,250$.

The formula for the difference between compound interest and simple interest at the same rate for 2 years is-

$$d = \frac{P \times R^2}{10000}$$

where d is the difference, P is the principal and R is the rate.

$$\Rightarrow 250 = \frac{25000 \times R^2}{10000}$$

$$\Rightarrow R^2 = 100$$

$$\Rightarrow R = 10\%$$

Hence, the correct option is (C).

32. Number of horizontal lines in chess board $= 9$
Number of vertical lines in chess board $= 9$
Calculation:
2 horizontal lines and 2 vertical lines will for 1 rectangle box
Number of rectangle $= {}^9C_2 \times {}^9C_2$
$$\Rightarrow 36 \times 36 = 1296$$
Hence, the correct option is (B).

33. Given,

BP = AC = 7 cm and BC = 10 cm

As we know,

Two tangents to a circle from the same point are always equal.

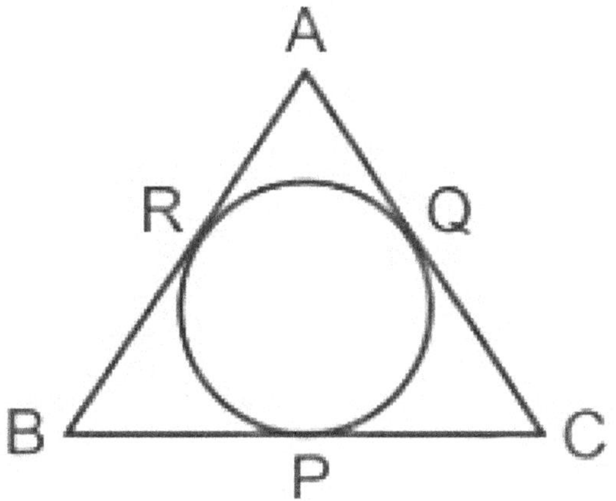

∴ BP = BR (Tangents to the circle from the same point B)

So,

BR = 7 cm

⇒ PC = BC – BP = 10 – 7 = 3 cm

Now,

QC = PC (Tangents to the circle from the same point C)

So,

QC = 3 cm

⇒ AQ = AC – QC = 7 – 3 = 4 cm

Now,

AR = AQ (Tangents to the circle from the same point A)

So,

AR = 4 cm

⇒ AB = AR + BR = 4 + 7 = 11 cm

∴ The length of AB is 11 cm.

Hence, the correct option is (C).

34. As we know,

$(x^n - a^n) \rightarrow$ divisible by $(x + a)$ if n is even number.

By using the formula, we get

$(x^n - a^n) \rightarrow$ divisible by $(x + a)$ if n is even number.
Where,

$$\Rightarrow \frac{(17^{2020} - 1^{2020})}{(17 + 1)} = \frac{(-1)^{2020}}{18}$$

When 17^{2020} is divided by 18 getting remainder 1,

$$= \frac{17^{2020}}{18}$$

$$= \frac{(18 - 1)^{2020}}{18}$$

$$= (-1)^{2020}$$

$$= 1$$

Hence, the correct option is (A).

35. Given,

$$18 + 5 - 2 \times 50 \div 5$$

Using the BODMAS rule to solve the above expression, we get

$$18 + 5 - 2 \times 10$$

$$= 18 + 5 - 20$$

$$= 23 - 20$$

$$= 3$$

Hence, the correct option is (A).

36. Given:

Discount = 8% and Ball's worth = Rs. 256

We know that,

$$\text{Discount \%} = \frac{Discount}{M.P.} \times 100$$

Let M.P be Rs. x

∴ 8% of x = 256

$$x = \left(\frac{256}{8}\right) \times 100$$

x = Rs. 3200

Price paid for bat = 3200 - 256 = Rs. 2944

Hence, the correct option is (C).

37. Given:

Sayma reaches bus stand at $9:35$ am

The previous bus has left at $9:25$ am as per her watch,

Zeenat's watch is 5 minutes fast

So, the right time when previous bus has left is $= 9:25$ am -5 minutes $= 9:20$ am

The frequency of bus is every 20 minutes

Thus, the next bus is come at $= 9:20$ am $+20$ minutes $= 9:40$ am

Sayma has to wait to catch the next bus $= 9:40$ am $-9:35$ am $= 5$ minutes

Hence, the correct option is (D).

38. Given,

The number is subtracted from each of $50, 61, 92$, and 117 to make it in proportion.

Let the number be x.

According to the question,

$$\frac{(50 - x)}{(61 - x)} = \frac{(92 - x)}{(117 - x)}$$

$$\Rightarrow (50 - x) \times (117 - x) = (92 - x) \times (61 - x)$$

$$\Rightarrow 5850 - 50x - 117x + x^2 = 5612 - 92x - 61x + x^2$$

$$\Rightarrow 238 = 14x$$

$$\Rightarrow x = 17$$

Hence, the correct option is (B).

39. The given series follows the following pattern:

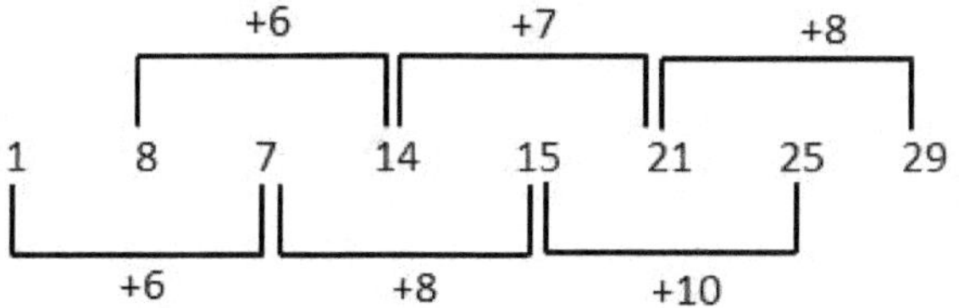

Hence, the correct option is (D).

40. According to the questions,

The highest three-digit number $= 999$

L. C. M of $3, 7$ and $21 = 21$

$\Rightarrow 999 \div 21$

$\Rightarrow$ Remainder $= 12$

So,

The greatest number divisible by $3, 7$ and $21 = 999 - 12 = 987$

The required number that will leave the remainder 2

$\Rightarrow 987 + 2 = 989$

$\therefore$ The highest three-digit number is 989.

Hence, the correct option is (D).

41. Let the number of students $= x$

Average weight of students $= 43$ kg

Total weight $= 43x$ kg

After admitted 4 new students the average weight $= 42.5$ kg

Average weight $= \dfrac{43 \times x + 42 + 36.5 + 39 + 42.5}{x+4} = 42.5$

$43x \times 160 = 42.5x + 170$

$43x - 42.5x = 10$

$0.5x = 10$

$x = \dfrac{10}{0.5}$

$x = \dfrac{100}{5}$

$\therefore$ number of students $(x) = 20$

Hence, the correct option is (C).

42. Possible event when a die is thrown: $1, 2, 3, 4, 5, 6$

$\therefore n(S) = 6$

Probability of getting a Prime number: $2, 3, 5$

$n(A) = 3$

$\therefore P(A) = \dfrac{n(A)}{n(S)} = \dfrac{3}{6} = \dfrac{1}{2}$

Hence, the correct option is (B).

43. Given,

Pipe A can fill the cistern in 3 hours and pipe B can fill the cistern in 4 hours.

As we know

Total work $=$ Time $\times$ Efficiency

Suppose total capacity of cistern $= 12$ units (LCM of 3 and 4)

So,

Efficiency of pipe $A = \dfrac{12}{3} = 4$ units

Efficiency of pipe $B = \dfrac{12}{4} = 3$ units

According to the question,

A starts first followed by B then by A.

Work completed in 3 hours $= 4 + 3 + 4 = 11$ units

Remaining 1 unit of work will be completed by B in $\dfrac{1}{3}$ hours.

$\therefore$ Total time $= 3 + \dfrac{1}{3} = \dfrac{10}{3}$ hours

Hence, the correct option is (A).

44. Let the number of hemispheres formed be n.
Then,
The volume of cuboidal gold bar $= n \times$ volume of a hemisphere
The volume of cuboid $=$ length $\times$ breadth $\times$ height
The volume of hemisphere $= \dfrac{2}{3} \times \dfrac{22}{7} \times$ radius ^{3}
$16 \times 11 \times 8 = n \times \dfrac{2}{3} \times \dfrac{22}{7} \times 2^3$
$n = 84$
Hence, the correct option is (A).

45. Given:

Gaurav earns per day $=$ Rs. 800

After a week, he earns $=$ Rs. 960

According to the question

Increase in his earnings $=$ Rs. $(960 - 800)$

$=$ Rs. 160

Now,

Percentage increase in his daily earnings $=$ Rs. $\left(\dfrac{160}{800} \times 100\right)$

$= 20\%$

$\therefore$ The required percentage increase in his earnings is 20%

Hence, the correct option is (B).

46. According to given conditions,

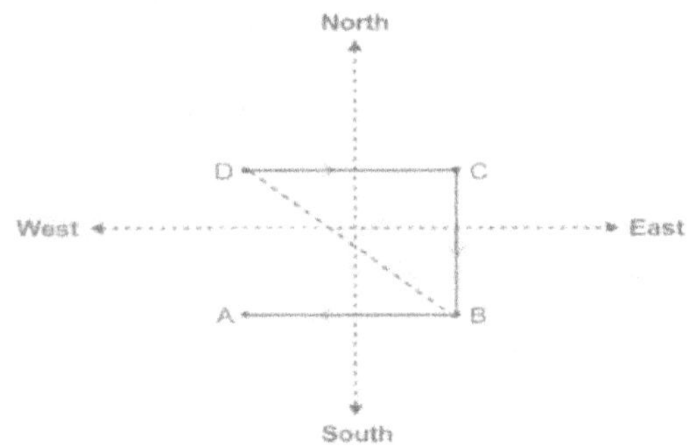

So, B's house is to the South-East of D's house.

Hence, the correct option is (B).

47. All follow the same pattern except 'VR'.

The pattern followed here is,

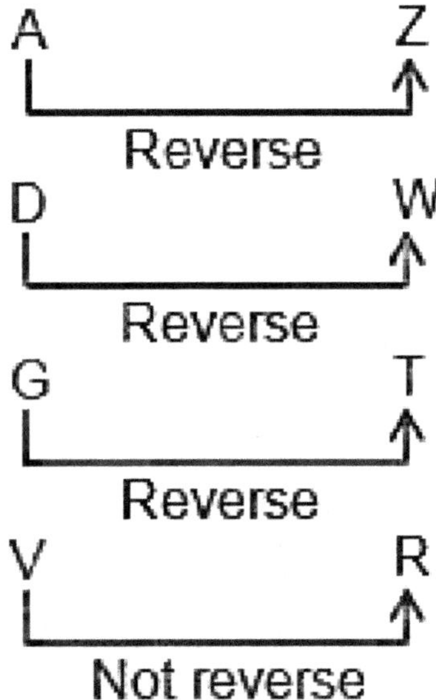

A is at 1st position, 1st position from the end is Z.

D is at 4th position, 4th position from the end is W.

G is at 7th position, 7th position from the end is T.

V is at 22nd position, 22nd position from the end is E.

∴ The odd letters from the given alternatives is 'VR'.

Hence, the correct option is (D).

48. By using the symbols in the table given below, we can draw the following family tree:

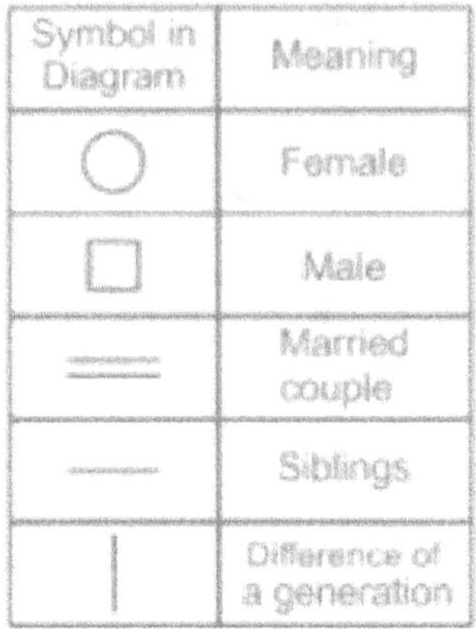

According to the given information,

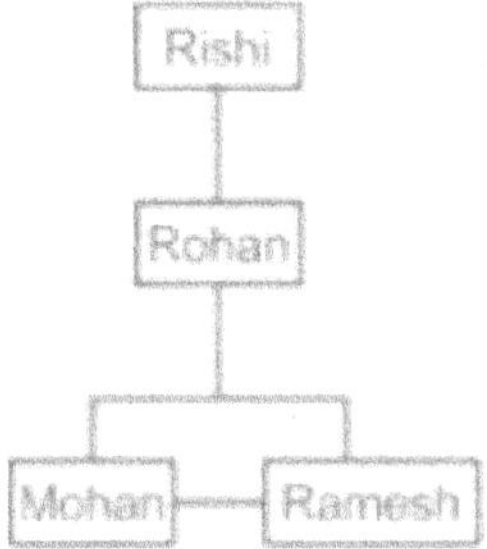

∴ Rishi is the father of Rohan.

Hence, the correct option is (A).

49. Given series: $AE, KQ, EI, LR, IO, ?, OU, NT$

The given series contains two series:

1) vowel series: each vowel moves to the next vowel letter.

$$AE = A + 1, E + 1 \rightarrow E, I$$

$$EI = E + 1, I + 1 \rightarrow I, O$$

$$IO = I + 1, O + 1 \rightarrow O, U$$

2) consonant series: each consonant moves to the next consonant letter.

$$KQ = K + 1, Q + 1 \rightarrow L, R$$

$$LR = L + 1, R + 1 \rightarrow M, S$$

$$MS = M + 1, S + 1 \rightarrow N, T$$

So, MS can replace the question mark (?).

Hence, the correct option is (C).

50. The code for TOUR is:

T	O	U	R
1	2	3	4

The code for CLEAR is:

C	L	E	A	R
5	6	7	8	4

The code for SPARE is:

S	P	A	R	E
9	0	8	4	7

Similarly,

The code for CARE is:

C	A	R	E
5	8	4	7

So, '5847' is the correct answer.

Hence, the correct option is (D).

Mock Test 02

General Knowledge

Q.1 The Peninsular rivers which do not join the Arabian Sea are _____.

A. Narmada and Tapi
B. Narmada and Cauvery
C. Godavari and Krishna
D. Tapi and Cauvery

Q.2 Who is the author of the book "The Kingdom of God is Within You"?

A. Leo Tolstoy
B. Henry David
C. Mahatma Gandhi
D. John Ruskin

Q.3 Who is the author of "The Namesake"?

A. Amitav Ghosh
B. Arundhati Roy
C. Jhumpa Lahiri
D. Kiran Desai

Q.4 World No Tabacco Day is observed on:

A. May 31
B. June 11
C. September 28
D. October 10

Q.5 'Satriya' is the Classical Dance of which state?

A. Arunachal Pradesh
B. Assam
C. Rajasthan
D. Bihar

Q.6 Where is the medieval Lingaraj Temple situated?

A. Bhubaneswar
B. Khajuraho
C. Madurai
D. Mount Abu

Q.7 Which of the following is the administrative capital of South Africa?

[RRB (NTPC), 2020]

A. Durban
B. Cape Town
C. Pretoria
D. Bloemfontein

Q.8 The Fourth Buddhist Council was held in Kashmir under the leadership of -

A. Bindusara
B. Ashoka
C. Kunal
D. Kanishka

Q.9 Who founded the ancient city of 'Bhagyanagar'?

A. Akbar
B. Aurangzeb
C. Quli Qutub Shah
D. Krishna Deva Raya

Q.10 In which year was Lakshmibai National Institute of Physical Education established?

[Madhya Pradesh Public Service Commission (MPPSC), 2018]

A. 1952
B. 1957
C. 1960
D. 1961

Q.11 How many Police personnel have been awarded the Police Medals on the occasion of Independence Day, 2022?

A. 2022
B. 1080
C. 1947
D. 1082

Q.12 The major portion of river Mahanadi lies in the state of _____.

A. Chhattisgarh
B. Jharkhand
C. Odisha
D. Madhya Pradesh

Q.13 Who has won a bronze medal in the men's freestyle 125 kg category at the Commonwealth Games 2022 in Birmingham?

A. Jeremy Lalrinnunga
B. Mohit Grewal
C. Achinta Sheuli
D. Sanket Mahadev Sargar

Q.14 The first woman foreign minister of India was:

A. Sushma Swaraj
B. Jayalalithaa
C. Pratibha Patil
D. Annie Besant

Q.15 'Fundamental Rights' are:

A. Justiciable
B. Non-justiciable
C. Flexible
D. Rigid

General Science

Q.16 Abnormal level of cholesterol is associated with:

[Uttarakhand Public Service Commission (UKPSC), 2011]

A. Hardening of arteries
B. Hardening of veins
C. Kidney stones formation
D. Liver cirrhosis

Q.17 What rays of sunlight are mostly utilized by chlorophyll in photo-synthesis?

[Uttarakhand Public Service Commission (UKPSC), 2011]

A. Red
B. Yellow
C. Green
D. Blue

Q.18 The venom of Cobra is:

[Uttarakhand Public Service Commission (UKPSC), 2011]

A. Neurotoxic
B. Haemotoxic
C. Both (A) and (B)
D. None of the above

Q.19 In surgery, what is arthoplasty?

[Uttarakhand Public Service Commission (UKPSC), 2011]

A. Open heart surgery
B. Hip-joint replacement
C. Kidney transplant
D. Blood Transfusion

Q.20 Water soluble vitamin is:

[Uttarakhand Public Service Commission (UKPSC), 2011]

A. Vitamin A
B. Vitamin C
C. Vitamin D
D. Vitamin E

Q.21 Flemings "Left hand Rule" is associated with which effect?

A. Electric field on current
B. Magnetic field on magnet
C. Electric field on magnet
D. Magnetic field on current

Q.22 Why do we use a galvanometer?
A. For measuring altitudes
B. For measuring small electrical current
C. For measuring potential difference between two points
D. For projecting pictures on the screen

Q.23 An air bubble in water acts as a _______.
A. Convex lens
B. Plain mirror
C. Concave lens
D. Concave mirror

Q.24 The apparatus used to measure the intensity of light is known is-
A. Anemometer
B. Colorimeter
C. Luxmeter
D. Altimeter

Q.25 Which of these has the highest frequency?
A. Gamma Rays
B. Radio Waves
C. Ultraviolet Light
D. Infrared Rays

Q.26 Which chemical substance is used for making rat poison?
A. Ethyl Alcohol
B. Methyl Isocyanate
C. Potassium Cyanide
D. Ethyl Isocyanide

Q.27 The gas used to inflate the tyres of an aircraft is-
A. Hydrogen
B. Nitrogen
C. Helium
D. Neon

Q.28 Red litmus paper is changed into blue in solution of __________.
A. Base
B. Acid
C. Salt
D. None

Q.29 The non-metal which is liquid in nature is:
A. Iodine
B. Bromine
C. Mercury
D. Chlorine

Q.30 A pungent smell often present near the urinals is due to:
A. Sulphur-di-oxide
B. Chlorine
C. Ammonia
D. Urea

Maths

Q.31 The difference between simple and compound interests compounded annually on a certain sum of money for 2 years at 4% per annum is Re. 1. The sum (in Rs.) is:
A. 625
B. 630
C. 640
D. 650

Q.32 In Daya's bag, there are 3 books of History, 4 books of Science and 2 books of Maths. In how many ways can Daya arrange the books so that all the books on the same subject are together?
A. 9000
B. 6000
C. 8640
D. 1728

Q.33 If $ABCDE$ is a regular pentagon, find the value of $\angle EBC$.
A. 108°
B. 72°
C. 84°
D. 96°

Q.34 If 123457Y is completely divisible by 8, then what will be the digit in place of Y?

[SSC MTS, 2017]

A. 4
B. 5
C. 8
D. 6

Q.35 Find the value of- $\dfrac{\sqrt[4]{0.0625}+\sqrt[3]{0.008}+\sqrt{0.09}-1}{\sqrt[3]{62.5\times\sqrt[5]{32}}}$.

A. 1.25
B. 2.40
C. 2.50
D. 0

Q.36 The cash difference between the selling price of an article at a profit of 4% and 6% is Rs. 3. The ratio of two selling prices is:

[RRB (NTPC), 2017]

A. $51:53$
B. $55:53$
C. $52:53$
D. $54:53$

Q.37 Ram and Shyam together can finish a job in 8 days. Ram can finish the same job on his own in 12 days. How long will Shyam alone take to finish that work?
A. 16 days
B. 20 days
C. 24 days
D. 30 days

Q.38 The missing term in the series 21, 41, 66, 96, ____, 171, 216, 266 is:

[UP Police ASI, 2018]

A. 142
B. 131
C. 125
D. 117

Q.39 The sum of two numbers is 192 and their HCF is 32. Find how many such pairs can be formed.
A. 5
B. 4
C. 3
D. 1

Q.40 The mean temperature from Monday to Wednesday was $37°C$ and on Tuesday to Thursday was $34°C$ if the temperature on Thursday was $\dfrac{4th}{5}$ that of Monday, then what was the temperature on Thursday?
A. $36.5°C$
B. $36°C$
C. $35.5°C$
D. $34°C$

Q.41 Three cards are drawn at random one after another from an ordinary pack of cards. Find the probability that they will consist of a king, a queen and an ace.
A. $\dfrac{16}{5525}$
B. $\dfrac{15}{5525}$
C. $\dfrac{16}{5335}$
D. $\dfrac{16}{6525}$

Q.42 A person crosses a road of length 1200 m in 10 minutes. What is the speed of the person?
A. 3 km/h
B. 5 km/h
C. 8.5 km/h
D. 7.2 km/h

Q.43 Find the volume of a cone which has a base radius of 7 cm and height 21 cm. ($\pi = \dfrac{22}{7}$)
A. 1008 cm ^{3}
B. 1078 cm ^{3}
C. 778 cm ^{3}
D. 1068 cm ^{3}

Q.44 Rishu saves $x\%$ of her income. If her income increases by 26% and the expenditure increases by 20%, then her savings increase by 50%. What is the value of x?

[SSC CGL, 2020]

A. 30
B. 10
C. 20
D. 25

Q.45 The ratio of the number of boys to the number of girls at a party is $5:9$. If there are 99 girls at the party, the total number of persons at the party are:

A. 99   **B.** 55   **C.** 132   **D.** 154

Logical Reasoning

Q.46 If Diwali was on 25 November, 2013 which was Sunday, what day it would have been on 25 November, 2014?

A. Monday   **B.** Tuesday

C. Wednesday   **D.** Thursday

Q.47 Select the letter-pair that can replace the question mark (?) in the following series?

AR, CV, EZ, GD, ?

A. JL   **B.** IH   **C.** IJ   **D.** KM

Q.48 In a row of children, Aarna is fourteenth from the left end of the row. If she is shifted towards the right end of the row by five places, she becomes seventh from the right end. How many children are there in the row?

A. 26   **B.** 24   **C.** 23   **D.** 25

Q.49 Qv is the husband of Es. Rx is son of Qv. Tw is the brother of Es. How is Rx related to Tw?

A. Niece   **B.** Nephew

C. Son   **D.** Daughter

Q.50 In a code language, LEAVE is written as RKGBK. How will FLOAT be written in that language?

[SSC Selection Post Phase IX, 2020]

A. MSUGZ   **B.** LRVGY   **C.** LRUFA   **D.** LRUGZ

// Smart Answer Sheet //

Correct — Indicates percentage of students who answered questions correctly.

Skipped — Indicates percentage of students who skipped questions.

Q.	Ans.	Correct / Skipped	Q.	Ans.	Correct / Skipped	Q.	Ans.	Correct / Skipped	Q.	Ans.	Correct / Skipped	Q.	Ans.	Correct / Skipped
1	C	32.28 % / 67.62 %	11	D	50.02 % / 43.08 %	21	D	89.18 % / 10.46 %	31	A	19.88 % / 68.49 %	41	A	11.41 % / 71.7 %
2	A	83.17 % / 16.11 %	12	C	51.16 % / 46.63 %	22	B	76.51 % / 10.15 %	32	D	45.61 % / 34.55 %	42	D	87.9 % / 10.11 %
3	C	80.74 % / 16.1 %	13	B	30.33 % / 69.22 %	23	C	40.13 % / 44.07 %	33	B	64.98 % / 34.87 %	43	B	78.15 % / 20.15 %
4	A	82.82 % / 10.38 %	14	A	60.8 % / 31.54 %	24	C	66.38 % / 30.5 %	34	D	43.69 % / 48.03 %	44	C	58.71 % / 35.81 %
5	B	42.25 % / 42.19 %	15	A	48.77 % / 43.21 %	25	A	43.68 % / 49.39 %	35	D	32.51 % / 67.19 %	45	D	66.79 % / 31.29 %
6	A	52.44 % / 30.13 %	16	A	77.59 % / 11.79 %	26	C	19.0 % / 68.73 %	36	C	14.75 % / 73.71 %	46	A	59.67 % / 33.73 %
7	C	18.3 % / 76.13 %	17	A	16.63 % / 75.63 %	27	B	82.56 % / 14.38 %	37	C	81.24 % / 13.05 %	47	B	65.05 % / 32.98 %
8	D	10.08 % / 71.39 %	18	C	20.59 % / 72.97 %	28	A	66.81 % / 32.15 %	38	B	43.49 % / 47.1 %	48	D	28.78 % / 68.32 %
9	C	63.03 % / 31.45 %	19	B	29.01 % / 67.21 %	29	B	89.7 % / 10.09 %	39	D	83.19 % / 11.79 %	49	B	54.28 % / 44.04 %
10	B	43.68 % / 35.73 %	20	B	78.55 % / 19.91 %	30	C	53.87 % / 38.94 %	40	B	20.94 % / 73.52 %	50	D	61.32 % / 35.25 %

Performance Analysis

Avg. Score (%)	38.0%
Toppers Score (%)	63.0%
Your Score	

//Hints and Solutions//

1. The Peninsular rivers which do not join the Arabian Sea are Godavari and Krishna.

On the basis of flow, peninsular rivers are divided into two categories: east-flowing and west-flowing rivers. East flowing rivers such as Godavari, Krishna, Kaveri, Mahanadi drained into Bay of Bengal and West flowing rivers such as the Narmada, the Tapi drained into the Arabian Sea.

Hence, the correct option is (C).

2. Leo Tolstoy is the author of the book "The Kingdom of God is Within You".

The book is based on the Tolstoyan proponents of nonviolence, nonviolent resistance, and the Christian anarchist movement.

The book was published in Germany in the Russian language in the year 1894.

The book was his true transformation process of Luke 17:21 from the bible.

Hence, the correct option is (A).

3. Jhumpa Lahiri is an Indian American author. Her first novel, The Namesake (2003), was adapted into the popular film of the same name.

Hence, the correct option is (C).

4. World No Tabacco Day is observed on May 31.

Every year, on 31 May, WHO and partners mark World No Tobacco Day (WNTD), highlighting the health and additional risks associated with tobacco use, and advocating for effective policies to reduce tobacco consumption.

Hence, the correct option is (A).

5. 'Satriya' is the Classical Dance of Assam. The Sattriya dance form was introduced in the 15th century A.D by the great Vaishnava saint and reformer of Assam, Mahapurusha Sankaradeva as a powerful medium for the propagation of the Vaishnava faith.

Hence, the correct option is (B).

6. Lingaraj Temple is situated in Bhubaneswar.

Lingraj Temple is the largest temple of Bhubaneswar. This is a Hindu temple dedicated to the Harihar form of Lord Shiva. It is believed that this temple was built by the kings of the Somvanshi dynasty, succeeding the Gang rulers.

Hence, the correct option is (A).

7. Pretoria is the administrative capital of South Africa.

- South Africa is the southernmost country on the African continent.
- South Africa has three capital cities namely, Pretoria, Bloemfontein, Cape Town.
- Pretoria is host to all foreign embassies to South Africa.
- Pretoria was founded in 1855 by Marthinus Pretorius.
- The city Pretoria is named after the Voortrekker leader Andries Pretorius.
- South Africa became Republic on 31 May 1961.

Hence, the correct option is (C).

8. The Fourth Buddhist Council was held at Kundalvana (presumed to be in or near Srinagar), Kashmir in 72 AD under the patronage of Kushan king Kanishka and the president of this council was Vasumitra, with Asvaghosa as his deputy. This council distinctly divided Buddhism into 2 sects Mahayana & Hinayana.

Fourth Buddhist Council is the name of two separate Buddhist council meetings. The first one was held in Sri Lanka and is traditionally attributed to the 1st century BCE. The second one was held by the Sarvastivada school, in Kashmir around the 1st century CE.

Hence, the correct option is (D).

9. Bhagyanagar is the ancient name of the city Hyderabad, which was founded by Mohammad Quli Qutub Shah, the greatest ruler of the Qutub Shahi dynasty. Bhagmathi, a local nautch (dancing) girl with whom he had fallen in love, converted to Islam and adopted the title Hyder Mahal. The city was renamed Hyderabad in her honour. He also built Charminar.

Hence, the correct option is (C).

10. The Lakshmibai National Institute of Physical Education, Gwalior was established by the Ministry of Education and Culture. It was set up as Lakshmibai College of Physical Education (LCPE) in August 1957 and it was the affiliated college of the Vikram University, Ujjain. Later it came to the folds of Jiwaji University, Gwalior in 1964.

Hence, the correct option is (B).

11. A total of 1082 Police personnel have been awarded Police Medals on the occasion of Independence Day, 2022. 347 personnel have been awarded for Gallantry while 87 have been awarded for Distinguished Service.

Hence, the correct option is (D).

12. The major portion of river Mahanadi lies in the state of Odisha.

The Mahanadi is a major river in East Central India. It drains an area of around 141,600 square kilometres (54,700 sq mi) and has a total course of 858 kilometres (533 mi) Mahanadi is also known for the Hirakud Dam.

Hence, the correct option is (C).

13. Mohit Grewal has won a bronze medal in the men's freestyle 125 kg category at the Commonwealth Games 2022 in Birmingham. He defeated Jamaica's Aaron Johnson. The Indian wrestler clinched the medal in only 3 minutes and 30 seconds.

Hence, the correct option is (B).

14. Sushma Swaraj was the first full-time woman foreign affairs minister of the country. Although Indira Gandhi also took charge of the Ministry of External Affairs twice but while being the Prime Minister.

Sushma Swaraj was born on 14 February 1952 in Ambala Cantonment of Haryana (then Punjab) state, to Hardev Sharma and Lakshmi Devi, her father was a prominent member of the Rashtriya Swayamsevak Sangh.

Hence, the correct option is (A).

15. 'Fundamental Rights' are Justiciable.

The Fundamental Rights are enshrined in Part III of the Constitution (Articles 12-35). Part III of the Constitution is described as the Magna Carta of India. The Fundamental Rights are justiciable because when violated the aggrieved individual can move the courts for their enforcement.

Hence, the correct option is (A).

16. Abnormal level of cholesterol is associated with Hardening of arteries.

Atherosclerosis, sometimes called "hardening of the arteries," occurs when fat, cholesterol, and other substances build up in the walls of arteries. These deposits are called plaques. Over time, these plaques can narrow or completely block the arteries and cause problems throughout the body.

Hence, the correct option is (A).

17. Red rays of sunlight are mostly utilized by chlorophyll in photo-synthesis.

Green plants are green because they contain a pigment called chlorophyll. Chlorophyll absorbs certain wavelengths of light within the visible light spectrum. Chlorophyll absorbs light in the red (long wavelength) and the blue (short wavelength) regions of the visible light spectrum. Green light is not absorbed but reflected, making the plant appear green. Chlorophyll is found in the chloroplasts of plants.

Hence, the correct option is (A).

18. The venom of Cobra is neurotoxic and hemotoxic.

Snake venoms are usually classified as hemotoxic or neurotoxic. Snakes of the Viperidae (vipers and rattlesnakes) family have venoms containing proteins that can disrupt the coagulation cascade, the hemostatic system, and tissue integrity.

Neurotoxicity occurs when the exposure to natural or manmade toxic substances (neurotoxicants) alters the normal activity of the nervous system. This can eventually disrupt or even kill neurons, key cells that transmit and process signals in the brain and other parts of the nervous system.

haemotoxins or hematotoxins are toxins that destroy red blood cells, disrupt blood clotting, and/or cause organ degeneration and generalized tissue damage. Injury from a hemotoxic agent is often very painful and can cause permanent damage and in severe cases death.

Hence, the correct option is (C).

19. In surgery, Hip-joint replacement is arthoplasty.

Arthroplasty is an orthopedic surgical procedure where the articular surface of a musculoskeletal joint is replaced, remodeled, or realigned by osteotomy or some other procedure. It is an elective procedure that is done to relieve pain and restore function to the joint after damage by arthritis or some other type of trauma.

Hence, the correct option is (B).

20. Water soluble vitamin is Vitamin C.

Vitamins are classified as either fat soluble (vitamins A, D, E and K) or water soluble (vitamins B and C). This difference between the two groups is very important. It determines how each vitamin acts within the body.

Water-soluble vitamins include vitamin C and the B vitamins: thiamine, riboflavin, niacin, pantothenic acid, B6, biotin, folic acid, and B12. Fat-soluble vitamins. These vitamins are stored in the body's cells and do not pass out of the body as easily as water-soluble vitamins do.

Hence, the correct option is (B).

21. Flemings "Left hand Rule" is associated with magnetic field on current.

It is found that whenever an current carrying conductor is placed inside a magnetic field, a force acts on the conductor, in a direction perpendicular to both the directions of the current and the magnetic field.

Hence, the correct option is (D).

22. Galvanometer is used for measuring small electrical current.

The galvanometer is an instrument for measuring a function of the current by deflection of a moving coil. The deflection is a mechanical rotation derived from forces resulting from the current. An ammeter is also used for measuring the magnitude of current.

Hence, the correct option is (B).

23. Inside water, the air bubble behaves like a Concave lens. The concave lenses are known as diverging lenses as the rays diverge after falling on the concave lens. The air bubble is a sphere with a convex surface and when light reaches it, the light is reflected within the water as in a concave lens.

Hence, the correct option is (C).

24. Luxmeter is used to measure the intensity of light, while a colorimeter is a device used to measure the intensity of color. An anemometer is an instrument that measures wind speed and wind pressure. An altimeter is a device that measures altitude a location's distance above sea level. Most altimeters are barometric, meaning they measure altitude by calculating the location's air pressure.

Hence, the correct option is (C).

25. Gamma Rays have the highest frequency out of the above options. The frequency of a wave is the number of waves that pass through a single point in one second Frequency is measured in unit of Hertz (Hz), 1 Hertz is equal to one wave passing a point per second Gamma Rays have frequencies in order of greater than 10^{19} Hz. The energy of a wave is directly related to its frequency which makes gamma rays the most high energy form of electromagnetic radiation

Hence, the correct option is (A).

26. Potassium Cyanide (KCN) or Zinc Phosphide is a highly toxic chemical used as a rodenticide a poison to kill the mouse. Zinc phosphide is highly toxic in acute exposure to humans. It may be consumed accidentally or intentionally as means of suicidal or homicidal acts. Other routes of entry into the body could be via inhalation or through the skin. Zinc phosphide is hydrolysed by the gastric acid and is transformed into phosphine gas.

Hence, the correct option is (C).

27. Nitrogen gas is used in the tyres of an aeroplane. This is because the nitrogen gas does not support combustion and can assist in preventing wheel fire when the aircraft lands.

Hence, the correct option is (B).

28. Red litmus paper is changed into blue in the solution of the base.

Red litmus restrains a weak diprotic acid. A weak acid used in acid-base indicator usually has a different colour between the acid form and the conjugate base ion form. This is the reason when adding a water-soluble base into it, it turns blue, and allows the colour of the conjugate base ion.

Hence, the correct option is (A).

29. The non-metal which is liquid in nature is bromine.

It is the only nonmetallic element that is liquid under ordinary conditions. It is a Red liquid. It is a brownish-red liquid at ambient temperature. It evaporates easily at standard temperature. It is less active chemically than chlorine and fluorine but is more active than iodine.

Hence, the correct option is (B).

30. Urine odour is caused by the presence of Ammonia. Urine is an aqueous solution of greater than 95% water. Urine may smell like ammonia when it becomes concentrated with waste products. A variety of conditions can cause waste products to build up in urine, such as bladder stones, dehydration, and urinary tract infections. In most cases, urine that smells like ammonia can be treated with fluids or antibiotic medications.

Hence, the correct option is (C).

31. Given,

Time = 2 years

Rate = 4%

Let the Principal be Rs. x.

Formula used:

$$\text{C.I.} = P\left(1 + \frac{r}{100}\right)^t - P$$

Then,

$$\text{C.I.} = \left[x\left(1 + \frac{4}{100}\right)^2 - x\right]$$

$$= \left(\frac{676}{625}x - x\right)$$

$$= \frac{51}{625}x$$

$$\text{S.I.} = \left(\frac{x \times 4 \times 2}{100}\right)$$

$$= \frac{2x}{25}$$

$$\therefore \frac{51x}{625} - \frac{2x}{25} = 1$$

$$\Rightarrow x = 625$$

Hence, the correct option is (A).

32. Given,

Number of history books $= 3$

Number of Science books $= 4$

Number of Maths books $= 2$

According to the question,

A number of ways history books can be arranged $= 3! = 3 \times 2 \times 1 = 6$

A number of ways science books can be arranged $= 4! = 4 \times 3 \times 2 \times 1 = 24$

A number of ways maths books can be arranged $= 2! = 2$

A number of ways all three books can be arranged $= 3! = 3 \times 2 \times 1 = 6$

$\therefore$ Total number of ways $= 6 \times 6 \times 24 \times 2 = 1728$

Hence, the correct option is (D).

33. Given,

$ABCDE$ is a regular pentagon.

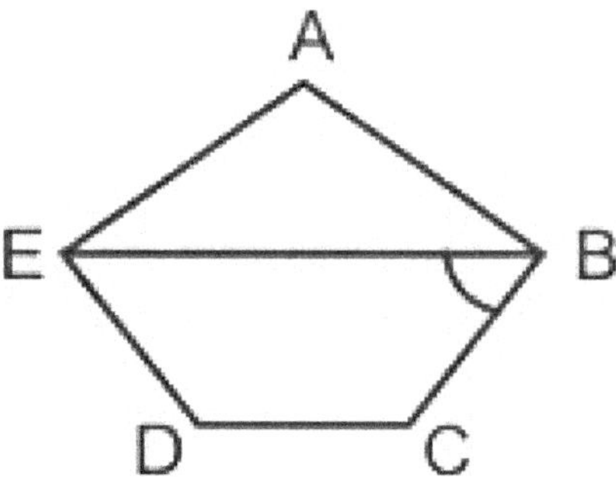

Angle of regular polygon $= \frac{(n-2)180}{n}$

Here, $n =$ number of sides

Angle of regular pentagon $= \frac{(5-2)180}{5}$

$\angle BCD = 108°$

$\angle BCD + \angle EBC = 180°$ (adjacent angles between two parallel lines)

$108° + \angle EBC = 180°$

$\angle EBC = 72°$

$\therefore$ Required answer $\angle EBC$ is $72°$.

Hence, the correct option is (B).

34. Given,

123457Y

If a number is completely divisible by 8, then the last three digits of the number must also be divisible by 8.

$\Rightarrow$ 57Y must be divisible by 8 and the only three-digit number starting with '57' which is divisible by 8 is = 576

$\Rightarrow$ Y=6

Hence, the correct option is (D).

35. Given-

$$\frac{\sqrt[4]{0.0625}+\sqrt[3]{0.008}+\sqrt{0.09}-1}{\sqrt[3]{62.5\times\sqrt[5]{32}}}$$

$$=\frac{\sqrt[4]{\frac{625}{10000}}+\sqrt[3]{\frac{8}{1000}}+\sqrt{\frac{9}{100}}-1}{\sqrt[3]{62.5\times\sqrt[5]{2^5}}}$$

$$=\frac{\sqrt[4]{\frac{5^4}{10^4}}+\sqrt[3]{\frac{2^3}{10^3}}+\sqrt{\frac{3^2}{10^2}}-1}{\sqrt[3]{62.5\times2}}$$

$$=\frac{\frac{5}{10}+\frac{2}{10}+\frac{3}{10}-1}{\sqrt[3]{125}}$$

$$=\frac{\frac{10}{10}-1}{5}$$

$$=\frac{1-1}{5}$$

$$=\frac{0}{5}$$

$$=0$$

Hence, the correct option is (D).

36. Let the cost price of an article be Rs. x.

At 4% profit,

Selling Price $=$ Cost Price $+4\%$ of Cost Price $= 1.04x$

At 6% profit,

Selling Price $=$ Cost Price $+6\%$ of Cost Price $= 1.06x$

Cash differences between selling price $=$ Rs. 3

$\Rightarrow 1.06x - 1.04x = 3$

$\Rightarrow 0.02x = 3$

$\Rightarrow x = 150$

Selling price of first article $= 1.04x = 1.04 \times 150 =$ Rs. 156

Selling price of second article $= 1.06x = 1.06 \times 150 =$ Rs. 159

The ratio of Selling Prices $= 156:159 = 52:53$

Hence, the correct option is (C).

37. Ram can complete the work in 12 days.

Ram's one-day work $= \dfrac{1}{12}$

Total time is taken by Ram and Shyam to complete the work $= 8$

Ram and Shyam's one-day work $= \dfrac{1}{8}$

Shyam's one day work $= \dfrac{1}{8} - \dfrac{1}{12}$

$$= \frac{3}{24} - \frac{2}{24}$$

$$= \frac{1}{24}$$

So, Shyam can complete the work in 24 days.

Hence, the correct option is (C).

38. Given:

21, 41, 66, 96, ____, 171, 216, 266

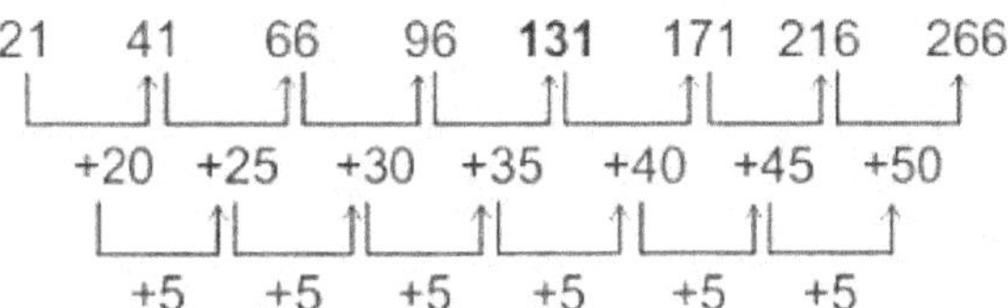

$\therefore$ The missing term is 131.

Hence, the correct option is (B).

39. If the HCF of two numbers is 32, then the two numbers are $32X$ and $32Y$ where X and Y are co-prime numbers.

Now the sum of the two numbers is 192.

So, we can say, $32X + 32Y = 192$

$\Rightarrow X + Y = 6$

The possible pairs of X and Y are: $(1,5), (2,4), (3,3)$

(As we are not considering the ordered pairs so $(4,2), (5,1)$ pairs have been excluded.)

Now, X and Y are co-prime numbers.

Two integers X and Y are said to be relatively prime or co-prime if the only positive integer that divides both of them is 1.

$\therefore$ Among the three pairs there is only one co-prime pair $(1,5)$.

$\therefore$ Only one such pair can be formed.

Hence, the correct option is (D).

40. Let the temperatures on Monday, Tuesday, Wednesday and Thursday be M, T, W and Th respectively.

Then $M + T + W = 3 \times 37°C = 111°C$ ....(i)

$T + W + Th = 3 \times 34°C - 102°C$ ....(ii)

From Eq (i)-Eq (ii), we get

$\Rightarrow M - Th = 111°C - 102°C = 9°C$

Also given $Th = \dfrac{4}{5} M$

$\Rightarrow M - \dfrac{4}{5} M = 9$

$\Rightarrow M = 40°C$

Therefore, temperature on $y = \dfrac{4}{5} \times 45°C = 36°C$

Hence, the correct option is (B).

41. Probability of getting the first card as king $= \dfrac{4}{52}$

Probability of getting the second card as queen $= \dfrac{4}{51}$

Probability of getting the third card as ace $= \dfrac{4}{50}$

So, Total probability $= 3! \times \dfrac{4}{52} \times \dfrac{4}{51} \times \dfrac{4}{50}$

$= 6 \times \dfrac{4}{52} \times \dfrac{4}{51} \times \dfrac{4}{50}$

$= \dfrac{384}{132600}$

$= \dfrac{48}{16575}$

$= \dfrac{16}{5525}$

Hence, the correct option is (A).

42. Given:

Length of road = 1200 m

Time taken to cross a road = 10 min

Formula Used:

Speed $= \dfrac{Distance}{Time}$

Speed $= \dfrac{1200 \times 60}{10 \times 1000} = 7.2$ km/hr

$\therefore$ The speed of the person is 7.2 km/hr.

Hence, the correct option is (D).

43. Given,

The radius of the cone $(r) = 7$ cm

Height of the cone $(h) = 21$ cm

As we know,

Volume of a cone $= \dfrac{1}{3} \pi r^2 h$

$\therefore$ Volume of the cone $= \dfrac{1}{3} \times \dfrac{22}{7} \times (7)^2 \times 21$

$= \dfrac{1}{3} \times \dfrac{22}{7} \times 49 \times 21$

$= 22 \times 7 \times 7$

$= 1078$ cm^3

So, the volume of the cone is 1078 cm^3.

Hence, the correct option is (B).

44. Given:

Rishu saves $x\%$ of her income

Increase in her income $= 26\%$

Increase in her expenditure $= 20\%$

Increase in saving $= 50\%$

As we know,

Income $=$ Saving $+$ Expenditure

Let income of Rishu be 100

Saving of Rishu $= 100 \times \left(\dfrac{x}{100}\right) = x$

Expenditure of Rishu $= 100 - x$

Rishu's salary after increment $= 100 \times \left(\dfrac{126}{100}\right) = 126$

Rishu's expenditure after increment $= (100 - x) \times \dfrac{120}{100}$

$= (100 - x) \times \dfrac{6}{5}$

New Saving $= 126 - (100 - x) \times \dfrac{6}{5} \dots (i)$

New saving after increment $= x \times \dfrac{150}{100}$

New saving after increment $= \dfrac{3x}{2} \dots (ii)$

From equation (i) and equation (ii)

$\Rightarrow 126 - (100 - x) \times \dfrac{6}{5} = \dfrac{3x}{2}$

$\Rightarrow 126 - 120 + \dfrac{6x}{5} = \dfrac{3x}{2}$

$$\Rightarrow 6 = \left(\frac{3x}{2}\right) - \left(\frac{6x}{5}\right)$$

$$\Rightarrow 6 = \frac{(15x - 12x)}{10}$$

$$\Rightarrow x = 20$$

$\therefore$ The value of x is 20.

Hence, the correct option is (C).

45. Let the number of boys be $5x$ and the number of girls be $9x$ at the party.

Given that there are 99 girls at the party,

So,

$$\Rightarrow 9x = 99$$

$$\Rightarrow x = 11$$

Total number of Persons at the party $=$ Number of boys $+$ Number of girls

Total number of Persons at the party $= 5x + 9x = 14x$

Total number of Persons at the party $= 14 \times 11 = 154$

Hence, the correct option is (D).

46. The logic follows here is:

In an ordinary year, there are 365 days and on dividing 365 by 7, we get remainder = 1 so this extra one day is taken as an odd day.

Similarly, in a leap year, there are 366 days and on dividing 366 by 7, we get remainder = 2 so these extra days are taken as the odd days.

Thus, the remainder, which we get after dividing the number of days by 7 is considered as odd days.

As Diwali was on 25 November 2013 which was Sunday.

Since 2013 is a non-leap year,

There are 365 days between 25 November 2013 and 25 November 2014.

When 365 is divided by 7,

The remainder is 1.

Thus 1 more day after Sunday.

So if 25 November 2013 was on Sunday,

25 November 2014 will be on Monday.

Hence, the correct option is (A).

47. The pattern followed here is:

A + 2 = C, C + 2 = E, E + 2 = G, G + 2 = I

R + 4 = V, V + 4 = Z, Z + 4 = D, D + 4 = H

Therefore, IH is the correct answer.

Hence, the correct option is (B).

48. According to the question,

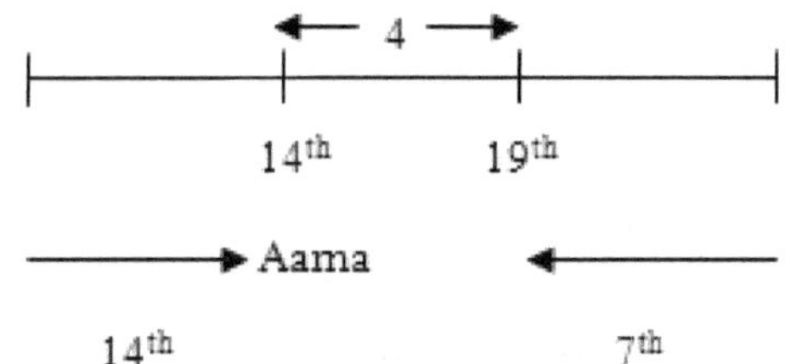

So, the total number of children in the row $= 19 + 7 - 1 = 25$

Hence, the correct option is (D).

49. Preparing the family tree using the following symbols:

Symbol in Diagram	Meaning
◯	Female
▢	Male
═	Married Couple
—	Siblings
│	Difference of a generation

A possible tree diagram will be:

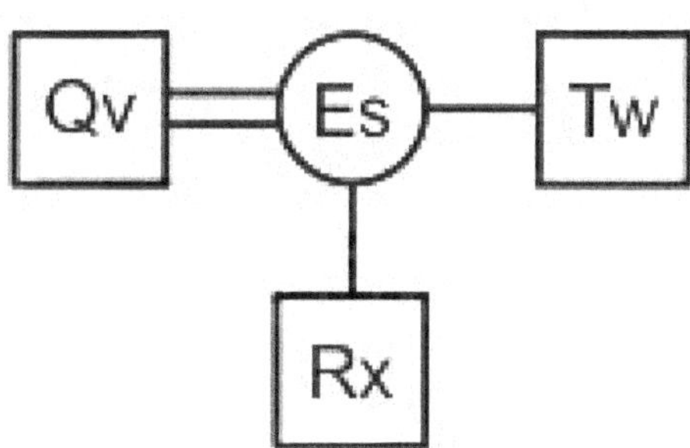

So, Rx is the nephew of Tw.

Hence, the correct option is (B).

50.

Alpha bets	A	B	C	D	E	F	G	H	I	J	K	L	M
Positi onal	1	2	3	4	5	6	7	8	9	10	11	12	13

value												
Positi onal value	2 6	2 5	2 4	2 3	2 2	2 1	2 0	1 9	1 8	1 7	1 6	1 5	1 4
Alpha bets	Z	Y	X	W	V	U	T	S	R	Q	P	O	N

The logic is as:

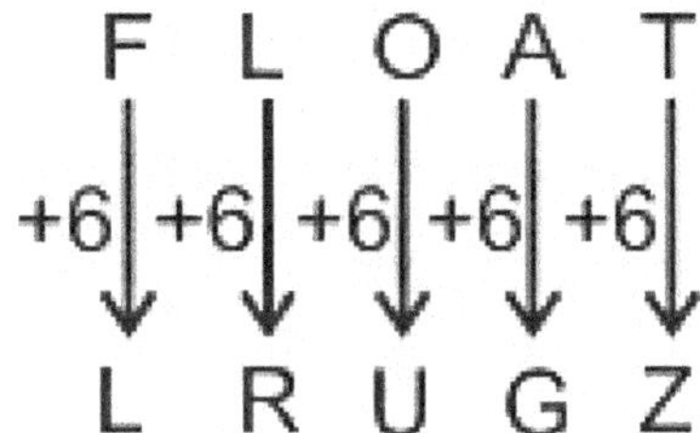

Similarly

F L O A T
+6 +6 +6 +6 +6
L R U G Z

Thus, FLOAT will be written as LRUGZ.

Hence, the correct option is (D).

General Knowledge

Q.1 Who has topped the Forbes' world's billionaires list for 2021?

A. Elon Musk
B. Jeff Bezos
C. Bill Gates
D. Warren Buffett

Q.2 Which one of the following statements about the Himalayas is not correct?

A. They are young fold mountains
B. They have geosynclinal rocks
C. Himalayan frontal faults (HFF) separates Himalaya from Tibet
D. Indus and Sutlej rivers form antecedent drainage in Himalaya

Q.3 Who wrote the book 'Panchatantra'?

A. Chanakya
B. Kalidas
C. Vishnu Sharma
D. Banabhatta

Q.4 Which of the following is not written by Munshi Premchand?

A. Gaban
B. Godan
C. Guide
D. Manasarovar

Q.5 Sabarimala Temple is located:

A. Kerala
B. Karnataka
C. Tamil Nadu
D. Odisha

Q.6 In which district of Haryana is the historic town of Gohana located?

A. Panipat **B.** Sirsa **C.** Sonipat **D.** Rewari

Q.7 Kalidas Samman award is presented by which state government?

A. Tamil Nadu
B. Karnataka
C. Andhra Pradesh
D. Madhya Pradesh

Q.8 Choose the correct pair of the country - capital from the given alternative.

A. Chile - Bogota
B. Costa Rica - Moroni
C. Cuba - Havana
D. Colombia - Santiago

Q.9 When is World Humanitarian Day observed?

A. 17 August
B. 18 August
C. 19 August
D. 20 August

Q.10 Match the following:

List-I	List-II
A. Kumaon Himalayas	1. Between the Indus and the Sutlej
B. Nepal Himalayas	2. Between the Kali and the Teesta
C. Punjab Himalayas	3. Between the Teesta and the
D. Assam Himalayas	4. Between the Sutlej and the Kali

A. A - 1, B - 2, C - 3, D - 4
B. A - 4, B - 3, C - 1, D - 4
C. A - 1, B - 2, C - 3, D - 1
D. A - 4, B - 2, C - 1, D - 3

Q.11 Saha Institute of Nuclear Physics is located in:

[RRB (NTPC), 2017]

A. Tamil Nadu
B. Delhi
C. Maharashtra
D. West Bengal

Q.12 The power of the Supreme Court of India to decide disputes between the Union and the States falls under its __________.

A. Advisory jurisdiction
B. Appellate jurisdiction
C. Original jurisdiction
D. Writ jurisdiction

Q.13 With which sport do you associate the name of Koneru Humpy ?

A. Chess
B. Volleyball
C. Table Tennis
D. Basketball

Q.14 Who was the Governor-General of India at the time of the Sepoy Mutiny of 1857?

A. Lord Hardings
B. Lord Canning
C. Lord Lytton
D. Lord Dalhousie

Q.15 Which of the following was the main objective behind introducing the Rowlatt Act?

A. To curb the growing nationalist upsurge in the country
B. To prevent the vernacular press from expressing criticism of British policies
C. To prevent the growth of Indian handicrafts
D. To give power to British Judges to try Indian offenders

General Science

Q.16 The maximum yield of ATP from the complete oxidation of sucrose via aerobic respiration is:

[Maharashtra Public Service Commission, 2018]

A. 37 **B.** 44 **C.** 60 **D.** 50

Q.17 The binomial system of classification was given by:

[Maharashtra Public Service Commission, 2018]

A. Carolus Linnaeus
B. Bentham and Hooker
C. Theophrastus
D. Hutchinson

Q.18 According to Sir J.C. Bose, an Indian scientist, ascent of sap takes place due to the of living cells of the innermost cortical layer.
A. Pulsatory activity
B. Transpiration pull theory
C. Cohesion theory
D. Root pressure theory

Q.19 Which of the following are hormones of the pituitary gland?
A. TSH
B. STH
C. HCG
D. ADH

[Maharashtra Public Service Commission, 2018]

A. A and B
B. B and C
C. A, B and D
D. A, B, and C

Q.20 Heating of ores in the absence of oxygen is called:
[RRB/RRC Group D, 2018]

A. Extraction
B. Calcination
C. Roasting
D. Corrosion

Q.21 which of the following is not correctly matched.
A. Aldehyde - OH
B. Amides - $CONH_2$
C. Amines - NH_2
D. Carboxylic Acid - COOH

Q.22 Atomic number of an element is:
[RRB/RRC Group D, 2018]

A. Number of electrons
B. Total number of protons and neutrons
C. Total number of electrons and neutrons
D. Number of neutrons

Q.23 What is 'amu' in the context of atoms and molecules?
[RRB/RRC Group D, 2018]

A. Avegadro Mass Unit
B. Atomic Unified Mass Unit
C. Atomic Mass Unit
D. Atomic Molecule Unit

Q.24 During which type of reaction, heat is evolved?
A. Exothermic reaction
B. Photochemical reaction
C. Endothermic reaction
D. None of the above

Q.25 What happens when sound enters from one medium to another?
A. Velocity changes
B. Velocity and wavelength changes
C. Frequency changes
D. All of the above

Q.26 What is the unit of acceleration?
[MP Jail Prahari, 2018]

A. km/sec   **B.** m/s^2 **C.** km/hr   **D.** kgm/s

Q.27 Ohm is a unit of measuring _______?
A. Resistance
B. Resistance
C. Current
D. None of the above

Q.28 Speed of sound wave is _____ in sea water concerning tap water.
A. Faster
B. Slower
C. The same for both medium
D. Sound cannot travel through water

Q.29 Which one of the following is commonly used for pulp bleaching in the paper industry?
A. Mild Sulphuric acid   **B.** Glucose isomerase
C. Hydrogen peroxide   **D.** Iodine and water

Q.30 Scientific name of Housefly is ___________.
A. Musca domestica   **B.** Acridotheres tristis
C. Grus leucogeranus   **D.** Pavo cristatus

Maths

Q.31 A person borrows certain amount of money at the rate of 2.5% per month. If he pays Rs. 13110 after 6 months to clear his dues then find the amount of interest paid by the person.
A. Rs. 1840   **B.** Rs. 1690   **C.** Rs. 1710   **D.** Rs. 1660

Q.32 In how many ways can 5 girls and 3 boys be seated in a row so that no two boys are together?
A. 14400   **B.** 12400   **C.** 14200   **D.** 15400

Q.33 In a right angled triangle, the square of the hypotenuse is twice the product of the other sides. The triangle is:
A. Equilateral
B. Isosceles
C. Of angles 30°, 60° and 90°
D. None of the above

Q.34 If the 8 digit number $267a3298$ is completely divisible by 11. What will be the digit at the place of 'a'?
[CTET Paper - I, 2022]

A. 7   **B.** 3   **C.** 5   **D.** 9

Q.35 Simplify the equation $\dfrac{(120 \div 20 \times y + 31)}{(8^2 - 6 \times 4 + y^2)} = 1$ and find the value of y.
[UP Police Sub Inspector, 2017]

A. 6   **B.** 3   **C.** 4   **D.** 2

Q.36 Mr. Mahesh buys a toy for Rs. 25 and sells it for Rs. 30. Find the gain percentage.
[RRB (NTPC), 2017]

A. 20%   **B.** 22%   **C.** 25%   **D.** 21%

Q.37 If 6 men can do a piece of work in 10 days. then 4 men will complete the same work in:
[Punjab Patwari, 2016]

A. 15 days   **B.** 20 days   **C.** 16 days   **D.** 14 days

Q.38 The radius of two right circular cylinders are in the ratio $3:2$ and the of their volumes is $27:16$. What is the ratio of their heights?

[SSC CGL, 2020]

A. $4:3$ **B.** $9:8$ **C.** $3:4$ **D.** $8:9$

Q.39 Direction : Select the number from among the given options that can replace the question mark (?) in the following series.

$1, 9, 25, 49, 81, ?$

A. 91   **B.** 111   **C.** 121   **D.** 94

Q.40 Find the smallest number divisible by all the odd numbers up to 15.

A. 19271   **B.** 34128   **C.** 45045   **D.** 29750

Q.41 The average weight of a certain number of persons in a group was 75.5 kg. Later on, 4 persons weighing 72.6 kg. 74 kg, 73.4 kg and 70 kg joined the group. As a result, the average weight of all persons in the group reduced by 500 g. The number of persons in the group, initially, was:

[SSC Constable (GD), 2019]

A. 20   **B.** 16   **C.** 18   **D.** 24

Q.42 Probability of Ankit passing in Maths, English and Science is $\frac{5}{8}, \frac{7}{9}$ and $\frac{3}{5}$ respectively. Find the probability of him failing in atleast two subjects.

A. $\frac{92}{360}$ **B.** $\frac{88}{360}$ **C.** $\frac{24}{90}$ **D.** $\frac{27}{90}$

Q.43 Two persons are standing on opposite ends of a field of length 1500 meters. If they are running towards each other at 10 km/hr and 20 km/hr respectively, after how much time will they meet each other?

A. 220 seconds   **B.** 120 seconds

C. 150 seconds   **D.** 180 seconds

Q.44 The slant height of a right circular cone is 10 m and its height is 8 m. Find the area of its curved surface.

A. $30\pi m^2$ **B.** $40\pi m^2$ **C.** $60\pi m^2$ **D.** $80\pi m^2$

Q.45 An certain number of students from school X appeared in an examination and 30% students failed. 150% more students than those from school X, appeared in the same examination from school Y. If 80% of the total number of students who appeared from X and Y passed, then what is the percentage of students who failed from Y?

[SSC CGL, 2020]

A. 24   **B.** 16   **C.** 20   **D.** 18

Logical Reasoning

Q.46 Direction: Four letter-clusters have been given, out of which three are alike in some manner and one is different. Select the letter-cluster that is different.

[SSC CHSL (Combined Higher Secondary Level), 2021]

A. KMPV   **B.** MIGF   **C.** BDMS   **D.** HKPT

Q.47 Seeta told Geeta, "The girl I met yesterday at the market was the youngest daughter of the brother-in-law of my friend, Namita's Mother." How is the girl related to Namita?

[UP Police ASI, 2018]

A. Sister   **B.** Daughter

C. Cousin   **D.** Aunt

Q.48 Two football players start running from the same point on the ground. Player A runs 10 km East, then turns to his left and runs 13 km. In the meanwhile, Player B runs 6 km South, then he runs 3 km East, the he turns to his left and runs 19 km. Where is Player A with respect to Player B?

A. 7 km West   **B.** 7 km East

C. 13 km East   **D.** 13 km West

Q.49 In a code language, if 'PLAYER' is coded as '119', then how will 'OPTIONS' be coded in the same language?

[SSC Selection Post Phase IX, 2019]

A. 150   **B.** 121   **C.** 131   **D.** 141

Q.50 Direction: Which letter cluster will replace the question mark (?) to complete the given series?

TRKM, XVIK, BZGI, ?, JHCE

[SSC Selection Post Phase IX, 2019]

A. FEGG   **B.** FDFG   **C.** FDEG   **D.** EDFH

// Smart Answer Sheet //

Correct   Indicates percentage of students who answered questions correctly.

Skipped   Indicates percentage of students who skipped questions.

Q.	Ans.	Correct / Skipped	Q.	Ans.	Correct / Skipped	Q.	Ans.	Correct / Skipped	Q.	Ans.	Correct / Skipped	Q.	Ans.	Correct / Skipped
1	B	29.59 % / 69.94 %	11	D	55.52 % / 30.79 %	21	A	89.88 % / 10.09 %	31	C	49.65 % / 40.49 %	41	A	10.26 % / 83.53 %
2	C	40.41 % / 58.02 %	12	C	67.7 % / 31.73 %	22	A	79.73 % / 12.3 %	32	A	86.15 % / 12.24 %	42	A	57.79 % / 38.2 %
3	C	79.17 % / 10.96 %	13	A	84.29 % / 13.13 %	23	C	88.62 % / 10.6 %	33	B	24.48 % / 73.73 %	43	D	65.8 % / 30.71 %
4	C	82.6 % / 13.83 %	14	B	46.23 % / 39.1 %	24	A	79.93 % / 13.16 %	34	C	55.96 % / 35.85 %	44	C	82.56 % / 11.78 %
5	A	23.77 % / 72.08 %	15	A	45.66 % / 43.86 %	25	B	61.04 % / 30.15 %	35	B	14.2 % / 84.15 %	45	B	28.4 % / 67.7 %
6	C	89.34 % / 10.07 %	16	C	44.54 % / 46.22 %	26	B	41.39 % / 30.23 %	36	A	40.04 % / 39.22 %	46	B	31.97 % / 67.1 %
7	D	22.47 % / 74.45 %	17	A	53.81 % / 39.75 %	27	A	86.2 % / 12.55 %	37	A	76.99 % / 13.08 %	47	C	18.57 % / 68.65 %
8	C	12.88 % / 70.83 %	18	A	88.41 % / 10.47 %	28	A	60.92 % / 34.63 %	38	C	51.33 % / 45.73 %	48	B	17.99 % / 74.59 %
9	C	81.87 % / 15.44 %	19	C	87.67 % / 10.38 %	29	C	61.93 % / 32.91 %	39	C	80.8 % / 17.23 %	49	A	66.33 % / 33.25 %
10	D	31.8 % / 67.53 %	20	B	84.03 % / 15.15 %	30	A	57.59 % / 31.39 %	40	C	57.45 % / 32.43 %	50	C	53.35 % / 38.7 %

Performance Analysis	
Avg. Score (%)	49.0%
Toppers Score (%)	63.0%
Your Score	

//Hints and Solutions//

1. Forbes' world's billionaires list for 2021 includes a record-breaking 2,755 billionaires.

- Jeff Bezos is the world's richest person for the fourth year running, worth $177 billion, up by $64 billion from 2020 as a result of surging Amazon shares.

- Elon Musk rocketed into the No. 2 spot with a $151 billion fortune, up by $126.4 billion in 2020 when he ranked No. 31.

Hence, the correct option is (B).

2. The Himalayan frontal faults is a series of reverse faults that demarcates the boundary of the Shivalik from the alluvial expanse of the Indo-Gangetic plains. Hence, Option 3 is NOT correct. The Himalayan frontal faults are also known as the Main Frontal Thrust (MFT).

The geology of the Himalayas is characterized by three major tectonic units:

- The Main Central Thrust (MCT)

- The Main Boundary Thrust (MBT)

- The Himalayan Frontal Thrust (HFT)/(MFT)

Main Central Thrust (MCT) Zone separates the Greater Himalayas in the north from lesser Himalayas in the south.

The Main Boundary Thrust (MBT) zone separates the outer Himalayas from the lesser Himalayas. The Himalayas are young fold mountains.

Hence, the correct option is (C).

3. Vishnu Sharma wrote the book 'Panchatantra'. It is one of the most famous non-religion books, translated in different languages and is known by different names in different cultures. The book was originally written in the Sanskrit language.

Hence, the correct option is (C).

4. The Guide is a 1958 novel written in English by the Indian author R. K. Narayan. Like most of his works, the novel is based on Malgudi, a fictional town in South India. The novel describes the transformation of the protagonist, Raju, from a tour guide to a spiritual guide and then one of the greatest holy men of India.

Hence, the correct option is (C).

5. Sabarimala is a famous Hindu temple located in the Periyar Tiger Sanctuary in Kerala. It has the largest annual pilgrimage in the world, which attracts about 2 crore devotees every year.

Sabarimala is a wonderful link between Shaivites and Vaishnavites. In Malayalam, 'Shabarimala' means mountain.

There is a temple of Lord Ayyappan in Sabarimala.
Hence, the correct option is (A).

6. The historic town named Gohana is located in the Sonipat district.

In ancient times, Gohana was considered a sacred place. Prithviraj Chauhan constructed a fort here, which was later destroyed by Muhammad Ghori after defeating Prithviraj in 1192.

Hence, the correct option is (C).

7. The Kalidas Samman is a prestigious arts award presented annually by the government of Madhya Pradesh in India. The award is named after Kalidasa, a renowned Classical Sanskrit writer of ancient India. The Kalidas Samman was first awarded in 1980.

Hence, the correct option is (D).

8. The correct pair of the country - capital are: Cuba - Havana

Cuba officially the Republic of Cuba is a country comprising the island of Cuba, as well as Isla de la Juventud and several minor archipelagos. Cuba is located where the northern Caribbean Sea, Gulf of Mexico, and Atlantic Ocean meet.

Havana is the capital and largest city of Cuba. The heart of the La Habana province, Havana is the country's main port and leading commercial center. The city has a population of 2.1 million inhabitants, and it spans a total of 781.58 km2 (301.77 sq mi) – making it the largest city by area, the most populous city, and the fourth largest metropolitan area in the Caribbean region.

Hence, the correct option is (C).

9. 19 August is World Humanitarian Day observed.

World Humanitarian Day is observed across the world on August 19 to pay tribute to workers who risk their lives in humanitarian services and to gather support for people affected by crises around the world. The day was designated by the UN General Assembly to commemorate the 19 August 2003 bombing of the United Nations headquarters in Baghdad, Iraq.

Hence, the correct option is (C).

10. Correct option is A - 4, B - 2, C - 1, D - 3

List-I	List-II
A. Kumaon Himalayas	4. Between the Sutlej and the Kali
B. Nepal Himalayas	2. Between the Kali and the Teesta
C. Punjab Himalayas	1. Between the Indus and the Sutlej
D. Assam Himalayas	3. Between the Teesta and the Brahmaputra

Hence, the correct option is (D).

11. Saha Institute of Nuclear Physics is located in West Bengal.

Saha Institute of Nuclear Physics (SINP) Research in the nuclear sciences, has its roots in the activities initiated and led by Prof. Meghnad Saha in 1940. The journey, which began with the design and construction of a small cyclotron and the measurement of a fission cross-section of 235U by a limited number of committed staff, has gone a long way in discovering the secrets of atoms, nucleus and molecules, using state-of-the-art techniques at present and involving various groups of people spread across the world. During this time, a 14.8 MeV neutron generator was also successfully installed in the Institute. The initial efforts in nuclear physics science, which began with the small cyclotron and the 14.8 MeV generator, were filled with the installation of the Variable Energy Cyclotron at VECC, Kolkata, West Bengal.

Hence, the correct option is (D).

12. The power of the Supreme Court of India to decide disputes between the Union and the States falls under its original jurisdiction.

Original jurisdiction means cases that can be directly considered by the Supreme Court without going to the lower courts before that. The Original Jurisdiction of the Supreme Court establishes it as an umpire in all disputes regarding federal matters.

Hence, the correct option is (C).

13. Koneru Humpy is an Indian Chess player from Gudivada, Andhra Pradesh, India.

- In 2002, she became the youngest woman ever to achieve the title of Grandmaster at the age of 15 years.
- In 2003 she was awarded Arjuna Award.
- In 2007 she was awarded Padma Shri.

She is an Asian games gold medalist winning 2 gold medals in the individual and mixed category that were held in Doha.

Hence, the correct option is (A).

14. Lord Canning (1856-62) was the Governor-General of India during the 1857 revolt. He served as the Governor-General of India from 1856 to 1862.

Lord Canning: During his tenure, the Government of India Act, 1858 was passed which created the office of the Viceroy to be held by the same person who was the Governor-General of India. Lord Canning also served as the first Viceroy of India.

The important events during his tenure include:

- Sepoy mutiny of 1857, which he was able to suppress successfully.
- The passing of the Indian Councils Act, 1861 introduced a portfolio system in India.

Hence, the correct option is (B).

15. The main objective behind introducing the Rowlatt Act was to curb the growing nationalist upsurge in the country.

The Rowlatt Act: This act authorised the British government to arrest anybody suspected of terrorist activities. It also authorised the government to detain such people arrested for up to 2 years without trial. It empowered the police to search a place without a warrant.

Hence, the correct option is (A).

16. The maximum yield of ATP from the complete oxidation of sucrose via aerobic respiration is 60.

Glycolysis produces only 4 ATP per sucrose metabolized, compared to 60 ATP per sucrose that are produced by aerobic respiration. Sucrose consist of Glucose and Fructose. On oxidation, Glucose gives 36 ATP and Fructose gives 24 ATP of energy. That's why the total energy given out by Sucrose is 60 ATP.

Hence, the correct option is (C).

17. The binomial system of classification was given by Carolus Linnaeus.

Carolus Linnaeus (1707- 1778), also known after his ennoblement as Carl von Linn was a Swedish botanist, zoologist, and physician who formalised binomial nomenclature, the modern system of naming organisms.

Linnaeus developed a simple two-part naming system. The first part of the name indicates the group to which the particular plant belongs (now known as the genus), and the second part indicates the species. For example, human beings belong to the genus Homo, and our species is sapiens - so the scientific name is Homo sapiens. This nomenclature system was given by him in his book 'Species Plantarum'. He published a book naming over 7,700 species using this binomial system. He is known as the "father of modern taxonomy".

Hence, the correct option is (A).

18. According to Sir J.C. Bose, an Indian scientist, ascent of sap takes place due to the "pulsatory activity" of living cells of the innermost cortical layer.

Sir J.C. Bose (1923) said that living cells of the innermost layer of the cortex of a plant, just outside the endodermis are in rhythmic pulsations. Such pulsations are responsible for pumping the water in an upward direction. According to him, the pulsatory cells pump the water into vessels.

Hence, the correct option is (A).

19. TSH, STH and ADH are hormones of the pituitary gland.

The anterior pituitary gland produces the following hormones and releases them into the bloodstream:

- Thyroid-stimulating hormone (TSH), which stimulates the thyroid gland to secrete thyroid hormones.
- Growth hormone (STH), which regulates growth, metabolism, and body composition.
- Anti-diuretic hormone (also called vasopressin (ADH)), which controls water balance and blood pressure.

Hence, the correct option is (C).

20. Heating of ores in the absence of oxygen is called Calcination.

Calcination:

- It is the process of heating the ore below its melting point absence of air to remove volatile impurities.
- It is the process of converting ore into an oxide by heating it strongly.
- In calcination, ores are heated strongly in the absence of air(Oxygen) to convert Metal Carbonates into Metal Oxides and Carbon Di Oxide.

Hence, the correct option is (B).

21. Aldehyde - OH is not a correct match.

- The -OH functional group is the hydroxyl group. OH is alcohol consisting of an oxygen atom bonded to a hydrogen atom.
- An amide functional group consists of a carbonyl group bonded to a nitrogen. In amides, two hydrogen atoms are bonded to the nitrogen ($-CONH_2$).

- Amines are compounds and functional groups that contain a basic nitrogen atom with a lone pair. NH_2 belongs to this group.

- Carboxylic acid is a homologous series in which the compounds contain a functional group called the carboxyl group (-COOH).

Hence, the correct option is (A).

22. Atomic number of an element is Number of electrons.

The total number of electrons present in an atom represents the atomic number of a particular atom.

The number of electrons = number of protons

Atomic Number = Number of Protons = Number of Electrons

The atomic number uniquely identifies a chemical element.

Hence, the correct option is (A).

23. Atomic Mass Unit is the full form of amu.

One Atomic Mass Unit: It is defined as the mass equal to one-twelfth the mass of one carbon- 12 atom.

And $1 \text{ amu} = 1.66056 \times 10^{-24}$ g

Hence, the correct option is (C).

24. Exothermic reactions are reactions or processes that release energy, usually in the form of heat or light. In an exothermic reaction, energy is released because the total energy of the products is less than the total energy of the reactants. In the presence of water, a strong acid will dissociate quickly and release heat, so it is an exothermic reaction. Other examples are the combustion of fuels, some polymerization reactions, decomposition of organic waste, etc.

Hence, the correct option is (A).

25. The velocity of sound is directly proportional to the wavelength. Thus, if the velocity of sound doubles when it travels from one medium to another, its wavelength also doubles.

The frequency of sound depends upon the source of the sound, not the medium of propagation. Therefore, it does not change. Hence, the correct option is (B).

26. Acceleration (a) is defined as the rate of change of velocity. Velocity is a vector quantity, and therefore acceleration is also a vector quantity. The SI unit of acceleration is meters/second^2 (m/s^2).
Hence, the correct option is (B).

27. The ohm is the SI unit of electrical resistance. The electrical resistance of an object is the measure of its obstruction to the flow of electric current. It mainly depends on the material it is made of, the cross-sectional area of a conductor, length and temperature. The resistance of a conductor of unit cross-sectional area and unit length is known as Resistivity. The unit of resistivity is ohm-metre.

Hence, the correct option is (A).

28. Speed of sound depends upon bulk modulus of material and density of the material, as we know that Salt water is about 2-4% denser than fresh water. But it also has a bulk modulus that's about 9% greater than that of fresh water. So overall the speed of sound in sea water is faster than tap water/fresh water.

Higher bulk modulus means the faster speed of sound. So, in sea water sound travel faster than tap water.

Hence, the correct option is (A).

29. Hydrogen peroxide is used in pulp bleaching in the paper industry. It's a colorless liquid and is slightly more viscous than water. It is used as an oxidizer, bleaching agent, and disinfectant.

Bleaching of wood pulp is done to lighten its color and also to whiten the pulp. The primary product obtained from wood pulp is paper, and the whiteness of paper is an important characteristic.

Hence, the correct option is (C).

30. The scientific name of Housefly is Musca domestica.

Birds name	Scientific name
Common myna	Acridotheres tristis
Siberian crane	Grus leucogeranus
Peacock	Pavo cristatus
House sparrow	Passer domesticus

Hence, the correct option is (A)

31. Given:

Rate of interest $= 2.5\%$ per month

Amount paid after 6 months $=$ Rs. 13110

Amount, $A = P + SI$

Simple interest, $SI = \dfrac{P \times R \times T}{100}$

Where $P \to$ Principal, $R \to$ rate of interest, $T \to$ time

Suppose the sum borrowed be Rs. x

$$SI = \dfrac{x \times 2.5 \times 6}{100} = 0.15x$$

$$A = x + 0.15x = 1.15x$$

$$1.15x = 13110$$

$$\Rightarrow x = 11400$$

$\Rightarrow$ Amount of interest $= 0.15 \times 11400$

$=$ Rs. 1710

Hence, the correct option is (C).

32. Let us first seat the 5 girls. This can be done in 5! ways. For each such arrangement, the three boys can be seated only at the cross marked places.

$$\times G \times G \times G \times G \times G \times$$

There are 6 crosses marked places and the three boys can be seated in $^6P_3$ ways.

Thus, by the multiplication principle, the total number of ways,

$$= 5! \times {}^6P_3 = 5! \times \dfrac{6!}{3!} \qquad \left[\because \text{Using } {}^nC_r = \dfrac{n!}{r!(n-r)!}\right]$$

$$= 4 \times 5 \times 2 \times 3 \times 4 \times 5 \times 6 = 14400.$$

Hence, the correct option is (A).

33. Given,

Right-angled triangle, the square of the hypotenuse is twice the product of the other sides.

As we know,

A triangle whose two sides are equal, called isosceles triangle.

A triangle whose one angle is equal to 90°, called right angled triangle.

Let given sides are p, b and h where p = perpendicular, b = base and h = hypotenuse.

Now, $p^2 + b^2 = h^2$ ---- (1) [Right angles triangle property]

According to question,

$h^2 = 2 \times p \times b$...(2)

Putting (2) in (1), we get

$P^2 + b^2 = 2pb$

$\Rightarrow p^2 + b^2 - 2pb = 0$

$\Rightarrow (p - b)2 = 0$

$\Rightarrow p = b$

The other two sides are equal. Therefore, the triangle is an isosceles triangle.

Hence, the correct option is (B).

34. Given,

The 8 digit number $= 267a3298$

As we know,

Divisibility rule of 11**:** A number will be divisible by 11 if the difference between the sum of digits at even places and the sum of digits at odd places is divisible by 11.

The given 8 digit number $= 267a3298$

The sum of digits at odd places $= 6 + a + 2 + 8$

$= 16 + a$

The sum of digits at even places $= 2 + 7 + 3 + 9$

$= 21$

Now, $21 - (16 + a) = (5 - a)$ is divisible by 0 or 11.

From the four option, if we put $a = 5,$

The $(5 - a)$ will be divisible by 0

The number will be 26753298

$\therefore$ The digit at the place of 'a' will be $5.$

Hence, the correct option is (C).

35. Given:

Equation $= \dfrac{(120 \div 20 \times y + 31)}{(8^2 - 6 \times 4 + y^2)} = 1$

$\Rightarrow \dfrac{(120 \div 20 \times y + 31)}{(8^2 - 6 \times 4 + y^2)} = 1$

$\Rightarrow (120 \div 20 \times y + 31) = (8^2 - 6 \times 4 + y^2)$

$\Rightarrow 6y + 31 = (64 - 24 + y2)$

$\Rightarrow 6y = y^2 + 40 - 31$

$\Rightarrow y^2 - 6y + 9 = 0$

$\Rightarrow y^2 - 3y - 3y + 9 = 0$

$\Rightarrow y(y - 3) - 3(y - 3) = 0$

$\Rightarrow (y - 3) (y - 3) = 0$

$\Rightarrow y - 3 = 0$

$\Rightarrow y = 3$

$\therefore$ The value of y is 3.

Hence, the correct option is (B).

36. Given,

Cost price of toy $=$ Rs. 25

Selling price of toy $=$ Rs. 30

As we know,

Profit $=$ Selling price $-$ Cost price

Profit $=$ Rs. $(30 - 25) =$ Rs. 5

Profit percentage $= \left(\dfrac{\text{Profit}}{\text{Cost price}}\right) \times 100$

Profit percentage $= \left(\dfrac{5}{25}\right) \times 100 = 20\%$

So, the gain percentage is 20%.

Hence, the correct option is (A).

37. Given:

Time taken by 6 men to complete a piece of work $= 10$ days

If a person takes x days to complete a work, part of the work completed by him in one-day $= \dfrac{1}{x}$

Time taken by 1 man $= 6 \times 10 = 60$ days

$\therefore$ The time taken by 4 men to complete the work $= \dfrac{60}{4} = 15$ days

Hence, the correct option is (A).

38. Given:

Ratio of radius of two right circular cylinders $= 3:2$

Ratio of their volumes $= 27:16$

As we know,

Volume of right circular cylinder $= \pi r^2 h$

let the height of both cylinder be h_1 and h_2

$$\Rightarrow \frac{\pi 3^2 \, h_1}{\pi 2^2 \, h_2} = 27:16$$

$$\Rightarrow \frac{9 \, h_1}{4 \, h_2} = 27:16$$

$$\Rightarrow 4 \, h_1 = 3 \, h_2$$

$$\Rightarrow h_1 : h_2 = 3:4$$

$\therefore$ The ratio of their heights is $3:4$.

Hence, the correct option is (C).

39. The logic followed here is:

$$1^2 = 1$$

$$3^2 = 9$$

$$5^2 = 25$$

$$7^2 = 49$$

$$9^2 = 81$$

$$11^2 = 121$$

Therefore, 121 is the correct answer.

Hence, the correct option is (C).

40. The smallest number which is divisible by all the odd numbers up to 15 would be the L.C.M of all the odd numbers up to 15.

$\therefore$ Required number $=$ L.C.M of $1,3,5,7,9,11,13,15$

$$= 45045$$

Hence, the correct option is (C).

41. Given:

Average weight $= 75.5kg$

Weight of new people $= 72.6kg, 74kg, 73.4kg$ and $70kg$

New Average weight $= 75kg$

FORMULA USED:

Total weight $=$ Average weight $\times$ Number of persons

CALCULATION:

Let the initial number of People be x

Total weight initially $= 75.5x$

New total weight $= 75.5x + 72.6 + 74 + 73.4 + 70 = 75.5x + 290$

According to question

$$\Rightarrow \frac{(75.5x + 290)}{(x+4)} = 75$$

$$\Rightarrow 75.5x + 290 = 75(x + 4)$$

$$\Rightarrow 75.5x + 290 = 75x + 300$$

$$\Rightarrow 0.5x = 10$$

$$x = 20$$

$\therefore$ The number of persons in the group, initially, was 20

Hence, the correct option is (A).

42. Given,

Probability of two or more incidents happening when they are not related to each other $= P_1 \times P_2 \times P_3$

We know that:

$$P' = 1 - P$$

P' is the probability of a thing not happening and P is of that happening.

Probability of Ankit failing in atleast two subject = Probability of him failing in 2 subject + Probability of him failing in 3 subjects.

Probability of failing in Maths $= 1 - \dfrac{5}{8} = \dfrac{3}{8}$

Probability of failing in English $= 1 - \dfrac{7}{9} = \dfrac{2}{9}$

Probability of failing in Science $= 1 - \dfrac{3}{5} = \dfrac{2}{5}$

Probability of him failing in 2 subject

$$= \frac{3}{8} \times \frac{2}{9} \times \frac{3}{5} + \frac{5}{8} \times \frac{2}{9} \times \frac{2}{5} + \frac{3}{8} \times \frac{7}{9} \times \frac{2}{5}$$

$$= \frac{(18+20+42)}{360}$$

$$= \frac{80}{360}$$

Probability of him failing in three subjects $= \dfrac{3}{8} \times \dfrac{2}{5} \times \dfrac{2}{9} = \dfrac{12}{360}$

Required probability $= \dfrac{80}{360} + \dfrac{12}{360}$

$$= \frac{92}{360}$$

Hence, the correct option is (A).

43. Relative speed, if opposite directions = (x + y) km/hr

Relative speed of both men, if they running opposite direction.

$$= 10 + 20 = 30 \text{ km/hr}$$

$$= 30 \times \frac{5}{18} \text{ m/s}$$

Time taken to meet each other $= \dfrac{1500}{\left(30 \times \frac{5}{18}\right)} = 180$ seconds

Hence, the correct option is (D).

44. length $(l) = 10\,m$

Height $(h) = 8\,m$

So, $r = \sqrt{l^2 - h^2} = \sqrt{(10)^2 - 8^2} = 6\,m$

$\therefore$ Curved surface area

$\pi r l = (\pi \times 6 \times 10)m^2$

$= 60\pi m^2$

Hence, the correct option is (C).

45. Given:

Students failed in school X $= 30\%$

Number of students in school Y $= 150\%$ more than number of students in school X

Students passed in both schools $= 80\%$

Let number of students in school X be $100x$.

Number of failed students in school X $= 30\%$ of $100x = 30x$

Number of passes students in school Y $= (100x - 30x) = 70x$

Number of students in school Y $= 100x + 150\%$ of $100x$

$= 100x + 150x = 250x$

Total number of students in school X and school Y $= 100x + 250x = 350x$

Number of passes students in both schools $= 80\%$ of $350x = 280x$

So, number of passed students in school Y $= 280x - 70x = 210x$

Number of failed students in school Y $= 250x - 210x = 40x$

Percentage of failed students in school Y $= \left(\dfrac{40x}{250x}\right) \times 100\%$

$= 16\%$

$\therefore$ The percentage of students who failed from school Y is 16%.

Hence, the correct option is (B).

46. Table show alphabet serial number:

Alpha bets	A	B	C	D	E	F	G	H	I	J	K	L	M

Positional value	1	2	3	4	5	6	7	8	9	10	11	12	13
Positional value	26	25	24	23	22	21	20	19	18	17	16	15	14
Alpha bets	Z	Y	X	W	V	U	T	S	R	Q	P	O	N

The pattern followed is,

K(11) M(13) P(16) V(22)	Alphabets in ascending order and all alphabets are consonants.
M(13) **I(9)** G(7) F(6)	Alphabets in descending order and one alphabet is vowel.
B(2) D(4) M(13) S(19)	Alphabets in ascending order and all alphabets are consonants.
H(8) K(11) P(16) T(20)	Alphabets in ascending order and all alphabets are consonants.

All follow the same pattern, except 'MIGF'.

Therefore, "MIGF" is the odd one.

Hence, the correct option is (B).

47. By using the symbols in the table given below, we can draw the following family tree:

Symbol in Diagram	Meaning
◯	Female
▢	Male
═══	Married Couple
───	Siblings
│	Difference of A Generation

There can be 2 possibilities:

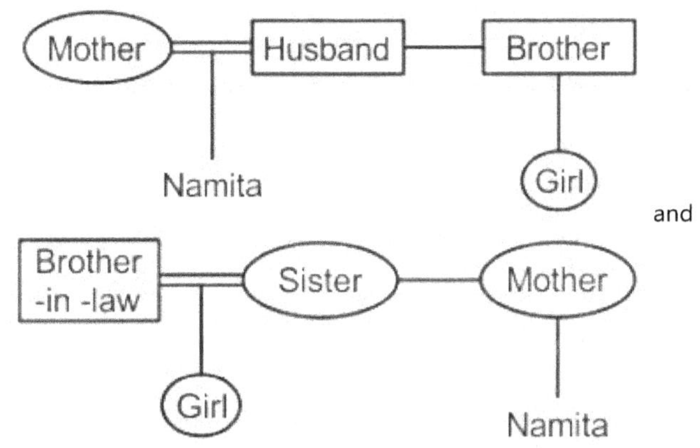

and

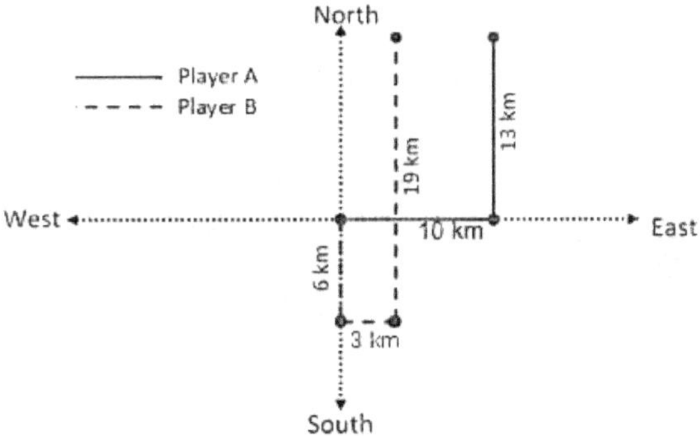

Clearly, the girl is Cousin of Namita in both the cases.

Hence, the correct option is (C).

48. We have drawn the following figure according to the information given in the question,

From the above figure, player A is 7 km east of B.

Hence, the correct option is (B).

49. According to the English alphabet series and its positional value:

Alpha bets	A	B	C	D	E	F	G	H	I	J	K	L	M
Positional value	1	2	3	4	5	6	7	8	9	10	11	12	13
Positional value	26	25	24	23	22	21	20	19	18	17	16	15	14
Alpha bets	Z	Y	X	W	V	U	T	S	R	Q	P	O	N

The pattern followed is,
PLAYER:
P + L + A + Y + E + R → 16 + 12 + 1 + 25 + 5 + 18 = 77
So, 77 + 42 = 119
Similarly,
OPTIONS:
O + P + T + I + O + N + S → 15 + 16 + 20 + 9 + 15 + 14 + 19 = 108
So, 108 + 42 = 150

Hence, the correct option is (A).

50. The pattern followed is,

In TRKM, XVIK, BZGI and JHCE, there is a gap of one alphabet between (1st, 2nd) and (3rd, 4th) alphabet of each group from left end.

Therefore,

Option (A): In FEGG, two alphabets are repeated.

Option (B): In FDFG, there is no gap between F and G.

Option (C): In FDEG, there is a gap of one alphabet.

Option (D): EDFH, there is no gap between E and D.

Hence, the correct option is (C).

General Knowledge

Q.1 Soj-e-Vatan is the book written by:
[Uttarakhand Public Service Commission (UKPSC), 2011]

A.   Mahadevi Verma

B.   Premchand

C.   Sumitra Nandan Pant

D.   Suryakant Tripathi 'Nirala'

Q.2 The author of the book 'Unstoppable: My Life So Far' is:

A. Maria Sharapova

B. Anirudh krishna

C. Rajal Gupta

D. Rajeev Maharishi

Q.3 15 January is celebrated as the -

A. Republic Day

B. Ugadhi

C. Teachers' Day

D. Army Day

Q.4 Where is the White Desert of India situated?

A. Kutch

B. Jodhpur

C. Bikaner

D. Jaisalmer

Q.5 The term 'Duckworth-Lewis' is associated with which sport?

A. Cricket   **B.** Squash   **C.** Hockey   **D.** Tennis

Q.6 What is the capital of Bulgaria?

A. Beirut

B. Bucharest

C. Sofia

D. Tashkent

Q.7 Find out the correct sequence of planetary winds found from the equator to pole:
[Maharashtra Public Service Commission, 2018]

A.   Westerlies, Trade winds, Polar winds

B.   Trade winds, Westerlies, Polar winds

C.   Trade winds, Polar winds, Westerlies

D.   Polar winds, Westerlies, Trade winds

Q.8 Which major river flows between the Vindhya and the Satpura Mountain ranges?

A. Narmada   **B.** Ken   **C.** Tapti   **D.** Sons

Q.9 Which is correctly matched?
[Rajasthan Teachers Eligibility Test - Level 1 Primary Level (RTET), 2017]

A.   Bombay Natural History Society – New Delhi

B.   Botanical Survey of India - Kolkata

C.   Wildlife Institute of India - Coimbatore

D.   National Botanical Research Institute - Jodhpur

Q.10 Ranbir Singh Bist is related to:
[Uttarakhand Public Service Commission (UKPSC), 2011]

A. Medicine

B. Painting

C. Military

D. Police

Q.11 Keisabadi is a popular dance form of _________.

A. Kerala

B. Gujarat

C. Maharashtra

D. Odisha

Q.12 Who was the first Indian to receive the Magsaysay Award for community leadership?

A. Indira Gandhi

B. TN Sheshan

C. Kiran Bedi

D. Vinoba Bhave

Q.13 In which of the following cases did the Supreme Court of India pronounce the verdict that the basic structure of the constitution cannot be amended by the parliament?
[Maharashtra Public Service Commission, 2018]

A.   Shankari Prasad vs Union of India

B.   Golaknath vs State of Punjab

C.   Kesavananda Bharti vs State of Kerala

D.   Minerva Mills Ltd. vs Union of India

Q.14 Famous Cave temples of Elephanta are ascribed to:
[Uttarakhand Public Service Commission (UKPSC), 2011]

A. Chalukyas

B. Cholas

C. Pallavas

D. Rashtrakoots

Q.15 Subhas Chandra Bose started the 'Azad Hind Radio' in which of the following countries?
[Officers Training Academy (OTA), 2018], [Indian Military Academy (IMA), 2018]

A. Japan

B. Austria

C. Germany

D. Malaysia

General Science

Q.16 Food chain is:
[Officers Training Academy (OTA), 2019], [Indian Military Academy (IMA), 2019]

A.   Relationship between autotrophic organisms.

B.   Exchange of genetic material between two organisms.

C.   Passage of food (and thus energy) from one organism to another.

D.   Modern enterpreneur establishment providing food outlets.

Q.17 Which one of the following is active transport?
[Officers Training Academy (OTA), 2019], [Indian Military Academy (IMA), 2019]

A.   It is the movement of a substance against a diffusion gradient with the use of energy from respiration.

B.   It is the movement of a substance against a diffusion gradient without the use of energy.

C.   It is the movement of a substance against a diffusion gradient with the use of energy from photosynthesis.

D.   It is the movement of a substance along a diffusion gradient with the use of energy from respiration.

Q.18 Chlorophyll in photosynthetic prokaryotic bacteria is associated with _______.

[*Officers Training Academy (OTA), 2019*], [*Indian Military Academy (IMA), 2019*]

A. Plastids
B. Membranous vesicles
C. Nucleoids
D. Chromosomes

Q.19 Which one of the following body parts/organs of the human body does not have smooth muscles?
[*Officers Training Academy (OTA), 2019*], [*Indian Military Academy (IMA), 2019*]

A. Ureters
B. Iris of eye
C. Bronchi of lungs
D. Biceps

Q.20 Which one of the following cell organelles is known as 'suicide bags' of a cell?
[*Officers Training Academy (OTA), 2019*], [*Indian Military Academy (IMA), 2019*]

A. Lysosomes
B. Plastids
C. Endoplasmic reticulum
D. Mitochondria

Q.21 Hydraulic lift works on which law?
A. Hooke's law
B. Pascal's Law
C. Newton's First Law of Motion
D. Archimedes' Law

Q.22 What is the SI unit of pressure?
A. Newton
B. Weber
C. Henry
D. Pascal

Q.23 Which one of the following is monatomic?
[*Officers Training Academy (OTA), 2019*], [*Indian Military Academy (IMA), 2019*]

A. Hydrogen
B. Sulphur
C. Phosphorus
D. Helium

Q.24 Employing Chromatography, one cannot separate:
[*Officers Training Academy (OTA), 2019*], [*Indian Military Academy (IMA), 2019*]

A. Radio-isotopes
B. Colours from a dye
C. Pigments from a natural colour
D. Drugs from blood

Q.25 RADAR is used for:
A. Locating submerged submarines
B. Receiving signals in a radio receiver
C. Locating geostationary satellites
D. Detecting and locating the position of objects such as airplanes

Q.26 Which of the following magnetic property of materials is said to be the universal property?
A. Diamagnetism
B. Paramagnetism
C. Ferromagnetism
D. Electromagnetism

Q.27 In which of the following devices, electrical energy is converted into mechanical energy?

A. Battery
B. Electric Generator
C. Electric Motor
D. Computer

Q.28 Which metal is protected by a layer of its own oxide?
A. Gold
B. Aluminum
C. Copper
D. Iron

Q.29 Which of the following metals can be extracted by smelting?
A. Aluminum
B. Magnesium
C. Iron
D. Silver

Q.30 Which one of the following element's isotope is used in the treatment of cancer?
[*UPSC NDA, 2020*]

A. Uranium
B. Cobalt
C. Sodium
D. Iodine

Maths

Q.31 If a certain amount doubles itself in 5 years at simple interest then find the rate of interest per annum at which the sum was invested?
A. 12.50%
B. 15%
C. 16.66%
D. 20%

Q.32 If $^9P_5 + 5 \cdot {}^9P_4 = {}^{10}P_r$ then the value of r is:
A. 2
B. 3
C. 5
D. 7

Q.33 If 790368p5 is divisible by 9 then what is the value of p ?
A. 8
B. 7
C. 6
D. 5

Q.34 Direction: What will come in place of question mark (?) in the following question:
$$(37)^2 = ? + [(11\sqrt{3} + 5\sqrt{3}) \times (9\sqrt{3} + 11\sqrt{3})]$$
A. 411
B. 415
C. 409
D. 406

Q.35 Amit bought an article for Rs. 310 and sold it at a loss of 25%. With this money, he bought another article and sold it at a gain of 40% What was his overall gain or loss percent?
[*SSC MTS, 2019*]

A. Loss of 4%
B. Gain 5%
C. Gain 8%
D. Loss of 2.5%

Q.36 20% of a number is 40% of another number. What is the ratio of the first number to second number?
A. 2 : 7
B. 2 : 1
C. 2 : 3
D. 2 : 5

Q.37 Direction : Identify the number that DOES NOT belong to the following series.
$$2,9,28,64,126,217,344,513$$
A. 28
B. 513
C. 344
D. 64

Q.38 Find the highest common factor of $\frac{25}{9}$ and $\frac{5}{18}$?
A. $\frac{5}{18}$
B. $\frac{5}{8}$
C. $\frac{12}{8}$
D. $\frac{18}{5}$

Q.39 The average of five consecutive odd numbers is 51. What is the difference between the highest and lowest number?
A. 3
B. 7
C. 8
D. 11

Q.40 A die is thrown once. The probability of getting an even number and a multiple of 3 is:

A. $\frac{1}{2}$ **B.** $\frac{1}{5}$ **C.** $\frac{1}{6}$ **D.** $\frac{1}{3}$

Q.41 The value of two adjacent angles of a quadrilateral are $125°$ and $35°$ and the other two angles are equal. Find out the value of equal angles.

A. $135°$ **B.** $80°$ **C.** $100°$ **D.** $90°$

Q.42 Heena and Karan together complete a work in 12 days, if Heena works alone, she completes it in 18 days. Karan alone can complete it in how many days?

A. 12 days **B.** 36 days **C.** 14 days **D.** 34 days

Q.43 A car travels some distance at a speed of 8 km/hr and returns at a speed of 12 km/hr. If the total time taken by the car is 15 hours, then what is the distance (in km)?

A. 48 **B.** 60 **C.** 56 **D.** 72

Q.44 Two cones have their heights in the ratio 1 : 3. If the radii of their bases are in the ratio 3 : 1, then the ratio of their volumes will be:

[Indian Military Academy (IMA), 2018]

A. 1 : 1 **B.** 2 : 1 **C.** 3 : 1 **D.** 9 : 1

Q.45 If 40% of a number is 112. Then, find the 15% of a number.

A. 42 **B.** 21 **C.** 54 **D.** 56

Logical Reasoning

Q.46 A series is given, with one term missing. Choose the alternative from the given ones that will complete the series.
BMY, DNW, FOU, ?

A. GHO **B.** HGO **C.** HPS **D.** HPT

Q.47 Direction: In the following question, select the odd word from the given alternatives.

A. Nestle **B.** Café Coffee Day
C. InMobi **D.** Peter England

Q.48 Direction: On the basis of the given information, answer the following question.
X and Y are brothers. R is the father of Y. S is the brother of T and maternal uncle of X. What is T to R?

A. Mother **B.** Wife **C.** Sister **D.** Brother

Q.49 Rahul put his timepiece on the table in such a way that at 6 P.M. hour hand points to North. In which direction the minute hand will point at 9.15 P.M.?

A. South-East **B.** South
C. North **D.** West

Q.50 If FLOWER is coded as 14 and DISTANCE is coded as 18, then how will BUREAUCRAT be coded as?

A. 22 **B.** 18 **C.** 20 **D.** 28

// Smart Answer Sheet //

Correct   Indicates percentage of students who answered questions correctly.

Skipped   Indicates percentage of students who skipped questions.

Q.	Ans.	Correct / Skipped	Q.	Ans.	Correct / Skipped	Q.	Ans.	Correct / Skipped	Q.	Ans.	Correct / Skipped	Q.	Ans.	Correct / Skipped
1	B	80.92 % / 17.96 %	11	D	57.72 % / 31.38 %	21	B	45.64 % / 32.54 %	31	D	59.7 % / 34.25 %	41	C	18.92 % / 74.22 %
2	A	62.64 % / 30.95 %	12	D	29.35 % / 68.53 %	22	D	81.98 % / 10.56 %	32	C	89.73 % / 10.26 %	42	B	11.96 % / 70.3 %
3	D	85.93 % / 10.1 %	13	C	17.63 % / 73.18 %	23	D	51.5 % / 42.39 %	33	B	84.7 % / 13.27 %	43	D	62.41 % / 32.87 %
4	A	42.34 % / 41.45 %	14	D	65.27 % / 31.52 %	24	A	42.69 % / 49.48 %	34	C	27.89 % / 70.22 %	44	C	50.91 % / 47.71 %
5	A	23.73 % / 73.65 %	15	C	19.56 % / 69.6 %	25	D	49.42 % / 40.5 %	35	B	63.34 % / 35.6 %	45	A	29.93 % / 69.37 %
6	C	20.56 % / 72.55 %	16	C	78.02 % / 18.38 %	26	A	26.87 % / 72.61 %	36	B	55.95 % / 37.27 %	46	C	40.34 % / 54.17 %
7	B	51.59 % / 44.93 %	17	A	60.24 % / 37.0 %	27	C	28.59 % / 67.5 %	37	D	78.1 % / 14.23 %	47	A	78.69 % / 15.27 %
8	A	53.13 % / 34.58 %	18	B	13.98 % / 70.0 %	28	B	66.37 % / 30.19 %	38	A	66.61 % / 32.61 %	48	B	76.4 % / 12.26 %
9	B	40.18 % / 30.15 %	19	D	47.74 % / 43.39 %	29	C	24.78 % / 67.0 %	39	C	76.94 % / 19.05 %	49	D	50.75 % / 44.46 %
10	B	83.09 % / 13.87 %	20	A	85.28 % / 13.94 %	30	B	11.54 % / 74.32 %	40	C	60.18 % / 36.17 %	50	A	25.76 % / 67.99 %

Performance Analysis

Avg. Score (%)	73.0%
Toppers Score (%)	75.0%
Your Score	

//Hints and Solutions//

1. Soj-e-Vatan is the book written by Premchand.

Dhanpat Rai Srivastava, better known by his pen name Premchand, was an Indian writer famous for his modern Hindustani literature. Premchand was a pioneer of Hindi and Urdu social fiction. He was one of the first authors to write about caste hierarchies and the plights of women and labourers prevalent in the society of late 1880s. He is one of the most celebrated writers of the Indian subcontinent, and is regarded as one of the foremost Hindi writers of the early twentieth century. He published his first collection of five short stories in 1907 in a book called Soz-e-Watan.

Hence, the correct option is (B).

2. The book Unstoppable: My Life So Far, written by Maria Sharapova, was released in September 2017. It is described in this book. How Sharapova became a tennis star from an ordinary person. And what problems they had to face in reaching this place, Mmaria Yuriyavna Sharapova was born on 19 April 1987 in the province of Siberia, Russia. Sharapova, who won the 2004 Wimbledon title at the age of just 17, won the US Open in 2006 and became the world's number one player, Sharapova won the Australian Open title in 2008 and the French Open title in 2012.

Hence, the correct option is (A).

3. Army Day is celebrated on 15 January every year in India as it is on this historic day that General K. M. Cariappa became the first Indian to take charge of the Indian Army in 1949.

Hence, the correct option is (D).

4. The White Desert of India is situated in Kutch, Gujarat. It is the largest salt desert in the world. The White Desert in Kutch is also known as the Great Rann of Kutch. One of the hottest regions in India, the desert is the site of the popular Rann Festival in Gujarat which is held from November to February every year. Camel rides, hot air balloon safari, jeep safaris, and watching cultural dances are popular things to do in the White Desert in Kutch.

Hence, the correct option is (A).

5. The Duckworth-Lewis (DLS) method is used in cricket to calculate the target score for a match interrupted by weather or other circumstances. It was created by two Britishers-Frank Duckworth and Tony Lewis.

- The method was formerly known as the Duckworth–Lewis method and it was adopted officially by the ICC in 1999.

- Tony Lewis, one of the men behind the Duckworth-Lewis-Stern method used in weather-affected limited-overs cricket matches passed away in April 2020.

Hence, the correct option is (A).

6. Sofia is the capital of Bulgaria and it is the 15th largest city in the European Union with a population of around 13 million people. It has been ranked by the Globalization and World Cities Research Network as a Beta city. Many of the major universities, cultural institutions, and commercial companies of Bulgaria are concentrated in Sofia.

Hence, the correct option is (C).

7. The correct sequence of planetary winds found from the equator to pole is Trade winds, Westerlies, Polar winds.

Trade winds:

- These are permanent winds flowing from east to west.
- They flow in the Earth's equatorial region.
- Between $30°N$ and $30°S$ latitudes.

Westerlies:

- These are prevailing winds that flow from the west towards the east.
- They flow in the Earth's middle latitudes
- Between 30 and 60 degrees latitude.
- They are also called anti-trade winds.

Polar winds:

- It is a prevailing wind blowing from the east.
- These winds are also called polar easterlies.
- Between 60 and 90 degrees latitude.

Hence, the correct option is (B).

8. Narmada river flows between the Vindhya and the Satpura Mountain ranges.

Vindhya Range is composed of horizontally bedded sedimentary rocks of ancient age. The Vindhyas ranges are continued eastwards as the Bharner and Kaimur hills.

Satpura Range is a series of Seven Mountains so it is called a Satpura range. Satpura Range contains some worked manganese and coal deposits in its southeastern flanks. It is largely forested, dissected plateau country, and it contains valuable teak stands in the west.

Hence, the correct option is (A).

9. Botanical Survey of India: Botanical Survey of India (BSI) located in Kolkata, West Bengal, India.

- It was founded on 13 February 1890, by the Government of India Ministry of Environment, Forest and Climate Change.

- It is an organization for the survey, research and conservation of plant wealth of India, flora and endangered species of India.

- It also includes collecting and maintaining germplasm and gene bank of endangered, patent and vulnerable plant species.

Hence, the correct option is (B).

10. Ranbir Singh Bist is related to painting.

Ranbir Singh Bisht was an Indian painter and the Principal of the College of Fine Arts, Lucknow University. He was also fellow of the UP State Lalit Kala Akademi (184) and UNESCO. The Government of India awarded him the fourth highest civilian award of the Padma Shri, in 1991. Bisht, who was the vice

president of the Uttar Pradesh State Lalit Kala Akademi, died in 1998, aged 70.

Hence, the correct option is (B).

11. Keisabadi is a popular dance form of Odisha.

The dance depicts the traditional love story of Lord Krishna and Radha. It is popular in the Sambalpur district of Odisha. Nritya, Nritta, and Natya are the main elements of the dance. The dance is performed by men.

Hence, the correct option is (D).

12. Acharya Vinoba Bhave was a nonviolence activist, freedom activist, social reformer and spiritual teacher. An avid follower of Mahatma Gandhi, Vinoba upheld his doctrines of non-violence and equality. He dedicated his life to serving the poor and the downtrodden and stood up for their rights. Most of his adult life he led an ascetic style of existence centred on spiritual beliefs of right and wrong.

Hence, the correct option is (D).

13. In Kesavananda Bharti vs State of Kerala case, the Supreme Court of India pronounce the verdict that the basic structure of the constitution cannot be amended by the parliament.

In the Keshavananda Bharti case, Supreme Court overruled its judgment in the Golak Nath case (1967). It upheld the validity of the 24th Amendment Act (1971) and stated that Parliament is empowered to abridge or take away any of the Fundamental Rights.

At the same time, it laid down a new doctrine of the basic structure of the constitution. The parliament reacted to it by enacting the 42nd Constitution Amendment Act, 1976, in which the Supreme Court held that the constituent power of Parliament under Article 368 does not enable it to alter the basic structure of the constitution.

Hence, the correct option is (C).

14. Famous Cave temples of Elephanta are ascribed to Rashtrakoots.

The caves of Ellora Elephanta were built by the Rashtrakuta rulers. They have been built by cutting the walls of high basalt steep rock walls. There are about 34 caves which are located 30 km away from the district in Aurangabad district of Maharashtra state, These are declared a World Heritage Site by UNESCO.

The Rashtrakuta contributions to art and architectural heritage of the Deccan are reflected in the splendid rock-cut cave temples at Ellora and Elephanta, areas also occupied by Jain monks, located in present-day Maharashtra. The Ellora site was originally part of a complex of 34 Buddhist caves probably created in the first half of the 6th century whose structural details show Pandyan influence.

Hence, the correct option is (D).

15. Azad Hind Radio was a radio service that was started by Netaji Subhas Chandra Bose in 1942 in Germany, while the Quit India Movement was in full swing in India.

Initially, it was based in Germany, but its headquarters later shifted to Singapore, and later Rangoon. Different languages were used to propagate nationalistic sentiments like English, Hindi, Tamil, Telugu, Bengali, Gujarati, and Poshto.

Hence, the correct option is (C).

16. Food Chain is the transfer of food energy from producers like plants through a series of organisms, where each stage is accompanied by one eating the other.

- Every step is called the 'trophic level'.
- There are two types of food chains - Detritus food chain, and the Grazing food chain.
- About 90% of energy is lost after each trophic level.
- Thus, only 10% of the energy is transferred.

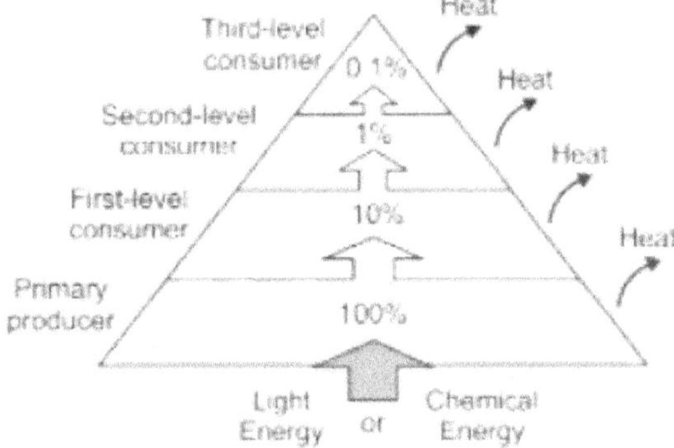

Hence, the correct option is (C).

17. Active Transport is the movement of a substance against a diffusion gradient with the use of energy from respiration.

Active Transport involves the transportation of a substance from a low concentration to a high concentration, against the diffusion gradient.

- The use of energy released through respiration helps in making the process sufficiently exergonic.
- This would help in making the transportation process favorable.

- Passive-mediated transport or facilitated diffusion is when the substance moves from the high concentration to the low concentration region.

Stomata	Located on leaf surface Responsible for gas exchange
Xylem	Located in stem Main function upward transport of water
Root Hair	Located in root Used to absorb water and minerals from soil
Phloem	Located in stem Main function is transporting sap which is a sugary solution

Hence, the correct option is (A).

18. Chlorophyll in Photosynthetic prokaryotic bacteria is associated with Membrane Vesicles.

- Chlorophyll in Photosynthetic Eukaryotes is associated with Plastids.

- Photosynthesis has two parts - the light-dependent reactions, and the Calvin Cycle.

- They take place in Chloroplasts.

- However, in Prokaryotic bacteria like the Cyanobacteria, membrane-bound organelles are not present, including the chloroplasts.

- Prokaryotic photosynthetic organisms have an unfolding of the plasma membrane for the chlorophyll attachment.

- It is in this membrane vesicle, that the cyanobacteria carry out photosynthesis.

Hence, the correct option is (B).

19. Smooth muscle is named so because the cells don't have striations.

- They are present in the walls of organs which are hollow.

- These include urinary bladder, uterus, stomach, intestines, in circulatory systems like arteries and veins.

- They are also present in the tracts of the respiratory system, reproductive systems, urinary system.

- Smooth muscles are present in the eyes, where they help in the change of the size of the iris.

- This helps in changing the shape of the lens.

- They alter the shape of the lens, and in the skin causing the hair to stand erect in response to any cold temperature.

- They are not found in Biceps.

Hence, the correct option is (D).

20. Lysosomes is the cell organelles is known as 'suicide bags' of a cell.

- Lysosomes are called suicidal bags of the cells, containing hydrolytic enzymes which undergo autolysis and burst open when the cell gets damaged.

- Plastids are double-membrane organelle found in plant cell and contain pigments which help the plant is photosynthesis. They are responsible for the storage and manufacture of food.

- Endoplasmic reticulum usually contains ribosomes which are involved in lipid and protein synthesis.

- Mitochondria is known as the powerhouse of the cell.

Hence, the correct option is (A).

21. A hydraulic lift works on the principle of Pascal's law. Pascal's law states that in a fluid that is at rest in a container, the pressure applied to one part of the fluid is uniformly transmitted to all the parts of the fluid. A hydraulic lift operates on this principle to lift heavy objects.

Hence, the correct option is (B).

22. The SI unit for pressure is the pascal (Pa), equal to one newton per square meter (N/m^2). Pascal's law is a principle in fluid mechanics given by Blaise Pascal that states that a pressure change at any point in a confined incompressible fluid is transmitted throughout the fluid such that the same change occurs everywhere.

Hence, the correct option is (D).

23. Helium is monatomic. Helium is a chemical element with the symbol He and atomic number 2. It is a colorless, odorless, tasteless, non-toxic, inert, monatomic gas and the first in the noble gas group in the periodic table.

Monatomic or monoatomic elements are elements that are stable as single atoms.

For an element to be stable, it needs to have a stable octet of valence electrons.

List of Monatomic Elements

- Helium (He)
- Neon (Ne)
- Argon (Ar)
- Krypton (Kr)
- Xenon (Xe)
- Radon (Rn)

Hence, the correct option is (D).

24. Chromatography cannot be used to divide into radio-isotopes. The isotope can be divided in six ways.

These include diffusion, distillation, centrifugation, thermal diffusion, exchange reactions, and electrolysis. None of it is chromatography.

All have been tried with some degree of success on either uranium or hydrogen or both.

According to IUPAC, chromatography is a physical method of separation in which the components to be separated are distributed between two phases, one of which is stationary while the other moves in a definite direction.

Hence, the correct option is (A).

25. Radar (Radio Detection and Ranging) is a detection system that uses radio waves to determine the distance (range), angle, or velocity of objects. It can be used to detect aircraft, ships, spacecraft, guided missiles, motor vehicles, weather formations, and terrain.

Radar systems transmit electromagnetic, or radio, waves. Most objects reflect radio waves, which can be detected by the radar system. The frequency of the radio waves used depends on the radar application.

Hence, the correct option is (D).

26. Diamagnetism is the universal property of all magnetic materials. It is present in all materials. The effect is so weak in most cases that it gets shifted by other effects like paramagnetism, ferromagnetism, etc.

Diamagnetic substances have a tendency to move from the stronger part to the weaker part of the external magnetic field. We can also say that the diamagnetic substances get repelled by a magnet.

Bismuth, Copper, Lead, Silicon, Nitrogen, Water, and Sodium chloride, etc. are some of the examples of diamagnetic materials.

Hence, the correct option is (A).

27. A device that converts electrical energy into mechanical energy is termed an electrical motor. The working principle of an electric motor depends on the magnetic and electric field interaction.

There are two varieties of the electric motor:

AC motor: Converts alternating current into mechanical power. Linear motor, synchronous motor, and induction motor are examples of AC motor.

DC motor: Converts direct current into mechanical power. Self-excited motor and separately excited are examples of DC motor.

Hence, the correct option is (C).

28. Aluminum metal is protected by a layer of its own oxide.

Oxides are chemical compounds that have at least one oxygen atom and at least one other element. Most of the Earth's surface is made up of oxides. Oxides are formed by the oxidation reaction of oxygen in the air of the elements. At normal temperatures, a thin layer of oxide is added to the surface of metals such as magnesium, aluminum, zinc, lead, etc. This layer of oxide protects metals from re-oxidation.

Here, Aluminum is protected due to formation of a layer of Al_2O_3 on its surface.

Hence, the correct option is (B).

29. Iron can be extracted by smelting.

Smelting is a type of extraction metallurgy. It is mainly used to make metals from ore. Silver, iron, copper, etc. are made by this method. The technique of smelting is being used some eight thousand years ago. Nevertheless, smelting is considered a high technological achievement. The process of smelting involves roasting, reducing, and separating dirt from the metal in the form of flux.

Hence, the correct option is (C).

30. Cobalt-60 isotope of Cobalt is used in cancer treatments.

Cobalt therapy is the medical use of gamma rays from the radioisotope cobalt-60 to treat conditions such as cancer. Beginning in the 1950s, cobalt-60 was widely used in external beam radiotherapy (teletherapy) machines, which produced a beam of gamma rays that was directed into the patient's body to kill tissue.

Hence, the correct option is (B).

31. Given:

Time = 5 years

$$SI = \frac{PRT}{100}$$

Where P is principal, R is rate of interest and T is time.

Sum doubles itself:

So, SI = 2P – P = P

$$\Rightarrow P = \frac{P \times R \times 5}{100}$$

$$\Rightarrow R = 20\%$$

So, rate of interest = 20%

Hence, the correct option is (D).

32. Given,

$$^9P_5 + 5 \cdot {}^9P_4 = {}^{10}P_r$$

$$^nP_r = \frac{n!}{(n-r)!}$$

$$^9P_5 + 5 \cdot {}^9P_4 = {}^{10}P_r$$

$$\frac{9!}{4!} + 5 \cdot \frac{9!}{5!} = \frac{10 \times 9!}{(10-r)!}$$

$$\Rightarrow \frac{2}{4!} = \frac{10}{(10-r)!}$$

$$(10 - r)! = 5!$$

$$\Rightarrow r = 5$$

Hence, the correct option is (C).

33. Sum of the digits = 7 + 9 + 0 + 3 + 6 + 8 + p + 5

= 38 + p

A number is divisible by 9 only if the sum of the digits is divisible by 9 an so

Adding 7 to 38 we get 45 and it is divisible by 9.

Hence, the correct option is (B).

34. $\Rightarrow (37)^2 = ? + [(11\sqrt{3} + 5\sqrt{3}) \times (9\sqrt{3} + 11\sqrt{3})]$

$\Rightarrow 1369 - [16\sqrt{3} \times 20\sqrt{3}] = ?$

$\Rightarrow 1369 - 16 \times 20 \times 3 = ?$

$\Rightarrow ? = 1369 - 960$

$\Rightarrow ? = 409$

Hence, the correct option is (C).

35. Given:

Amit bought an article for Rs. 310 and sold it at a loss of 25%.

he bought another article and sold it at a gain of 40%.

Let cost price(CP) of the article bought by Amit be Rs. 100.

Selling price(SP) of the article $= 100 \times \left[\dfrac{75}{100}\right] = 75$

In Rs. 75 he bought another article,

So, SP of another article $= 75 \times \left(\dfrac{140}{100}\right) = 105$

Profit $= 100 - 105 = 5$

Profit percentage $= \left[\dfrac{5}{100}\right] \times 100 = 5\%$

Hence, the correct option is (B).

36. Given:

20% of a number $= 40\%$ of another number

Let, first number $= x$

Second number $= y$

According to the question,

$\Rightarrow x \times \left(\dfrac{20}{100}\right) = y \times \left(\dfrac{40}{100}\right)$

$\Rightarrow \left(\dfrac{x}{5}\right) = \left(\dfrac{2y}{5}\right)$

$\Rightarrow \left(\dfrac{x}{y}\right) = \dfrac{2}{1}$

$\therefore$ required ratio $= 2:1$

Hence, the correct option is (B).

37. The pattern followed is,

$1^3 + 1 = 2$

$2^3 + 1 = 9$

$3^3 + 1 = 28$

$4^3 + 1 = 65$, not 64

$5^3 + 1 = 126$

$6^3 + 1 = 217$

$7^3 + 1 = 344$

$8^3 + 1 = 513$

' 65' should be in the place of ' 64'.

Therefore, " 64" does not belong to the series.

Hence, the correct option is (D).

38. Given:

The given fractions are $\dfrac{25}{9}$ and $\dfrac{5}{18}$.

We know that,

$\text{HCF of fraction} = \left(\dfrac{\text{HCF of numerators}}{\text{LCM of denominators}}\right)$

$\text{HCF of numerator} = \text{HCF of } (25 \text{ and } 5) = 5$

And, $\text{LCM of denominator} = \text{LCM of } (9 \text{ and } 18) = 18$

$\therefore \text{HCF of } \left(\dfrac{25}{9} \text{ and } \dfrac{5}{18}\right) = \dfrac{\text{HCF of } (25 \text{ and } 5)}{\text{LCM of } (9 \text{ and } 18)}$

$= \dfrac{5}{18}$

Hence, the correct option is (A).

39. Let the numbers be $x, x + 2, x + 4, x + 6$ and $x + 8$.

According to question,

$\dfrac{[x+(x+2)+(x+4)+(x+6)+(x+8)]}{5} = 51$

$\Rightarrow 5x + 20 = 255$

$\Rightarrow x = 47$

So, required difference $= (47 + 8) - 47 = 8$

Hence, the correct option is (C).

40. even outcomes $= 2,4,6 = 3$

and multiple of 3 also $= 6 = 1$ only

Number of possible outcomes $= \{ 6\}$

n(A)$= 1$

Number of Total outcomes$= 1,2,3,4,5,6$

n(S)$= 6$

$\therefore \quad P(A) = \dfrac{n(A)}{n(S)} = \dfrac{1}{6}$

Hence, the correct option is (C).

41. Given,

Two angles of quadrilateral are $125°$ and $35°$.

As we know,

Sum of all the angle in quadrilateral $= 360°$

$\therefore x + x + 125° + 35° = 360°$

$\Rightarrow 2x + 160° = 360°$

$\Rightarrow 2x = 360° - 160°$

$\Rightarrow 2x = 200°$

$\therefore x = 100°$

Value of each equal angle $= 100°$.

Hence, the correct option is (C).

42. Given:

Number of days taken, if Heena and Karan work together $= 12$ days

Heena alone completes the work in 18 days.

Let the number of days taken by Karan to complete work be x.

Work done in 1 days by Heena $= \left(\dfrac{1}{18}\right)$

Work done in 1 day by Karan $= \left(\dfrac{1}{x}\right)$

Work done in 1 day when both work together $= \left(\dfrac{1}{12}\right)$

According to question:

$\left(\dfrac{1}{18}\right) + \left(\dfrac{1}{x}\right) = \dfrac{1}{12}$

$\Rightarrow \dfrac{1}{x} = \dfrac{(3-2)}{36} = \dfrac{1}{36}$

$\Rightarrow x = 36 \text{ days}$

$\therefore$ Karan completes the work in 36 days.

Hence, the correct option is (B).

43. Let the distance be $d\ km$.

We know that,

Distance $=$ Speed x Time

$\Rightarrow \dfrac{d}{8} + \dfrac{d}{12} = 15$

$\Rightarrow \dfrac{3d+2d}{24} = 15$

$\Rightarrow d = 72\ km$

Hence, the correct option is (D).

44. Given:

Two cones have their heights in the ratio $1:3$.

The radii of their bases are in the ratio $3:1$.

$\because$ Volume of cone $= \left(\dfrac{1}{3}\right)\pi \times (\text{base radius})^2 \times \text{height}$

Ratio of the volume of two cones $=$
$(\text{Ratio of base radii})^2 \times \text{Ratio of heights}$

Given, ratio of base radii $= 3:1$ and Ratio of heights $= 1:3$

$\therefore$ Ratio of their volumes $= \left(\dfrac{3}{1}\right)^2 \times \left(\dfrac{1}{3}\right) = \dfrac{9}{3} = 3:1$

Hence, the correct option is (C).

45. Given:

40% of a number is 112.

Let the number is x.

$\left(\dfrac{40}{100}\right) \times x = 112$

$x = \dfrac{(112 \times 100)}{40}$

$x = 280$

So, 15% of $280 = 42$

$\therefore 15\%$ of a number is 42.

Hence, the correct option is (A).

46. Here the relation between the letters is as follows,

B + 2 = D, D + 2 = F, F + 2 = H

M + 1 = N, N + 1 = O, O + 1 = P

Y – 2 = W, W – 2 = U, U – 2 = S

Thus, the required term is HPS.

Hence, the correct option is (C).

47. Café Coffee Day, InMobi, and Peter England are brands of Indian origin whereas Nestle is a brand from Switzerland.

Thus Nestle is the odd word.

Hence, the correct option is (A).

48.

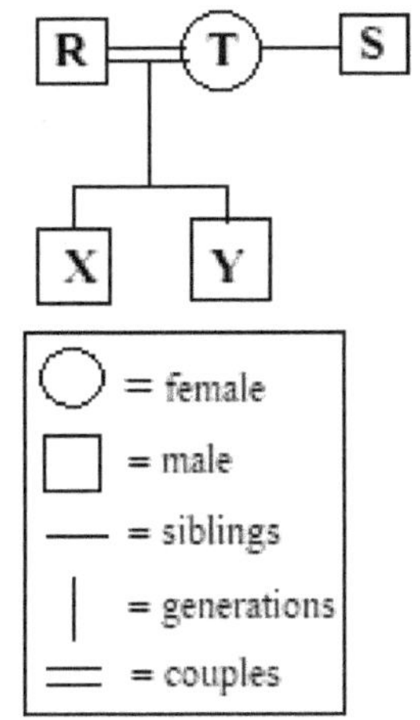

According to the figure, we can conclude T is the wife of R.

Hence, the correct option is (B).

49.

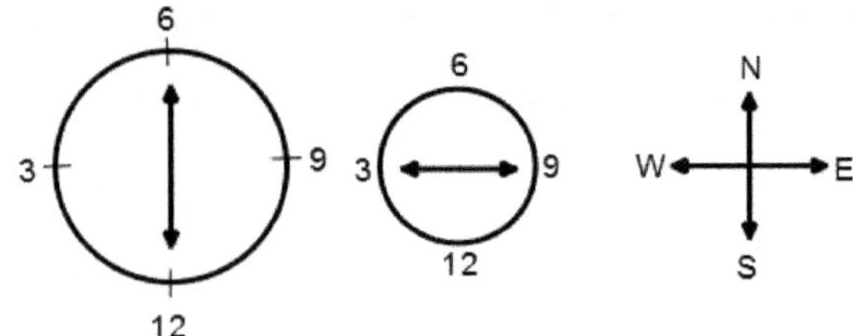

At 9.15 P.M., the minute hand will point towards west.

Hence, the correct option is (D).

50. FLOWER $= 6$ alphabets

So, $6 \times 2 + 2 = 14$

DISTANCE $= 8$ alphabets

So, $8 \times 2 + 2 = 18$

BUREAUCRAT $= 10$ alphabets

So, $10 \times 2 + 2 = 22$

Hence, the correct option is (A).

General Knowledge

Q.1 Which famous personality said the following?

"Don't take rest after your first victory because if you fail in second, more lips are waiting to say that your first victory was just luck?"

A. APJ Abdul Kalam

B. Amartya Sen

C. Homi Bhabha

D. Atal Bihari Vajpayee

Q.2 Silent valley national park is located in __________.

A. Tamil Nadu   **B.** Kerala

C. Orissa   **D.** Chhattisgarh

Q.3 Which one of the following pairs is/are not correctly matched?

Name of the author	Title of the Book
1. R.C. Dutt	Economic History of India
2. Bal Gangadhar Tilak	The Drain of Wealth and Indian Nationalism at the turn of the century
3. W. Digly	Prosperous British India
4. V. Anstey	The Economic Development of India

A. 1 and 2 only   **B.** 2 only

C. 1 and 3 only   **D.** 2 and 3 only

Q.4 In which language did 'Dr. Masti Venkatesh Iyengar' write?

A. Malayalam   **B.** Tamil

C. Kannada   **D.** Telugu

Q.5 In which of the following districts of Madhya Pradesh is the 'Mahamrityunjay ka Mela' held every year?

A. Narsinghpur   **B.** Khargone

C. Sheopuri   **D.** Rewa

Q.6 In which state/UT is the Chaukhandi Stupa located?

[Rajasthan Police Constable, 2020]

A. Ladakh   **B.** Himachal Pradesh

C. Karnataka   **D.** Uttar Pradesh

Q.7 During which years Maharana Pratap Khel Award was instituted?

[Rajasthan Police Constable, 2020]

A. During 1986-87   **B.** During 1982-83

C. During 1992-93   **D.** During 1989-90

Q.8 Elvera Britto has passed away, was a former captain of which sports team of India?

A. Cricket   **B.** Polo

C. Volleyball   **D.** Hockey

Q.9 Vienna is the national capital and largest city of:

A. Austria   **B.** Russia   **C.** Spain   **D.** Syria

Q.10 20 August is celebrated as -

A. Earth Day   **B.** Sadbhavana Diwas

C. No Tobacco Day   **D.** None of these

Q.11 The second highest peak in the world is __________.

A. Kanchenjunga   **B.** K - 2

C. Nandadevi   **D.** Lhotse

Q.12 Consider the following pairs:

Magazines/Newspaper	Editors
1. Bharat Ke Dost	Fardun Ji Marzban
2. Matra Bhumi	K.P. Keshav
3. The Leader	Pt. Madan Mohan Malviya

Choose the correct pairs using the codes given below?

A. 1 and 2 only   **B.** 1 and 3 only

C. 2 and 3 only   **D.** All are correct

Q.13 Consider the following statements with respect to Tanjore paintings :

1. The paintings were created on paper or cloth.

2. They used gemstones and cut glass.

Which of the statements given above is/are correct?

A. 1 only   **B.** 2 only

C. Both 1 and 2   **D.** Neither 1 nor 2

Q.14 In which city is the headquarter of MIDHANI (MIDHANI-Alloy Nigam Limited) located?

[Rajasthan Police Constable, 2020]

A. Ahmedabad   **B.** Kota

C. Hyderabad   **D.** Chennai

Q.15 In 1946, who among the following was made the interim president of the Indian Constituent Assembly?

A. Sachindranath Sanyal

B. Sarojini Naidu

C. S. Subramania Iyer

D. Sachchidananda Sinha

General Science

Q.16 Which of the following diseases are caused by the consumption of water contaminated by mercury and nitrate?

[UPSC Central Armed Police Forces AC, 2017]

A. Minamata disease and Osteoporosis

B. Osteoporosis and Blue Baby Syndrome

C. Minamata disease and Blue Baby Syndrome

D. Osteoporosis and Minamata disease

Q.17 Which enzyme converts sucrose into glucose & fructose?

A. Isomerase   **B.** Invertase

C. Amylase   **D.** Maltase

Q.18 Amarbel (Cuscuta) is an example of:

[Haryana Primary Teacher (PRT), 2019]

A. Autotroph   **B.** Parasite
C. Saprotroph   **D.** Host

Q.19 Plants are divided into ____ groups.
A. 6   **B.** 7   **C.** 5   **D.** 4

Q.20 Saffron is obtained from _________.

[UPTET Social Studies, 2022]

A. bud   **B.** leaf
C. flower stigma   **D.** calyx

Q.21 Myopia and hypermetropia can be corrected by:
A. Concave and plano-convex lens
B. Concave and convex lens
C. Convex and concave lens
D. Plano-concave lens for both defects

Q.22 The magnetic field produced by a current carrying solenoid is similar to the magnetic field produced by a?
A. Ring magnet   **B.** Rod magnet
C. Horse shoe magnet   **D.** Bar Magnet

Q.23 The force of friction acts in a direction ____ to the direction of motion of an object.
A. Same   **B.** Downwards
C. Perpendicular   **D.** Opposite

Q.24 The moment of the force measures:
A. Moment of inertia of the body about any axis
B. The tendency of rotation of the body along an axis
C. Work is done by the force on the body
D. None of these

Q.25 The pH of the solution is given. Which of the solutions has the highest concentration of hydrogen ions?

[RRB/RRC Group D, 2018]

A. 10.1   **B.** 4.7   **C.** 2.4   **D.** 8.0

Q.26 Electric bulbs are usually filled with chemically-inactive gases like _______.

[RRB/RRC Group D, 2018]

A. Hydrogen   **B.** Oxygen
C. Nitrogen   **D.** Chlorine

Q.27 Who classified elements based on atomic numbers?

[RRB/RRC Group D, 2018]

A. Newlands   **B.** Mendeleev
C. Dobereiner   **D.** Moseley

Q.28 A chemical reaction in which heat is generated is called a/an _______.

[RRB/RRC Group D, 2018]

A. endothermic reaction
B. exothermic reaction
C. combustion reaction
D. displacement reaction

Q.29 The correct formula of calcium hydroxide is:

[RRB/RRC Group D, 2018]

A. $CaOH_2$ **B.** Ca_2OH **C.** $Ca(OH)_2$ **D.** $CaOH$

Q.30 What type of waves are light wave?
A. Transverse wave   **B.** Longitudinal wave
C. Both A & B   **D.** None

Maths

Q.31 A jar contains 10 red marbles and 30 green ones. How many red marbles must be added to the jar so that 60% of the marbles will be red?
A. 25   **B.** 30   **C.** 35   **D.** 40

Q.32 The integers 34041 and 32506 when divided by a three-digit integer n leave the same remainder. What is n?
A. 339   **B.** 332   **C.** 305   **D.** 307

Q.33 Three men and 4 women can do a piece of work in 7 days, whereas 2 men and 1 woman can do it in 14 days. Seven women will complete the same work in:

[SSC CGL, 2020]

A. 8 days   **B.** 9 days   **C.** 10 days   **D.** 12 days

Q.34 In the following number series, a wrong number is given. Find out the wrong number.
850, 843, 829, 808, 788, 745, 703
A. 843   **B.** 829   **C.** 808   **D.** 788

Q.35 Two numbers have equal LCM and HCF, then they must be?
A. Prime   **B.** Co prime
C. Natural   **D.** Equal

Q.36 It is given that in a group of 3 students, the probability of 2 students not having the same birthday is 0.992. What is the probability that the 2 students have the same birthday?
A. 0.08   **B.** 0.008   **C.** 0.009   **D.** 0.006

Q.37 The area of a circular field is 124.74 hectares. The cost of fencing it at the rate of 80 paise per metre is :
A. Rs. 3168   **B.** Rs. 1584
C. Rs. 1729   **D.** None of these

Q.38 The compound interest on a sum of money for 2 years at 10% per annum is Rs. 16800 . Find the simple interest for 3 years at the same rate of interest and the same sum.
A. 24000   **B.** 12000   **C.** 22000   **D.** 14000

Q.39 The base of a right-angled triangle is $12cm$ and the difference between the other two sides is $6cm$. What will be the perimeter of the triangle?
A. 18 cm   **B.** 30 cm   **C.** 54 cm   **D.** 36 cm

Q.40 The selling price of glass is Rs 1965 and the loss percentage is 25%. If the selling price is Rs 3013, then what will be the profit percentage?
A. 13 %   **B.** 10 %   **C.** 15 %   **D.** 21 %

Q.41 If a : b : c = 3 : 4 : 7, then the ratio (a + b + c) : c is equal to:

A. 2 : 1   **B.** 14 : 3   **C.** 7 : 2   **D.** 1 : 2

Q.42 Average of 60 observations is 42 . If a number of the value of 50 is replaced by 20 . Find the new average of 60 observations.

A. 46   **B.** 44   **C.** 45.5   **D.** 41.5

Q.43 To cover a distance of 333 km in 2 hours by a car, what should be the average speed of the car in m/sec?

A. 165.5   **B.** 46.25   **C.** 83.25   **D.** 92.5

Q.44 The difference between two complementary angles is 40^0 . The angles are:

A. $65°, 35°$ **B.** $70°, 30°$
C. $65°, 25°$ **D.** $70°, 110°$

Q.45 If A 's salary is 60% more than B 's salary, then by what percentage is B 's salary less than that of A ?

[SSC Sub Inspector (CPO), 2020]

A. 47.7%   **B.** 33.3%   **C.** 37.5%   **D.** 45%

Logical Reasoning

Q.46 After walking 4 km, X turned to the right and then walked 3 km. After that he turned to the left and walked 5 km. In the end, he was moving towards the north. From which direction did he start the journey?

[UP Police Constable, 2019]

A. North   **B.** East   **C.** West   **D.** South

Q.47 In the following question, select the odd word from the given alternatives.

A. Fatigue : Interest   **B.** Cause : Forestall
C. Curb : Restrain   **D.** Lessen : Reassure

Q.48 In a code language, if 'MANDATE' is coded as '2612881405' then how will 'TECHNIQUE' be coded in the same language?

[SSC Selection Post Phase IX, 2019]

A. 40106162893442   **B.** 40561614917215
C. 20561628183422   **D.** 40561628934215

Q.49 A series is given with one term missing. Select the correct alternative from the given ones that will complete the series.

A. G   **B.** H   **C.** K   **D.** L

Q.50 P walked 15 m towards West, took a left turn, and walked 10 m. He took a right turn and walked 5 m. He took a left turn and walked 10 m. He again took a left turn and walked 20 m. How far and which direction is he from his starting point?

A. 25 m, West   **B.** 20 m, South
C. 30 m, East   **D.** 35 m, North

// Smart Answer Sheet //

Correct Indicates percentage of students who answered questions correctly.

Skipped Indicates percentage of students who skipped questions.

Q.	Ans.	Correct / Skipped
1	A	30.18 % / 68.89 %
2	B	66.7 % / 32.23 %
3	B	49.74 % / 30.63 %
4	C	46.52 % / 31.39 %
5	D	64.95 % / 32.5 %
6	D	64.3 % / 33.82 %
7	B	43.43 % / 52.85 %
8	D	47.92 % / 38.13 %
9	A	21.75 % / 71.17 %
10	B	77.6 % / 15.01 %

Q.	Ans.	Correct / Skipped
11	B	83.57 % / 16.0 %
12	C	44.7 % / 49.11 %
13	B	65.15 % / 33.43 %
14	C	49.5 % / 43.4 %
15	D	56.86 % / 33.09 %
16	C	76.33 % / 14.85 %
17	B	14.52 % / 74.44 %
18	B	64.05 % / 32.5 %
19	C	49.32 % / 46.72 %
20	C	49.2 % / 31.94 %

Q.	Ans.	Correct / Skipped
21	B	86.58 % / 11.26 %
22	D	47.22 % / 46.99 %
23	D	48.8 % / 35.31 %
24	B	66.78 % / 31.8 %
25	C	88.36 % / 10.45 %
26	C	53.53 % / 31.55 %
27	D	80.28 % / 14.63 %
28	B	57.65 % / 34.26 %
29	C	41.09 % / 45.63 %
30	A	50.88 % / 43.63 %

Q.	Ans.	Correct / Skipped
31	C	54.36 % / 45.35 %
32	D	89.38 % / 10.3 %
33	C	44.83 % / 30.78 %
34	D	53.18 % / 37.45 %
35	D	64.08 % / 34.26 %
36	B	51.81 % / 35.36 %
37	A	85.13 % / 10.83 %
38	A	84.89 % / 14.61 %
39	D	41.22 % / 39.52 %
40	C	62.4 % / 35.02 %

Q.	Ans.	Correct / Skipped
41	A	82.02 % / 13.98 %
42	D	77.13 % / 17.62 %
43	B	77.52 % / 22.2 %
44	C	86.94 % / 10.37 %
45	C	40.39 % / 46.53 %
46	A	42.84 % / 43.72 %
47	C	14.17 % / 76.64 %
48	D	40.52 % / 57.06 %
49	B	63.68 % / 30.75 %
50	B	50.72 % / 32.6 %

Performance Analysis

Avg. Score (%)	72.0%
Toppers Score (%)	74.0%
Your Score	

//Hints and Solutions//

1. APJ Abdul Kalam full name was Avul Pakir Jainulabdeen Abdul Kalam. He served as the 11th President of India from 2002 to 2007. He was famously known as the Missile Man of India.

APJ Abdul Kalam said, "Don't take rest after your first victory because if you fail in second, more lips are waiting to say that your first victory was just luck".

Hence, the correct option is (A).

2. Silent valley national park is located in Kerala.

Silent Valley National Park:

- Located in the Palakkad district in the Nilgiri Mountains of Kerala.
- It is at the heart of Nilgiri Biosphere Reserve and consists of areas of South Western Ghats rain forests and tropical wet evergreen jungle.
- River Kunthi passes through it.
- Silent Valley Park is known for many highly endangered species such as lion-tailed macaque, tiger, gaur, leopard, wild boar, panther, Indian Civet, and Sambhar.

Hence, the correct option is (B).

3.

Name of the author	Title of the Book
R.C. Dutt	• Romesh Chandra Dutt, a retired ICS officer, published The Economic History of India at the beginning of the 20th century in which he examined in minute detail the entire economic record of colonial rule since 1757.
Dadabhai Naoroji	• Poverty and Unbritish Rule in India book was written by Dadabhai Naoroji.
W. Digly	• 'Prosperous' British India, more completely titled Prosperous' British India: A Revelation from Official Records, was a book published in 1901 by British author William Digby that described the economic conditions prevailing in British India in the latter half of the nineteenth century under British rule.
V. Anstey	• The Economic Development of India by V. Anstey lucidly explains the journey of the Indian economy pre and post-independence and its gradual transition to a relatively market-friendly economy today.

Hence, the correct option is (B).

4. Maasthi Venkatesa Iyengar was a well known writer of Kannada language.Maasti Venkatesha Iyengar was the fourth writer from Kannada literature to receive the prestigious Jnanpith Award, the highest award for Indian literature awarded by Indian government. He won the Award in the year 1983 for his novel Chikkavira Rajendra.

Hence, the correct option is (C).

5. In the Rewa district of Madhya Pradesh, the 'Mahamrityunjay ka Mela' is held every year.

- There is a temple of Maha Mrityunjay in Rewa.
- The fair is held every year on Basant Panchami and Shivratri.
- Bhairavnath of Bhagat Panchami is a famous Shiv Temple in Devtailab Birsinghpur.

Hence, the correct option is (D).

6. Chaukhandi Stupa is located in Sarnath, Uttar Pradesh. It was built in the period of the 4th and 5th century A.D during the Gupta period. It is believed that Buddha first time met his five disciples here. It was built to mark the site where Lord Buddha and his first disciples met while traveling from Bodh Gaya to Sarnath. It is declared as a 'protected area of national importance' in 2019. The Archaeological Survey of India declared Chaukhandi Stupa as a monument of national importance in June 2019.

Hence, the correct option is (D).

7. Maharana Pratap Khel Award was instituted during 1982-83.

Maharana Pratap Khel Award is given by the State Sports Council for outstanding achievements at the National and International levels. It was instituted in the year 1982-1983. The awards consist of:

- A Citation
- Bronze Statue of Maharana Pratap
- Cash prize of INR 1,00,000

Hence, the correct option is (B).

8. Former Indian women's hockey team captain, Elvera Britto has passed away at 81 due to old-age-related problems on April 2022. Elvera Britto led Karnataka's domestic team to win seven national titles. She ruled the domestic circuit from 1960 to 1967. She also represented India against Japan, Sri Lanka, and Australia. She is the second women hockey player to be conferred with the Arjuna Award(1965) after Anne Lumsden.

Hence, the correct option is (D).

9. Vienna is the national capital and largest city of Austria.

Vienna is the most populous city in Austria. The official language of Austria is German. Danube river is the longest river of Austria which flows through the cities of Linz, Krems, and Vienna Schönbrunn Palace is located in Hietzing, Vienna.

Hence, the correct option is (A).

10. Rajiv Gandhi's birthday is celebrated as Sadbhavana Diwas on 20 August.

Every year India observes Sadbhavana Diwas on August 20 to commemorate the birth anniversary of late erstwhile Prime Minister, Rajiv Gandhi. This year on 20th August 2022, we are going to celebrate the 78th birth anniversary of former Prime Minister Rajiv Gandhi. The Indian National Congress instituted Rajiv Gandhi Sadbhavana Award in 1992, a year after his death.

Hence, the correct option is (B).

11. K2 is the second-highest mountain on Earth.

It is located on the border of Pakistan and China. It is also known as the Savage Mountain due to the difficulty of ascent and also known for the second-highest fatality rate near "eight thousanders" for those who climb it.

Hence, the correct option is (B).

12. The correct match:

Magazine/Newspaper	Year of Publication	Language	Editor/Publisher
Bharat Ke Dost	1818	English	J.C Marshman
Matra Bhumi	1923	Malayalam	K.P. Keshav
The Leader	1918	English	Pt. Madan Mohan Malviya

Only pairs 2 and 3 are correct.
Hence, the correct option is (C).

13. Tanjore school of paintings is famous for its special style of decorative paintings. The Maratha rulers patronized them during the 18th century. The paintings were usually created on glass and board instead of cloth and vellum. Therefore, statement 1 is incorrect.

They were unique because of the use of brilliant colour patterns and the use of the gold leaf. They used many types of gemstones and cut glasses. Therefore, statement 2 is correct.

Paintings were based on religious themes. The school reached its zenith under the patronage of Sarfoji Maharaj. Tanjore paintings have been recognized as a Geographical indication by the Government of India in 2007-08.

Hence, the correct option is (B).

14. The headquarter of MIDHANI (MIDHANI-Alloy Nigam Limited) is located in Hyderabad.

Mishra Dhatu Nigam Limited (MIDHANI) was established in the year 1973 under the Ministry of Defence as Government of India Enterprise.

- MIDHANI has been set up with a view to achieving self-reliance in the production and supply of various superalloys, special steels, materials to Defence, other Strategic Sectors for Nuclear, aeronautical and Space applications.

- The guiding factors for setting up of MIDHANI were the demand for Defence oriented technologies, which come under the national priorities.

- Presently, more than seventy per cent of MIDHANI's products (value-wise) cater to strategic customers viz. Ordnance Factory Board (OFB), Defence Research & Development Organisation (DRDO), Indian Space Research Organisation (ISRO), Hindustan Aeronautics Ltd. (HAL), and Department of Atomic Energy (DAE) etc. In addition, MIDHANI also supplies special alloys and products to the commercial sector including Larsen & Toubro, BHEL, Titanium equipment, etc.

Hence, the correct option is (C).

15. Dr. Satchidanand Sinha, the oldest member of the assembly, was elected the president of the assembly. After him, Dr. Rajendra Prasad was elected as the President of the Constituent Assembly on December 11, 1946.

On December 9, 1946, the first meeting of the Constituent Assembly was held in the Library Building of the Council Chamber in New Delhi.

Hence, the correct option is (D).

16. Minamata disease caused by the mercury contaminated water. It was first discovered in Minamata city of Japan that's why it is called as Minamata Disease.

Blue baby syndrome caused by the nitrate contaminated water. Hence, the correct option is (C).

17. Sucrose is converted into glucose and fructose by the enzyme, invertase, and these two monosaccharides readily enter the glycolytic pathway. Glucose and fructose are phosphorylated to give rise to glucose-6- phosphate by the activity of the enzyme hexokinase. This phosphorylated form of glucose then isomerizes to produce fructose-6- phosphate. Subsequent steps of the metabolism of glucose and fructose are the same. In glycolysis, a chain of ten reactions, under the control of different enzymes, takes place to produce pyruvate from glucose.

Therefore Invertase is the enzyme that converts sucrose into glucose & fructose.

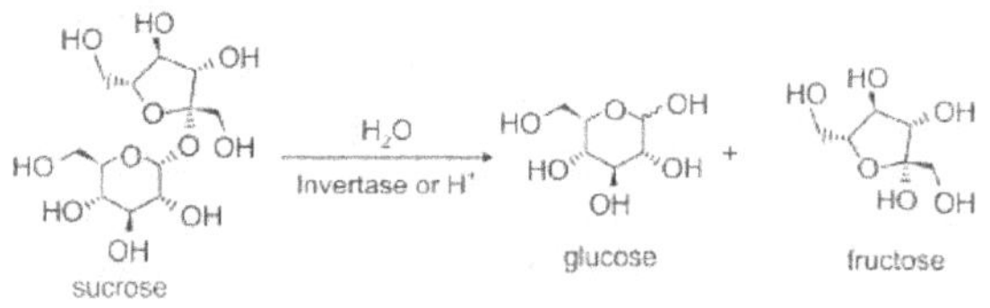

Hence, the correct option is (B).

18. Cuscuta is a parasitic plant. Since Cuscuta does not have chlorophyll, it cannot synthesize its own food by photosynthesis. It uses the nutrients of host plants for its growth.

Hence, the correct option is (B).

19. Based on whether plants have a well-differentiated body and the presence or absence of specialized tissues for transport, and the ability to bear seeds Kingdom Plantae (Plant Kingdom) is can be classified into 5 different groups.

Thallophyta: The plant body is not differentiated from roots, stems and leaves. They are commonly called algae.

Bryophyta: These are small terrestrial plants. They show differentiation in the body design, with stem, leaf-like structures, and root-like structures.

Pteridophyta: The plant body is differentiated into roots, stems, and leaves, apart from having a specialized tissue for conduction.

Gymnosperms: Gymnosperms are plants with naked seeds.

Angiosperms: Angiosperms are seed-bearing plants. Seeds develop inside tissues that get modified to form the fruit of the plant.

Hence, the correct option is (C).

20. Saffron is obtained from flower stigma.

Flower stigma: It is the part of the pistil where pollen germinates.

Bud: It is a small lateral or terminal protuberance on the stem of a vascular plant that can develop into a flower or leaf. The buds are produced from the meristem tissue.

Leaf: It is a green outgrowth from the stem of a vascular plant. Leaves help in manufacturing food for plants during the photosynthesis process. Botanically, leaves are an integral part of the stem system.

Calyx: It is a group of sepals.

Hence, the correct option is (C).

21. Myopia is corrected by using of suitable power of concave lens while hypermetropia is corrected by convex lens.

Hence, the correct option is (B).

22. The magnetic field produced by a current-carrying solenoid is similar to the magnetic field produced by a bar magnet.

The magnetic field of a solenoid carrying current is similar to a bar magnet as it also has the poles on either side and field lines(magnetic) curve outside and straight inside the solenoid.

Hence, the correct option is (D).

23. Frictional force offers resistance to the applied force opposing its motion. Thus, it always acts in the direction opposite to that of the object in motion. If force is applied to the left, then friction acts in the right.

Hence, the correct option is (D).

24. The moment of the force measures the tendency of the rotation of the body along with any axis whether it be the centroid axis of the body or any of the outside axis. The couple moment is produced by two forces, not by a single force. The total work done is the dot product of force and distance, not the cross.

Hence, the correct option is (B).

25. The pH level is a measure of the number of Hydrogen ions in a solution.

- The lower the solution or compound on the pH scale, the higher will be the concentration of hydrogen ions.
- Therefore the solution having a pH of 2.4 will have the highest concentration of hydrogen ions.
- The pH scale ranges from 0 to 14.
- A pH value of 7 is considered neutral, example - water and pH value > 7 is Basic > pH value < 7 is Acidic

Hence, the correct option is (C).

26. Electric bulbs are usually filled with chemically inactive gases like nitrogen and argon because these gases do not react with the hot tungsten filament and so prolong the life of the filament of the electric bulb.

Hence, the correct option is (C).

27. Henry Moseley classified elements based on Atomic numbers.

- In 1913 A.D. the English scientist Henry Moseley demonstrated, with the help of the experiments done using X-ray tube, that the atomic number (Z) of an element corresponds to the positive charge on the nucleus or the number of protons in the nucleus of the atom of that element.
- This revealed that 'atomic number' is a more fundamental property of an element than its atomic mass.

Hence, the correct option is (D).

28. A chemical reaction in which heat is generated is called a/an exothermic reaction.

Exothermic reaction: An exothermic reaction is a reaction in which heat is released or generated.

Examples of exothermic reactions:

- Combustion reactions of fuels or a substance ex: Burning of natural gas:
$$CH_4 + 2O_2 \rightarrow CO_2 + 2H_2O$$
- The thermite reaction
- The Haber process of ammonia production

Hence, the correct option is (B).

29. Calcium Hydroxide is $Ca(OH)_2$ which is also known as Slaked lime.

- It is an inorganic compound.
- It is a white powder or colorless crystal which is obtained when Quicklime (calcium oxide) is mixed with water.
- It is used in the Cement Industry.

Hence, the correct option is (C).

30. Wave: The disturbance that transfers energy from one place to another is called a wave.

There are mainly two types of waves:

1. Transverse waves: The wave in which the movement of the particles is at right angles to the motion of the energy is called a transverse wave. Light is an example of a transverse wave.
2. Longitudinal wave: The wave in which the movement of the particles is parallel to the motion of the energy is called a longitudinal wave. The sound wave is an example of a longitudinal wave.

Light-wave is a transverse wave because its components vibrate perpendicular to its direction of propagation.

Hence, the correct option is (A).

31. Let, x red marbles be added,

$\therefore \dfrac{10+x}{40+x} \times 100 = 60$

$\Rightarrow \dfrac{(10+x)\times 5}{40+x} = 3$

$\Rightarrow 50 + 5x = 120 + 3x$

$\Rightarrow 5x - 3x = 120 - 50$

$\Rightarrow 2x = 70$

$\Rightarrow x = \dfrac{70}{2} = 35$

Hence, the correct option is (C).

32. The difference of the numbers = 34041 – 32506 = 1535

The number that divides both these numbers must be a factor of 1535.

307 is the only 3 digit integer that divides 1535.

Hence, the correct option is (D).

33. Given:

3 men and 4 women can do a piece of work in 7 days and, 2 men and 1 woman can do it in 14 days

As we know,

$M_1 D_1 = M_2 D_2$, where M_1 and M_2 = Number of person, D_1 and D_2 = Number of days

Total Work $=$ Efficiency $\times$ Time

$M_1 D_1 = M_2 D$

$\Rightarrow (3 \text{ men } + 4 \text{ women }) \times 7 = (2 \text{ men } + 1 \text{ women }) \times 14$

$\Rightarrow (3 \text{men } + 4 \text{ women }) = (2 \text{ men } + 1 \text{ women }) \times 2$

$\Rightarrow 3 \text{ men } + 4 \text{ women } = 4 \text{ men } + 2 \text{ women }$

$\Rightarrow 2 \text{ women } = \text{men}$

$\Rightarrow (\text{women : men}) = 1 : 2$

$\Rightarrow$ Efficiency Ratio of (women : men) $= 1 : 2$

$\Rightarrow$ Total Work $=$ Efficiency $\times$ Time

$\Rightarrow (3 \text{ men } + 4 \text{ women }) \times 7 = (2 \text{ men } + 1 \text{ women }) \times 14$

$\Rightarrow (3 \times 2 + 4 \times 1) \times 7 = (2 \times 2 + 1 \times 1) \times 14$

$= 70$

$\Rightarrow$ Total Work $= 70$

$\Rightarrow$ number of days to complete the work by 7 women $= \dfrac{\text{Total work}}{\text{Efficiency}}$

$= \dfrac{70}{(7 \times 1)}$

$= 10$ days

$\therefore$ Required number of days to complete the work by 7 women is 10 days.

Hence, the correct option is (C).

34. The pattern of given series is:

850 – 843 = 7 [7 x 1]

843 – 829 = 14 [7 x 2]

829 – 808 = 21 [7 x 3]

808 – 788 = 20 [28 = 7 x 4]

788 – 745 = 43 [35 = 7 x 5]

745 – 703 = 42 [7 x 6]

If we replace 788 by 780, then 808 – 780 = 28 & 780 – 745 = 35

So the wrong term is 788.

Hence, the correct option is (D).

35. Let the number be a and b

We know that $LCM \times HCF =$ product of numbers

Given:

$LCM = HCF$

$\Rightarrow LCM \times LCM = a \times b$

$\Rightarrow LCM^2 = a \times b$

It will be possible only when $a = b$

$\therefore$ When HCF and LCM are equal then the number will also be equal,

Hence, the correct option is (D).

36. Given,

$P(E) = 0.992$

Let the event wherein 2 students having the same birthday be E.

As we know that,

$P(E) + P(\text{ not } E) = 1$

Or, $P(\text{ not } E) = 1 - 0.992 = 0.008$

$\therefore$ The probability that the 2 students have the same birthday is 0.008.

Hence, the correct option is (B).

37. $\pi r^2 = 124.74$ hectare

$\pi r^2 = 1247400 \; m^2$

$r = 630\ m$

$2\pi r = 3960$

Cost $= 3960 \times 0.8 = 3168$

Hence, the correct option is (A).

38. Given,

Compound interest in 2 years $= 16800$

Rate $= 10\%$

Simple interest for Time $= 3$ years

As we know,

Compound interest $=$ Principal $\left[\left(1 + \dfrac{\text{Rate}}{100}\right)^{\text{Time}} - 1\right]$

$\Rightarrow 16800 = P \times \left[\left(1 + \dfrac{10}{100}\right)^2 - 1\right]$

$\Rightarrow 16800 = P \times \left[\left(\dfrac{11}{10} \times \dfrac{11}{10}\right) - 1\right]$

$\Rightarrow 16800 = P \times \dfrac{121 - 100}{100}$

$\Rightarrow 16800 = P \times \dfrac{21}{100}$

$\Rightarrow P = $ Rs. 80,000

Simple interest $= \dfrac{\text{Principal} \times \text{Rate} \times \text{Time}}{100} = \dfrac{80000 \times 10 \times 3}{100} =$ Rs. 24,000

∴ The simple interest is Rs. 24,000 .

Hence, the correct option is (A).

39. Given:

Base $= 12cm$

$P^2 + b^2 = h^2$

Let height be $x cm$

So, hypotenous is $(x + 6)cm$

$(x + 6)^2 - x^2 = 144$

$\Rightarrow x^2 + 36 + 12x - x^2 = 144$

$\Rightarrow 12x = 108$

x=9

Height $= 9cm$

So, hypotenous is $15cm$

Perimeter $= 9 + 12 + 15$

$= 36cm$

∴ The perimeter of the triangle is $36cm$.

Hence, the correct option is (D).

40. According to the question,

Selling price of glass $=$ Rs. 1965

And loss $= 25\%$

∴ $CP = \dfrac{1965}{75} \times 100 =$ Rs. 2620

If selling price $=$ Rs. 3013

∴ Profit $\% = \dfrac{(3013 - 2620)}{2620} \times 100$

$= \dfrac{3930}{269} = 15\%$

Hence, the correct option is (C).

41. Given,

a : b : c = 3 : 4 : 7

$\Rightarrow$ 3x + 4x + 7x =14x

∴ a + b + c = 14x

$\Rightarrow$ c = 7x

∴ (a + b + c) : c

= 14x :7x

= 2 : 1

Hence, the correct option is (A).

42. Given,

Average of 60 observations $= 42$

As we know,

Average $= \dfrac{\text{Sum of all observations}}{\text{Total number of all observations}}$

Average of 60 observations $= 42$

Sum of all 60 observations $= 60 \times 42 = 2520$

New sum of all 60 observations if 50 is replaced by 20

$= 2520 - 50 + 20 = 2490$

∴ New average of 50 observations $= \dfrac{2490}{60} = 41.5$

Hence, the correct option is (D).

43. We know that,

$1 km = 1000 m$

1 hour $= 60 \times 60 sec$

According to the question,

Distance $= 333 km = 333 \times 1000 m$

Time $= 2$ hour $= 2 \times 60 \times 60 sec$

We know that,

$$\text{Speed} = \frac{\text{Distance}}{\text{Time}}$$

So,

$$= \frac{(333 \times 1000)}{(2 \times 60 \times 60)}$$

$$= 46.25 m/sec$$

Hence, the correct option is (B).

44. Let the two angles be A and B.

As we know,

Sum of two complementary angle $= 90°$

$$\angle A + \angle B = 90° \dots (1)$$

$$\angle A - \angle B = 40° \dots (2) \text{ (Given)}$$

From equation (1) and (2), we get

$$\angle A = 65°, \angle B = 25°$$

Hence, the correct option is (C).

45. Given,

A 's salary $= 60\%$ more than B 's salary.

Let the salary of B be 100.

A 's salary $= 100 + 60\%$ of $100 = 160$

B 's salary $= (160 - 100) = 60$ less than A

$$= \left[\frac{60}{\text{Salary of A}} \right] \times 100 \text{ percent less than } A$$

$$= \left[\frac{60}{160} \right] \times 100 \text{ percent less than } A$$

$$= 37.5\%$$

$\therefore$ The salary of B is 37.5% less than the salary of A.

Hence, the correct option is (C).

46. As X took one right and one left turn.

Starts from A to B 4km, right turn B to C 3 km, and left C to D 5 km.

$\Rightarrow$ Overall change in his direction = 90° - 90° = 0°.

Thus, his initial direction would be the same as his final direction.

The arrangement is as,

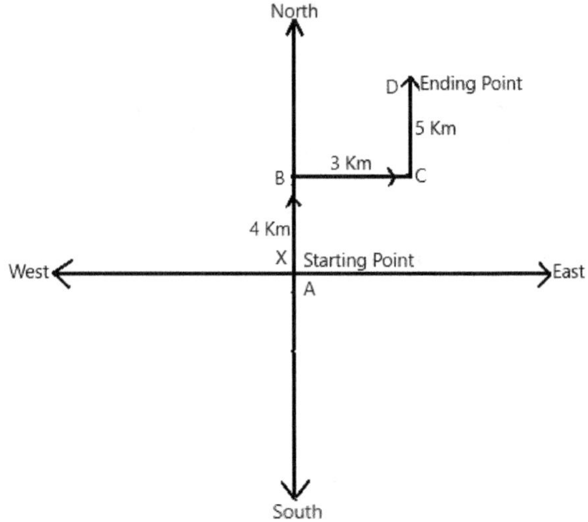

Thus, he started his journey from the North.

Hence, the correct option is (A).

47. All word-groups except option (C) are antonyms of each other while curb and restrain has same meaning i.e. Prevention.

Thus, Curb : Restrain is the odd one out.

Hence, the correct option is (C).

48. The logic is:

Alpha bets	A	B	C	D	E	F	G	H	I	J	K	L	M
Positional value	1	2	3	4	5	6	7	8	9	10	11	12	13
Positional value	26	25	24	23	22	21	20	19	18	17	16	15	14
Alpha bets	Z	Y	X	W	V	U	T	S	R	Q	P	O	N

Consonants place value is doubled and that of vowels is kept the same.

13	1	14	4	1	20	5
M	A	N	D	A	T	E
×2	×1	×2	×2	×1	×2	×1
26	1	28	8	1	40	5

Similarly,

20	5	3	8	14	9	17	21	5
T	E	C	H	N	I	Q	U	E
×2	×1	×2	×2	×2	×1	×2	×1	×1
40	5	6	16	28	9	34	21	5

Hence, the correct option is (D).

49. The followed pattern is:

$$D \xrightarrow{-2} B \xrightarrow{+5} G \xrightarrow{-2} E \xrightarrow{+5} J \xrightarrow{-2} H$$

Hence, the correct option is (B).

50. Drawing the diagram according to the given information,

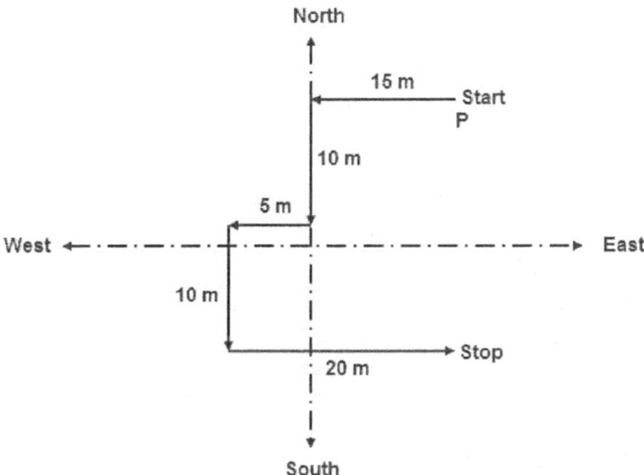

He is 20 m, South of his starting point.

Hence, the correct option is (B).

General Knowledge

Q.1 Who of the following painted the famous painting Guernica?

A. Vincent van Gogh   **B.** Rembrandt
C. Raphael   **D.** Pablo Picasso

Q.2 Which of the following river is famous for changing its path?

A. Narmada   **B.** Kosi
C. Brahmaputra   **D.** Damodar

Q.3 Whose autobiography is "My Life"?

A. Nelson Mandela   **B.** Bill Clinton
C. Margaret Thatcher   **D.** J.M. Lyngdoh

Q.4 Which of the following books has been written by Vikram Seth?

A. My God Died Young
B. Islamic Bomb
C. Look Back in Anger
D. A Suitable Boy

Q.5 The oldest form of composition of Hindustani vocal music is–

A. Ghazal   **B.** Dhrupad
C. Thumri   **D.** None of the options

Q.6 The Centre for Cellular and Molecular Biology is situated at:

A. Patna   **B.** Jaipur
C. Hyderabad   **D.** New Delhi

Q.7 'Teachers' Day' is observed on which of the date?

A. 5 September   **B.** 11 January
C. 14 November   **D.** 2 October

Q.8 _________ is the currency of North Korea.

A. Yen   **B.** Dinar   **C.** Dollar   **D.** Won

Q.9 Which one of the following statements about the atmosphere is correct?

A. The atmosphere has definite upper limit but gradually thins until it becomes imperceptible.
B. The atmosphere has no definite upper limit but gradually thins until it becomes imperceptible.
C. The atmosphere has definite upper limits but gradually thickens until it becomes imperceptible.
D. The atmosphere has no definite upper limits but gradually thickens until it becomes imperceptible.

Q.10 The organization which publishes the 'Red Data Book' of species is:

[Rajasthan Teachers Eligibility Test - Level 1 Primary Level (RTET), 2021]

A. ICFRE   **B.** WWF   **C.** IUCN   **D.** UNEP

Q.11 Eisenhower Cup is associated with which among the following sports?

A. Tennis   **B.** Chess   **C.** Football   **D.** Golf

Q.12 How many members of Rajya Sabha are nominated by the President?

A. 12   **B.** 18   **C.** 20   **D.** 22

Q.13 Who among the following persons has been conferred with the highest civilian award of Assam state 'Assam Baibhav' in February 2022?

A. Ratan Tata   **B.** Mukesh Ambani
C. Ajim Premji   **D.** Narendra Modi

Q.14 The period between ____ is known as the period of the Delhi Sultanate.

A. 1106 AD and 1326 AD
B. 1606 AD and 1826 AD
C. 1206 AD and 1526 AD
D. 1006 AD and 1326 AD

Q.15 Muhammad Bin Tughlaq changed his capital from Delhi to:

A. Lahore   **B.** Munger
C. Agra   **D.** Daulatabad

General Science

Q.16 During favourable conditions, Amoeba reproduces by:

A. Multiple fission   **B.** Binary fission
C. Budding   **D.** Fragmentation

Q.17 Cause of vitamin D deficiency:

A. Rickets   **B.** Night blindness
C. Goiter   **D.** None of these

Q.18 Which of the following is the most important role played by ribosomes in cells?

A. Synthesis of RNA
B. Synthesis of DNA
C. Protein synthesis
D. Carbohydrate metabolism

Q.19 At least genetic power is a feature of which of the following cells of the human body?

A. Brain   **B.** Bones   **C.** Skin   **D.** Liver

Q.20 Amflora is a genetically modified _____.

A. Rose   **B.** Potato   **C.** Lotus   **D.** Tomato

Q.21 Which force helps swimmers float in water?

A. Frictional force   **B.** Magnetic force
C. Muscular force   **D.** Buoyant force

Q.22 During inelastic collision between two bodies, which of the following quantities always remains conserved?

[Maharashtra Public Service Commission, 2019]

A. Total kinetic energy
B. Total mechanical energy
C. Total linear momentum
D. Speed of each body

Q.23 The following are some of the properties of the colloidal sols:

a. Tyndall effect
b. Brownian motion
c. Maxwell distribution
d. Van der Waals forces

[Maharashtra Public Service Commission, 2019]

A. a, b and c   B. a and b
C. a and c   D. b and d

Q.24 The point at which all rays converge is termed as _____.

[RRB/RRC Group D, 2018]

A. Principal axis   B. Pole
C. Aperture   D. Focus

Q.25 What is the formula of average velocity?

[RRB/RRC Group D, 2018]

A. $V_{av} = \frac{(u-v)}{2}$ B. $U_{av} = \frac{(u+v)}{2}$
C. $V_{ay} = u + v$ D. $V = \frac{s}{t}$

Q.26 Which hydrocarbons are the constituents of LPG?

A. Methane and Ethane
B. Propane and Butane
C. Pentane and Benzene
D. Only Methane

Q.27 Which one of the following statements is correct about camphor and ammonium chloride?

A. Both of them are inorganic compounds
B. Both of them are organic compounds
C. Both of them undergo sublimation
D. Both (A) and (B)

Q.28 The chemical used for making tooth pastes white is:

A. Calcium carbonate   B. Sodium carbonate
C. Titanium dioxide   D. Zinc oxide

Q.29 When lead nitrate is heated, the brown fumes observed are of:

A. Nitrogen Dioxide   B. Nitrogen Trioxide
C. Oxygen   D. Lead oxide

Q.30 According to Mendeleev's periodic law, the physical and chemical properties of elements are periodic functions of their:

[UPSESSB TGT Science, 2019]

A. Atomic numbers
B. Atomic weights
C. Number of electrons
D. Number of protons

Maths

Q.31 A person lent out a certain sum at 12% p.a. simple interest. In 10 years, the interest was Rs. 2,148 more than the sum. The sum was:

[SSC Selection Post Phase IX, 2020]

A. Rs. 10,740   B. Rs. 11,540
C. Rs. 10,850   D. Rs. 10,600

Q.32 A circle of radius 25 cm has a chord of length 48 cm. What is the length of perpendicular drawn from the centre of the circle to the chord?

A. 5 cm   B. 5.5 cm   C. 6.5 cm   D. 7 cm

Q.33 What will come in the place of the question mark '?' in the following question?

$$240 \div 6 + \sqrt{529} \times 17 = ? + 150\% \text{ of } 80$$

A. 311   B. 310   C. 309   D. 312

Q.34 A series is given with one term missing. Select the correct alternative from the given options that will complete the series.

16, 17, 14, 19, ?, 21

A. 19   B. 24   C. 17   D. 12

Q.35 Find the HCF of 3341 and 3328.

[RRB (NTPC), 2017]

A. 257   B. 13   C. 337   D. 31

Q.36 3 years ago, the average age of a family of 5 members was 16 years. A baby having been born, the average of the family is the same today. Find the age of the child in years.

A. 2   B. 2.5   C. 1   D. 1.5

Q.37 The probability of getting a number on a roll of one die having total of 6 outcomes is p. A pair of die is rolled. The mean is equal to 0.5. Find the probability of not getting number 5 on at most one die on roll of the pair of dice.

A. $\frac{1}{12}$ B. $\frac{11}{12}$ C. $\frac{143}{144}$ D. $\frac{1}{144}$

Q.38 A can do a piece of work in 12 hours, while B can do it in 8 hours. If A and B both work together, so in how many hours the work will be completed?

A. 10 hours   B. 4 hours
C. 5 hours 15 minutes   D. 4 hours 48 minutes

Q.39 A right circular cone of maximum volume is inserted into a cylinder of the same height. If the radius of the cylinder is 7 cm and the slant height of the cone is 25 cm, then find the volume ((in cm ^{3}) of the cylinder.

A. $1176\pi cm^3$ B. $1216\pi cm^3$
C. $1387\pi cm^3$ D. $1495\pi cm^3$

Q.40 If X is 25% more than Y then by what percentage is Y less than X?

A. 25%   B. 20%   C. 12.5%   D. 16%

Q.41 A box contains 5 red, 4 white and 3 blue balls. Three balls are drawn at random. Find out the number of ways of selecting the balls of different colours.

A. 24   B. 32   C. 60   D. 30

Q.42 A number when divided by 342 gives a remainder 47. When the same number is divided by 19, what would be the remainder?

A. 6   **B.** 8   **C.** 7   **D.** 9

Q.43 Find the mean proportional of 6 and 54.

A. 9   **B.** 3   **C.** 18   **D.** 16

Q.44 A jeep moves at the speed of 60 km/h. What is the speed of the jeep in m/sec?

A. 26.67   **B.** 16.67   **C.** 18.67   **D.** 15.67

Q.45 Sumit purchased an item for Rs. 6500 and sold it at the gain of 24%. From that amount, he purchased another item and sold it at a loss of 20%. What is his overall gain/loss?

A. Loss of Rs. 42

B. Gain of Rs. 42

C. Loss of Rs. 52

D. Neither gain nor loss

Logical Reasoning

Q.46 P is taller than Q and R is taller than S. If S is taller than Q but shorter than P and P is shorter than R, who is the tallest?

A. S   **B.** R   **C.** P   **D.** Q

Q.47 Direction: Select the combination of letters that when sequentially placed in the gaps of the given letter series will complete the series.

K _ CT _ BLUC _ M _ M _ C _ MB

[SSC Selection Post Phase IX, 2019]

A. UMTBUT   **B.** MTUMT

C. UMTUUT   **D.** UMTUM

Q.48 In a code language, if BOX is written as 725 and GLAND is written as 16493, then how will BOND be written in the same language?

[SSC Selection Post Phase IX, 2020]

A. 7276   **B.** 7553   **C.** 9293   **D.** 7293

Q.49 What was the day on 25th January 1975?

A. Friday   **B.** Saturday   **C.** Sunday   **D.** Monday

Q.50 'A' is the sister of 'B'. 'B' is married to 'D'. 'D' is the brother of 'K'. 'B' and 'D' have one daughter 'G'. How is 'A' related to 'D'?

A. Sister   **B.** Brother-In-Law

C. Daughter-In-Law   **D.** Sister-In-Law

// Smart Answer Sheet //

Correct   Indicates percentage of students who answered questions correctly.

Skipped   Indicates percentage of students who skipped questions.

Q.	Ans.	Correct / Skipped	Q.	Ans.	Correct / Skipped	Q.	Ans.	Correct / Skipped	Q.	Ans.	Correct / Skipped	Q.	Ans.	Correct / Skipped
1	D	55.7 % / 36.15 %	11	D	52.71 % / 40.61 %	21	D	76.2 % / 12.65 %	31	A	87.11 % / 10.49 %	41	C	61.6 % / 37.07 %
2	B	68.77 % / 30.29 %	12	A	56.49 % / 33.64 %	22	C	45.03 % / 52.51 %	32	D	49.47 % / 38.48 %	42	D	55.54 % / 35.19 %
3	B	62.38 % / 37.16 %	13	A	89.09 % / 10.66 %	23	B	56.48 % / 37.14 %	33	A	89.38 % / 10.08 %	43	C	57.7 % / 32.45 %
4	D	14.2 % / 67.49 %	14	C	46.08 % / 38.88 %	24	D	78.58 % / 12.19 %	34	D	42.47 % / 45.03 %	44	B	57.13 % / 36.98 %
5	B	59.56 % / 31.79 %	15	D	55.19 % / 33.5 %	25	B	83.38 % / 12.19 %	35	B	81.55 % / 13.05 %	45	C	56.69 % / 30.99 %
6	C	87.95 % / 11.8 %	16	B	26.33 % / 69.57 %	26	B	67.42 % / 30.25 %	36	C	53.08 % / 38.53 %	46	D	57.2 % / 39.44 %
7	A	81.9 % / 15.89 %	17	A	83.51 % / 11.26 %	27	C	84.08 % / 14.66 %	37	C	68.83 % / 30.96 %	47	A	51.44 % / 43.88 %
8	D	15.22 % / 67.68 %	18	C	64.74 % / 30.25 %	28	C	58.4 % / 36.37 %	38	D	20.6 % / 70.53 %	48	D	82.06 % / 15.89 %
9	B	42.72 % / 55.48 %	19	A	31.63 % / 67.63 %	29	A	49.71 % / 47.87 %	39	A	17.95 % / 74.65 %	49	B	50.76 % / 33.85 %
10	C	66.63 % / 32.15 %	20	B	13.29 % / 72.29 %	30	B	48.92 % / 30.95 %	40	B	55.31 % / 40.84 %	50	D	68.72 % / 30.93 %

Performance Analysis

Avg. Score (%)	**62.0%**
Toppers Score (%)	**72.0%**
Your Score	

//Hints and Solutions//

1. Spanish abstractionist Pablo Picasso increasingly reacted to social problems, reflecting his ideas in his works. One of his most famous painting is Guernica. This painting reflects the artist's worldview, his vision of the world and his attitude to the events around him.

Hence, the correct option is (D).

2. Kosi river is famous for changing its path.

Kosi river also known as "Sorrow of Bihar" carries huge amount of water and sediments and when it enters plains it changes its coarse regularly and huge amount of sediments deposit in very less time leading to overflow of water which causes devastating floods in Bihar specially in Monsoons.

Hence, the correct option is (B).

3. My Life is a 2004 autobiography written by former President of the United States Bill Clinton, who left office on January 20, 2001. It was released on June 22, 2004. The book was published by the Knopf Publishing Group; the book sold in excess of 2,250,000 copies. Clinton had received what was at the time the world's highest book advance fee, believed to have been worth US$12 million; at the announcement of media personality Oprah Winfrey's future weight loss book, it was said that her undisclosed advance fee had broken this record. In April 2008, the Clintons' tax records confirmed that the advance for My Life was actually $15 million.

Hence, the correct option is (B).

4. A Suitable Boy is a novel by Vikram Seth, published in 1993. A Suitable Boy by Vikram Seth is the story of ordinary people caught up in a web of love and ambition, humour and sadness, prejudice and reconciliation, the most delicate social etiquette and the appalling violence. Vikram Seth is an Indian poet, novelist, travel writer, librettist, children's writer, biographer and memoirist.

Hence, the correct option is (D).

5. Dhrupad is a vocal genre in Hindustani classical music, said to be the oldest still in use in that musical tradition. Its name is derived from the words Dhruva and Pad (verse), where a part of the poem (dhruva) is used as a refrain.

Hence, the correct option is (B).

6. The Centre for Cellular and Molecular Biology is situated at Hyderabad.

The Center for Molecular Biology (CMB) was established in the fall of 2002 with funding provided by Smith College and the Howard Hughes Medical Institute. The goal of the Center for Molecular Biology is to provide first-class support for molecular biology research, training, and education to all that are interested in the Smith community.

Hence, the correct option is (C).

7. Teachers day is observed on 5 September.

September 5th is the birth anniversary of a great teacher Dr Sarvepalli Radhakrishnan, who was a staunch believer of education and was a well-known diplomat, scholar, the President of India and above all, a teacher.

Hence, the correct option is (A).

8. North Korean Won is the currency of North Korea. It is subdivided into 100 chon. Vaughan is issued by the Central Bank of the Democratic People's Republic of Korea. Won is associated with the Chinese Yuan and the Japanese Yen.

Hence, the correct option is (D).

9. The atmosphere has no definite upper limit but gradually thins until it becomes imperceptible. The atmosphere becomes thinner and thinner with increasing altitude, with no definite boundary between the atmosphere and outer space.

Hence, the correct option is (B).

10. The organization which publishes the 'Red Data Book' of species is IUCN.

It also deals with fungi as well as some local subspecies that exist within the territory of the state or country. This book provides central information for studies and monitoring programs on rare and endangered species and their habits. The International Union for Conservation of Nature (IUCN) Red List was founded in 1964.

Hence, the correct option is (C).

11. Eisenhower Cup is associated with Golf.

Golf:

- Canada Cup
- Ryder Cup
- Walker Cup
- Eisenhower Cup

Hence, the correct option is (D).

12. Parliament- also called the Sansad, is the legislature of the Union. It has the President, and two houses- the Upper House and the Lower House. The Upper House is also called the Rajya Sabha or the Council of States while the Lower House is called the Lok Sabha or the House of the people.

Rajya Sabha	Lok Sabha
Maximum 250 members, out of which 12 are nominated by the President from fields like literature, science, art, and social service; the rest 238 are representatives of the States and the UTs.	Maximum 552 members (530 states, 20 UTs, and a maximum 2 Anglo-Indian representatives nominated by the President)
Indirect election: members elected by elected members of legislative assemblies of the States by the system of proportional representation using the single transferable vote while UT's representatives are elected by the law parliament prescribes.	Chosen directly based on adult suffrage
Not subject to dissolution since one-third of members retire every second	Dissolved every five years and fresh elections

year.	are held.

So, we see from the above table that 12 members of the Rajya Sabha are nominated by the President.

Hence, the correct option is (A).

13. Assam Chief Minister Himanta Biswa Sarma conferred the state's highest civilian award 'Assam Baibhav' to Tata Trust's Chairman Ratan Tata in Mumbai on 16 Feb 2022. He has been awarded for his exceptional contribution to furthering cancer care in Assam. The award carries a citation, a medal, and a cash amount of Rs five lakh.

Hence, the correct option is (A).

14. Delhi Sultanate, five short-lived dynasties, based in Delhi, from 1206 to 1526 AD, when it fell to the Mughal Empire.

During this period of over three hundred years, five dynasties ruled in Delhi.

1. The Slave dynasty (1206-90)
2. Khilji dynasty (1290-1320)
3. Tughlaq dynasty (1320-1413)
4. Sayyid dynasty (1414-51)
5. Lodhi Dynasty (1451-1526)

Hence, the correct option is (C).

15. Muhammad bin Tughlaq, in 1327, shifted his capital from Delhi to Daulatabad in the Deccan, in present-day Maharashtra. He thought that moving the capital to a central location will help him rule the whole Indian Sub-continent efficiently.

- Muhammad bin Tughluq was the Sultan of Delhi from 1325 to 1351.
- He was the eldest son of Ghiyas-ud-Din -Tughlaq, the founder of the Tughluq dynasty.
- Ibn Battuta, the famous traveller, and jurist from Morocco was a guest at his court and wrote about his empire in his book.

Hence, the correct option is (D).

16. During favourable conditions, Amoeba reproduces by binary fission. Binary fission, asexual reproduction by a separation of the body into two new bodies. In the process of binary fission, an organism duplicates its genetic material, or deoxyribonucleic acid (DNA), and then divides into two parts (cytokinesis), with each new organism receiving one copy of DNA.

Hence, the correct option is (B).

17. Deficiency of vitamin D can cause a decrease in bone density, resulting in osteoporosis and fractures (broken bones). Vitamin D deficiency in children can cause rickets.

Hence, the correct option is (A).

18. The most important carbohydrate metabolic role played by ribosomes in cells is the synthesis of proteins. Ribosomes are made up of specialized proteins and nucleic acids.

Hence, the correct option is (C).

19. The human brain is the central organ of the human nervous system, and forms the central nervous system along the spinal cord. It is considered to have the least generative power.

Hence, the correct option is (A).

20. Amflora which is also known as EH92-527-1 is a genetically modified potato cultivar developed by BASF Plant Science. It is developed to produce a specific natural starch (amylopectin) needed for industrial applications.

Hence, the correct option is (B).

21. The buoyant force comes from the pressure exerted on the object by the fluid.

the buoyant force is important in swimming because it helps the swimmer to stay closer to the surface. This is because the pressure experienced by the swimmer under the water is more than the pressure experienced above. This is also the reason why swimmers can float on the surface of the water.

Hence, the correct option is (D).

22. An inelastic collision is such a type of collision that takes place between two objects in which some energy is lost. In the case of inelastic collision, momentum is conserved but the kinetic energy is not conserved. Most of the collisions in daily life are inelastic in nature. Since no external forces are acting on the colliding bodies during collision, thus total linear momentum is always conserved in all type of collisions but kinetic energy in not conserved in all collisions.

Kinetic energy is conserved in perfectly elastic collision only but some kinetic energy is lost in inelastic collisions. So, total kinetic energy is not conserved in inelastic collision.

Hence, the correct option is (C).

23. Properties of a Colloidal sol are-

- Colloidal particles show the Tyndall effect as they scatter light. Small-sized colloidal particles cannot be seen with naked eyes but they are big enough to scatter a beam of light.
- Colloidal particles show Brownian motion since the colloidal particles show random movement in the solution.

Hence, the correct option is (B).

24. The point at which all the rays converge is termed focus. The straight line that goes through the center of the lens at right angles to the lens surface is called the principal axis. Pole is the midpoint of the Lens. The circular arc of any mirror is called the aperture of that mirror.

Hence, the correct option is (D).

25. If final Velocity v and Initial velocity u, are known, we make use of the formula:

$$U_{\text{av}} = \frac{(u+v)}{2}$$

Where, u = Initial Velocity and v = Final Velocity.

Hence, the correct option is (B).

26. LPG stands for liquefied petroleum gas. Like all fossil fuels, it is a non-renewable source of energy.

It is extracted from crude oil and natural gas. LPG is composed hydrocarbons containing three or four carbon atoms. The normal components of LPG thus, are propane (C_3H_8) and butane (C_4H_{10}).

Hence, the correct option is (B).

27. Both camphor and ammonium chloride are solid at room temperature. But they are vaporized (gas phase) when heat is applied. This property is called Sublimation.

The heat of sublimation - Heat required to change a unit mass of solid directly into vapour, at a given temperature, is called the heat of sublimation at that temperature.

Hence, the correct option is (C).

28. The chemical used for making toothpaste white is Titanium dioxide. Titanium dioxide is having a "high refractive index".

Titanium oxide or titanium dioxide is the mineral that occurs naturally in crystalline form. The chemical properties of titanium oxide make it a viable ingredient of toothpaste as a "whitening agent".

Hence, the correct option is (C).

29. When lead nitrate is heated, the brown fumes observed are of Nitrogen Dioxide.

Heating of lead nitrate is an example of a decomposition reaction:

$2Pb(NO_3)_2(s) \rightarrow 2PbO(s) + 4NO_2(g) + O_2(g)$

Hence, the correct option is (A).

30. According to Mendeleev's periodic law, 'The elements, if arranged according to their atomic weight, exhibit an apparent periodicity of properties'. The demerits of his periodic table include:

- Unable to locate Hydrogen
- The increase in the atomic mass was not regular.
- Discovery of isotopes

Hence, the correct option is (B).

31. Given:

Rate of $SI = 12\%$ p.a.

Time of investment $= 10$ years

Simple interest $= (P + $ Rs 2,148 $)$ where P is the principal.

We know that:

$$SI = \frac{(P \times R \times T)}{100}$$

Let the Principal = 'P'

$$\therefore SI = \frac{(P \times R \times T)}{100}$$

$$\Rightarrow 2,148 + P = \frac{(P \times 12 \times 10)}{100}$$

$$\Rightarrow (2148 + P) \times 100 = 120P$$

$$\Rightarrow 214800 + 100P = 120P$$

$$\Rightarrow 120P - 100P = 214800$$

$$\Rightarrow 20P = 214800$$

$$\Rightarrow P = \frac{214800}{20}$$

$$\Rightarrow P = \text{Rs. } 10,740$$

Hence, the correct option is (A).

32. Given:

Radius = 25 cm

Length of chord = 48 cm

Pythagoras Theorem: Hypotenuse^2 = Base^2 + Perpendicular^2

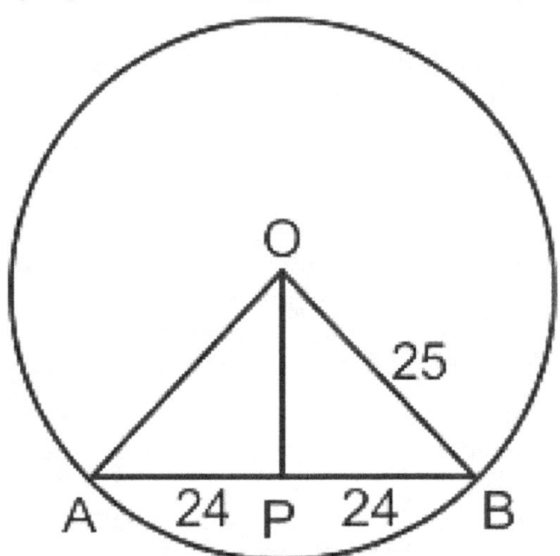

OA = OB = 25 cm (Radius of circle)

AB = 48 cm

$$PB = \frac{AB}{2} = \frac{48}{2}$$

Using the above concept

PA = PB = 24 cm

Applying Pythagoras theorem in ΔOPB,

OB^2 = OP^2 + PB^2

$\Rightarrow$ 25^2 = OP^2 + 24^2

$\Rightarrow$ OP2 = 625 - 576

$\Rightarrow$ OP^2 = 49

$\Rightarrow$ OP = 7 cm

∴ The length of perpendicular drawn from the centre of the circle to the chord is 7 cm.

Hence, the correct option is (D).

33. We know that:

Follow the BODMAS rule according to the table given below:

B	Brackets in order ( ), { }, [ ]	ब्रैकेट ( ), { }, [ ] क्रम में
O	of	का
D	Division $(\div)$	विभाजन $(\div)$
M	Multiplication (x)	गुणा (x)
A	Addition (+)	जोड़ (+)
S	Subtraction (-)	घटाव (–)

Given:

$$240 \div 6 + \sqrt{529} \times 17 = ? + 150\% \text{ of } 80$$

$$\Rightarrow 40 + 23 \times 17 = ? + 120$$
$$\Rightarrow 40 + 391 = ? + 120$$
$$\Rightarrow 431 - 120 = ?$$
$$\Rightarrow ? = 311$$

$\therefore$ The value of $?$ is 311.

Hence, the correct option is (A).

34. The pattern followed here is:

16 + 1 = 17

17 - 3 = 14

14 + 5 = 19

19 - 7 = 12

12 + 9 = 21

Here, 1, 3, 5, 7, and 9 are consecutive odd numbers in the increasing order.

Hence, the correct option is (D).

35. Factors of 3341 and 3328:

$$3341 = 257 \times 13$$
$$3328 = 2^8 \times 13$$

The common factor is only 13.

$\therefore$ HCF of 3341 and 3328 is 13.

Hence, the correct option is (B).

36. As we know,

$$\text{Average} = \frac{\text{Sum of ages}}{\text{Total number of member}}$$

$\therefore$ Sum of ages $=$ Average $\times$ Total number of member

Given,

3 years ago, the average age of 5 members $= 16$ years

$\therefore$ 3 years ago, sum of the ages of 5 members $= 16 \times 5 = 80$

Sum of the ages of 5 members today $= 80 + 3 \times 5 = 95$

Sum of the ages of 6 members today $= 16 \times 6 = 96$

$\therefore$ Age of the child $= 96 - 95 = 1$ year

Hence, the correct option is (C).

37. Given:

The probability of getting a number on a roll of one die having total of 6 outcomes is p. The mean is equal to 0.5

We know that:

Mean = n × probability of each outcome

Caculation:

The mean is equal to 0.5

$$\Rightarrow n \times p = 0.5$$
$$\Rightarrow 6p = 0.5$$
$$\Rightarrow p = \frac{1}{12}$$

Probability of not getting number 5 on at most one die $= 1 - p$ (Getting number 5 on both dice)

$$= 1 - \left(\frac{1}{12} \times \frac{1}{12}\right)$$
$$= \frac{143}{144}$$

$\therefore$ Probability of not getting number 5 on at most one die is $\frac{143}{144}$.

Hence, the correct option is (C).

38. Given:

A can complete the work in 12 hours

A's one - hour work $= \frac{1}{12}$

B can complete the work in 8 hours

B's one - hour work $= \frac{1}{8}$

Let the total time taken by A and B to complete the work be x hours

A and B's one - hour work $= \frac{1}{12} + \frac{1}{8}$

$$\frac{1}{12} + \frac{1}{8} = \frac{1}{x}$$

$\Rightarrow x = 4.8$ hr $= 4$ hr and (0.8×60) min $= 4$ hours 48 minutes

The total time is taken by A and B to complete the work is 4 hours and 48 minutes

Hence, the correct option is (D).

39. The volume of the cone will be maximum if the height and the radius of the cone are the same as that of the cylinder.

Let the height and radius of the cylinder be h, r and l be slant height respectively.

As, we know

$$l^2 = h^2 + r^2$$
$$h = \sqrt{25^2 - 7^2}$$
$$h = 24 \text{ cm}$$

Volume of cylinder

$$V = \pi r^2 h$$
$$= \pi \times 7^2 \times 24$$
$$= 1176\pi \text{ cm}^3$$

Hence, the correct option is (A).

40. Given:

We have to find 15% of Rs. 34

As X is 25% more than Y

∴ If Y = 100 then X = 125

Thus Y is less than X by 25 where X is 125.

$\Rightarrow$ Percentage by which Y is less than X = $\left(\dfrac{25}{125}\right)$ × 100 = 20%

Hence, the correct option is (B).

41. 1 red ball can be selected in $^5C_1$ ways

1 white ball can be selected in $^4C_1$ ways

1 blue ball can be selected in $^3C_1$ ways

∴ Total number of ways = $^5C_1 \times {}^4C_1 \times {}^3C_1$ = 5 × 4 × 3 = 60

Hence, the correct option is (C).

42. Given:

A number when divided by 342 leaves a remainder 47

Formula:

Dividend = Divisor × Quotient + Remainder

Let k be the quotient so on dividing the given number by 342, leaves 47 as remainder

$\Rightarrow$ number = 342k + 47

When this number is divided by 19 then

$\Rightarrow$ 342k + 47 = (19 × 18k + 19 × 2 + 9)

= 19 (18k + 2) + 9

∴ When the given is divided by 19 , gives (18k + 2) as quotient and 9 as remainder.

Hence, the correct option is (D).

43. Let 'x' be the mean proportional, then the ratio between the numbers are:

$$= 6 : x : x : 54$$
$$\Rightarrow \frac{6}{x} = \frac{x}{54}$$
$$\Rightarrow x^2 = 6 \times 54$$

$$\Rightarrow x^2 = 324$$
$$\Rightarrow x = \sqrt{324}$$
$$\Rightarrow x = 18$$

Therefore, the mean proportional of 6 and 54 is 18.

Hence, the correct option is (C).

44. Given:

Speed of the jeep = 60 km/h

Formula:

To convert km/h into $m/\sec$ = Speed $\times \dfrac{5}{18}$

To convert $m/\sec$ into km/h = Speed $\times \dfrac{18}{5}$

Calculation:

Jeep moves at the speed of 60 km/h

Speed of the jeep in m/s is,

$$= 60 \times \frac{5}{18}$$
$$= 3.33333 \times 5$$
$$= 16.666666 \ m/s$$

Approximately $16.67 \ m/s$

Hence, the correct option is (B).

45. Given:

Sumit purchased item for Rs.6500

Profit = 24%

Formula:

$$SP = CP \times \frac{100+P\%}{100}$$
$$SP = CP \times \frac{100-L\%}{100}$$

Here SP is selling price, CP is cost price, P% is profit% and L% is loss%

Calculation:

The selling price of item $= \dfrac{6500 \times 124}{100}$

= Rs. 8060

Sumit purchases another item at Rs. 8060

Sell at = 20% loss

The selling price of another item $= \dfrac{8060 \times 80}{100}$

= Rs. 6448

Gain/loss of Sumit in the whole transaction = 6448 – 6500

= - Rs. 52

Sumit loss in whole transition = 52

Hence, the correct option is (C).

46. The logic followed here is:

1) P is taller than Q.

P > Q

2) R is taller than S.

R > S

3) S is taller than Q but shorter than P and P is shorter than R.

R > P > S > Q

Thus, R is the tallest in all.

So, the correct answer is "R".

Hence, the correct option is (D).

47. The pattern followed here,

K | U C | T M B | L | U C | T M B | M | U C | T M B

The alphabets K, L and M are increasing alphabetical order while UC and TMB remain constant.

Hence, the correct option is (A).

48. In a code language, if BOX is written as 725

B	O	X
7	2	5

and GLAND is written as 16493,

G	L	A	N	D
1	6	4	9	3

Then BOND be written as

B	O	N	D
7	2	9	3

BOND is written as 7293.

Hence, the correct option is (D).

49. Counting the years 1600 + 300 + 74

In 1600 years, there are zero odd days.

In 300 years, there is one odd day.

In 74 years, there are 18 leap years and 56 normal years, so the odd days are:

18(2) + 56(1) = 36 + 56 = 92,

Which are 13 weeks and 1 odd day.

In 25 days of January 1975, there are 3 weeks and 4 odd days.

Total odd days = 0 + 1 + 1 + 4

Six odd days, so it was a Saturday.

Hence, the correct option is (B).

50. We have to draw a family tree and then find the relations between family members as asked.

Symbol in Diagram	Meaning
○	Female
□	Male
═══	Married Couple
──	Siblings
│	Difference of A Generation

The family tree as per the given conditions is as follows:

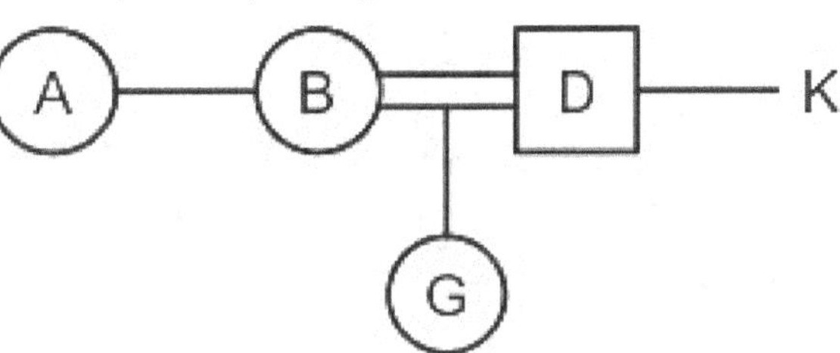

As it can be seen that "A" is "the sister in law "of "D".

Therefore, the correct answer should be "Sister in law".

Hence, the correct option is (D).

Mock Test 07

General Knowledge

Q.1 The International Nurses Day marks the birth anniversary of which social reformer?
- **A.** Mother Teresa
- **B.** Clara Barton
- **C.** Florence Nightingale
- **D.** Marie Curie

Q.2 Which day is observed as Parakram Diwas, birth anniversary of Netaji Subhas Chandra Bose?
- **A.** January 24
- **B.** January 23
- **C.** January 19
- **D.** February 22

Q.3 In which district of Rajasthan 'Ranthambore Fort' is located?
- **A.** Jodhpur
- **B.** Sawai Madhopur
- **C.** Chittor
- **D.** Jaisalmer

Q.4 'En Passant' is related to which game?

[Madhya Pradesh Public Service Commission (MPPSC), 2018]

- **A.** Billiards
- **B.** Snooker
- **C.** Carrom
- **D.** Chess

Q.5 In Uttarakhand, IIM is located at _____.
- **A.** Kashipur
- **B.** Khatima
- **C.** Pauri
- **D.** Rishikesh

Q.6 Balboa is the official currency of:
- **A.** Panama
- **B.** Belarus
- **C.** Austria
- **D.** Both (A) and (B)

Q.7 Which one of the following articles were called the 'heart and soul of the Constitution' by Dr B.R. Ambedkar?
- **A.** Article 32
- **B.** Article 19
- **C.** Article 350
- **D.** Article 363

Q.8 Which of the following describes the Geostationary Orbit (GEO) correctly?

[Maharashtra Public Service Commission, 2018]

- **A.** Altitude of 20,000 km above the sea level and the orbital period is 12 hours.
- **B.** Altitude of 36,000 km above the sea level and the orbital period is 24 hours.
- **C.** Altitude of 400 km above the sea level and the orbital period is 90 minutes.
- **D.** None of these

Q.9 Which state/ UT of India is known as the land of paradise?
- **A.** Uttar Pradesh
- **B.** Jammu and Kashmir
- **C.** Haryana
- **D.** Assam

Q.10 Name the highest Sports Award given by Haryana Government.

[HSSC Canal Patwari, 2021]

- **A.** Vikramaditya Award
- **B.** Eklavya Award
- **C.** Guru Vashisht Award
- **D.** Bhim Award

Q.11 Who among the following built the city of Tughlaqabad?
- **A.** Tughluq Khan
- **B.** Muhammad bin Tughlaq
- **C.** Firuz Shah Tughlaq
- **D.** Ghiyasuddin Tughlaq

Q.12 Which one of the following statements about the Gupta period is NOT correct?

[UPSC Central Armed Police Forces AC, 2017]

- **A.** Forced labour (Vishti) became more common than before in this period
- **B.** A passage in the Vishnu Purana refers to the Guptas enjoying all the territories along the Ganga up to Prayaga
- **C.** The Mehrauli inscription suggests that Chandragupta fought against a confederacy of enemies in Bengal and also led a campaign into the Punjab
- **D.** Saurashtra was not a part of the Gupta Empire

Q.13 The writer of the book 'India's Second Freedom' is:

[Uttarakhand Public Service Commission (UKPSC), 2011]

- **A.** Soli Sorabji
- **B.** Loknayak Jaiprakash Narain
- **C.** Lalkrishna Advani
- **D.** Atal Behari Bajpai

Q.14 The book titled 'Social Harmony' is written by:
- **A.** Atal Bihari Vajpayee
- **B.** Shyama Prasad Mukherjee
- **C.** Narendra Modi
- **D.** Lal Krishna Advani

Q.15 In which state is the Ponung folk dance practised?
- **A.** Sikkim
- **B.** Manipur
- **C.** Assam
- **D.** Arunachal Pradesh

General Science

Q.16 Cell wall is not present in cells of:

[Officers Training Academy (OTA), 2021], [Indian Military Academy (IMA), 2021]

- **A.** Bacteria
- **B.** Plants
- **C.** Fungi
- **D.** Humans

Q.17 A child receives a tall beautiful plant as a birthday gift from his father with a quiz. The father asked her how she would verify whether this tall plant was the progeny of both the tall parents or one tall and one short parent plant. She could verify this through?

[Officers Training Academy (OTA), 2021], [Indian Military Academy (IMA), 2021]

"

A. cross-pollination
B. self-pollination
C. tissue culture
D. negative propagation

Q.18 A student was doing an experiment on increasing the cell division among plants. She asked her supervisor to suggest the specific plant hormone for the same. Had you been her Supervisor, which plant hormone would you suggest?

[Officers Training Academy (OTA), 2021], [Indian Military Academy (IMA), 2021]

A. Abscisic acid
B. Gibberellins
C. Cytokinin
D. Auxin

Q.19 An antibiotic is not useful against a virus whereas a vaccine is. Which one of the following is the most appropriate reason for this?

[Officers Training Academy (OTA), 2021], [Indian Military Academy (IMA), 2021]

A. An antibiotic can break RNA only, whereas virus has DNA.
B. An antibiotic is a carbohydrate in its chemical nature, whereas a vaccine is a protein which works well to kill a virus.
C. Only a vaccine can break the genetic material of a virus.
D. A virus does not use biochemical pathways which can be blocked by an antibiotic. But a vaccine can boost an immune system to fight the virus.

Q.20 'Sleeping sickness' is caused by:

[Officers Training Academy (OTA), 2021], [Indian Military Academy (IMA), 2021]

A. Trypanosoma
B. Leishmania
C. Plasmodium
D. Paramecium

Q.21 How many calories are there in a Joule?
A. 0.24 gram
B. 0.48 gram
C. 0.72 gram
D. 0.96 gram

Q.22 The correct relationship between Moment of Inertia, Torque, and Angular acceleration is ________.
A. Angular acceleration = Torque × Moment of inertia
B. Angular acceleration = Torque / Moment of inertia
C. Moment of inertia = Angular acceleration × Torque
D. Moment of inertia = Angular acceleration + Torque

Q.23 The image formed in a compound microscope is:
A. Sometimes erect, sometimes inverted
B. Erect
C. Inverted
D. None of these

Q.24 The element M in the Dobereiner triad Ca, M and Ba is:

[Maharashtra Public Service Commission, 2018]

A. Be
B. Mg
C. Sr
D. I

Q.25 Wood grain alcohol is nothing but:

[Maharashtra Public Service Commission, 2018]

A. Methanol
B. Ethanol
C. Benzyl alcohol
D. Isopropyl alcohol

Q.26 Water is often treated with chlorine to:

[Maharashtra Public Service Commission, 2018]

A. Increase oxygen content
B. Kill germs
C. Remove sedimentation
D. Remove insoluble impurities

Q.27 Corrosion takes place as a result of:

[Maharashtra Public Service Commission, 2018]

A. Only physical reactions
B. Only chemical reactions
C. Both (A) and (B)
D. None of the above

Q.28 Which of the following law states that 'the ratio of the sine of the angle of incidence to the sine of the angle of refraction is a constant'?
A. Lenz's law
B. Faraday's law
C. Hook's law
D. Snell's law

Q.29 What does the amplitude of sound wave determine?
A. Loudness
B. Pitch
C. Frequency
D. Amplitude

Q.30 Which one of the following substances is used in the preservation of food stuff?
A. Citric Acid
B. Potassium Chloride
C. Sodium Benzoate
D. Sodium Chloride

Maths

Q.31 What sum of money will amount to Rs. 7000 in 4 years at 10% per annum on simple interest?
A. Rs, 4000
B. Rs. 5000
C. Rs. 7000
D. Rs. 5500

Q.32 There are 20 points in a plane, how many triangles can be formed by these points if 5 are colinear?
A. 1130
B. 550
C. 1129
D. 1140

Q.33 Let ΔABC be a triangle whose area is $10\sqrt{3}$ units with side lengths |AB| = 8 units and |AC| = 5 units. Find possible values of angle A.
A. 60° or 120°
B. 45° or 135°
C. 30° only
D. 90° only

Q.34 Simplify $16 - 2 \div 14 + 6 \times 2$.
A. $27\frac{12}{14}$
B. $29\frac{5}{7}$
C. $26\frac{5}{7}$
D. $27\frac{5}{8}$

Q.35 The cash difference between the selling price of an article at a profit of 4% and 8% is Rs. 3. The ratio of two selling prices is:

[RRB (NTPC), 2017]

A. 25 : 27
B. 26 : 27
C. 26 : 31
D. 26 : 29

Q.36 Amitabh covered a distance of 96 km two hours faster than he had planned to, thus he achieved by travelling 1 km more every hour than he intended to cover every 1 hour 15

minutes. What was the speed at which Amitabh travelled during the journey?

A. 16 km/hr   **B.** 26 km/hr   **C.** 36 km/hr   **D.** 30 km/hr

Q.37 If the ratio of A : B is 3 : 6 and ratio of B : C is 7 : 28, then find the ratio of A : B : C.

A. 3 : 7 : 28   **B.** 1 : 2 : 8   **C.** 2 : 1 : 8   **D.** 6 : 7 : 28

Q.38 Which number from the options will replace the question mark (?) in the following series?

0, 8, 24, 48, ?

A. 81   **B.** 74   **C.** 82   **D.** 80

Q.39 Two numbers are in the ratio $3 : 5$ and their HCF is 20. Their LCM is:

[RRB (NTPC), 2017]

A. 60   **B.** 300   **C.** 30   **D.** 10

Q.40 A number is selected at random from the numbers $7, 3, 9, 7, 9, 5, 7, 9, 9, 5$. The probability that the selected number is their average is:

A. $\frac{7}{10}$ **B.** $\frac{5}{10}$ **C.** $\frac{3}{10}$ **D.** $\frac{1}{10}$

Q.41 50 employees in a company can complete a work in 23 days. They start work together and after every 5 days, 5 employees more join them. Then in how much time work will be completed?

A. 25 days   **B.** 15 days   **C.** 20 days   **D.** 30 days

Q.42 A tank is made of the shape of a cylinder with a hemispherical depression at one end. The height of the cylinder is $1.45\ m$ and the radius is $30\ cm$. The total surface area of the tank is:

A. 30 m ^{2} **B.** 3.3 m ^{2}
C. 30.3 m ^{2} **D.** 3300 m ^{2}

Q.43 If 7% of a number is equal to the 11% of other number. The sum of the two numbers is 216. Find the numbers?

A. 162 and 54   **B.** 132 and 84
C. 116 and 100   **D.** 155 and 61

Q.44 The difference between the two numbers is 335. When the larger number is divided by the smaller number, the quotient is 13 and the remainder is 11. What is the larger number?

A. 390   **B.** 362   **C.** 350   **D.** 346

Q.45 Average of 40 numbers is 71. If the number 100 replaced by 140, then average is increased by:

A. 3   **B.** 4   **C.** 2   **D.** 1

Logical Reasoning

Q.46 Find the odd word from the given alternatives.

A. Tornado   **B.** Hurricane
C. River   **D.** Cyclone

Q.47 Sunil told that Mohit was the son of the only brother of Sunil father's wife. How is Mohit related to Sunil?

[UP Police ASI, 2018]

A. Cousin   **B.** Maternal Uncle
C. Son   **D.** Brother

Q.48 Direction: Select the combination of letters that when sequentially placed in the gaps of the given letter series will complete the series.

Z O M _ Q _ Y O _ S Q _ X _ M S _ N

[SSC Selection Post Phase IX, 2019]

A. SNMOQO   **B.** QMSNOQ
C. SNMNOQ   **D.** SMNOQM

Q.49 If SEVEN is coded as 23136 and EIGHT as 34579, what will be the code for NINE?

[Territorial Army Officer, 2021]

A. 6463   **B.** 6364   **C.** 6436   **D.** 6436

Q.50 Aman running towards South turns to his right and runs. Then he turns to his right and finally turns to his left. Towards which direction is he running now?

A. East   **B.** North   **C.** West   **D.** South

// Smart Answer Sheet //

Correct Indicates percentage of students who answered questions correctly.

Skipped Indicates percentage of students who skipped questions.

Q.	Ans.	Correct / Skipped
1	C	65.54 % / 30.71 %
2	B	76.12 % / 20.18 %
3	B	77.7 % / 15.4 %
4	D	25.91 % / 72.24 %
5	A	45.86 % / 40.74 %
6	A	15.3 % / 73.89 %
7	A	88.52 % / 10.05 %
8	B	18.88 % / 77.15 %
9	B	48.35 % / 44.35 %
10	D	18.0 % / 68.59 %
11	D	56.3 % / 40.35 %
12	D	69.75 % / 30.01 %
13	B	24.66 % / 70.83 %
14	C	25.71 % / 71.48 %
15	D	28.04 % / 67.64 %
16	D	68.13 % / 31.15 %
17	B	27.99 % / 67.83 %
18	C	14.44 % / 77.33 %
19	D	60.63 % / 36.49 %
20	A	57.7 % / 30.74 %
21	A	78.89 % / 14.5 %
22	B	47.8 % / 42.54 %
23	C	63.46 % / 32.43 %
24	C	85.01 % / 12.0 %
25	A	81.32 % / 17.53 %
26	B	89.12 % / 10.39 %
27	B	69.81 % / 30.17 %
28	D	59.82 % / 36.03 %
29	A	57.93 % / 33.61 %
30	C	40.46 % / 45.89 %
31	B	51.04 % / 45.2 %
32	A	62.53 % / 31.81 %
33	A	40.38 % / 31.88 %
34	A	30.38 % / 68.48 %
35	B	46.8 % / 43.47 %
36	A	26.87 % / 72.85 %
37	B	30.94 % / 67.29 %
38	D	20.98 % / 75.73 %
39	B	82.38 % / 14.59 %
40	C	14.83 % / 67.67 %
41	C	61.84 % / 36.7 %
42	B	67.05 % / 30.47 %
43	B	48.66 % / 43.42 %
44	B	49.14 % / 37.81 %
45	D	82.31 % / 10.59 %
46	C	10.1 % / 69.41 %
47	A	20.98 % / 76.16 %
48	C	63.26 % / 35.53 %
49	A	53.39 % / 33.73 %
50	C	45.45 % / 53.1 %

Performance Analysis

Avg. Score (%)	49.0%
Toppers Score (%)	56.0%
Your Score	

//Hints and Solutions//

1. International Nurses Day marks the birth anniversary of nursing pioneer Florence Nightingale, who was born on May 12, 1820.

Florence Nightingale was an English social reformer, statistician, and the founder of modern nursing. Nightingale came to prominence while serving as a manager and trainer of nurses during the Crimean War, in which she organized to care for wounded soldiers at Constantinople.

Hence, the correct option is (C).

2. Parakram Diwas is celebrated annually on 23 January. It is a national event celebrated in India to mark the birthday of the prominent Indian freedom fighter Netaji Subhas Chandra Bose. He played a pivotal role in Indian independence movement. He was the head of Indian National Army (Azad Hind Fouj). He was the founder-head of the Azad Hind Government.

Hence, the correct option is (B).

3. Ranthambore Fort is located in the Sawai Madhopur district of Rajasthan. Fort was held by the Chauhans until the 13th century till the Delhi Sultanate captured it. Ranthambore Fort lies within the Ranthambore National Park. There are three Hindu temples dedicated to Ganesha, Shiva, and Ramlalaji temple inside the fort. Ranthambore is also famous for its tiger conservation park(tiger reserve of Rajasthan). This park being the former hunting grounds of the Maharajahs of Jaipur. It is a UNESCO World Heritage Site.

Hence, the correct option is (B).

4. The en passant rule is a special pawn capturing move in chess.

- "En passant" is a French expression that translates to "in passing," which is precisely how this capture works.

- Pawns can usually capture only pieces that are directly and diagonally in front of it on an adjacent file.

- It moves to the captured piece's square and replaces it.

Hence, the correct option is (D).

5. Indian Institute of Management Kashipur also known as IIM Kashipur, is a public business school located in Kashipur, Uttarakhand. It is one of the 13 Indian Institutes of Management the government has set up during the Eleventh Five-Year Plan. On 29 April 2011, the foundation stone of the institute was laid.

Hence, the correct option is (A).

6. Balboa is the official currency of Panama.

Panama

- It is known as a transit country because of the Panama Canal.

- It is located on the Isthmus of Panama, connects North and South America.

Hence, the correct option is (A).

7. Dr. B. R. Ambedkar called Article 32 of the Indian Constitution i.e. Right to Constitutional remedies as ' the heart and soul of the Constitution'.

It was made so because the mere declaration of the fundamental right without a piece of effective machinery for enforcement of the fundamental rights would have been meaningless.

Also, a right that does not have a remedy is a worthless declaration.

Thus, the framers of our constitution adopted the special provisions in article 32 which provided remedies to the violated fundamental rights of citizens.

Hence, the correct option is (A).

8. Altitude of $36,000$ km above the sea level and the orbital period is 24 hours.

A Geostationary Orbit (GSO) is a geosynchronous orbit with an inclination of zero, meaning, it lies on the equator. Such satellites complete a revolution around orbit once a day and move in the same direction as the Earth.

Such satellites appear stationary from the earth, as they stay above the same point on the earth's surface. They are placed at an altitude of $35,790$ km. As the height of a satellite increases, the time for the satellite to complete the revolution increases. At a height of 35790 km, it takes 24 hours for the satellite to complete the orbit. This type of orbit is known as a geosynchronous orbit, i.e. it is synchronized with the Earth.

Hence, the correct option is (B).

9. Jammu and Kashmir, the state of India is a land of paradise.

Kashmir is the northwestern region of the Indian subcontinent. Historically the term Kashmir was used to refer to the valley lying between the Great Himalayas and the Pir Panjal range. Kashmir throughout the ages has remained another name for Paradise.

Hence, the correct option is (B).

10. The highest sports award given by the Haryana government is the Bhim Award. The Haryana government on 19 February 2017 conferred the Bhim awards to 42 sportspersons of the state, recognizing them for their outstanding performance at the national and international level between the years 2013 and 2017.

Hence, the correct option is (D).

11. Ghiyasuddin Tughlaq (1320 - 1325 AD) built the city of Tughlaqabad.

He was also known as Ghazi Malik. Ghiyasuddin Tughlaq was the founder of the Tughlaq dynasty. This dynasty was also known as the dynasty of the Qaraunah Turks. He was the first sultan of Delhi who took up the title of Ghazi or slayer of the infidels. He made policies for the Construction of canals and the formulation of a famine. He started the barter system or sharing of crops. He built the city of Tughlaqabad near Delhi and made it his capital.

Hence, the correct option is (D).

12. Vishti or forced labour was already common before the Gupta rule, there was a passage in Vishnu purana refers that the Gupta's enjoyed all the territories along the Ganga up to Pragya.

Mehrauli inscription suggests that Chandragupta fought against a Confederacy of enemies in Bengal and also led a campaign into the Punjab.

Saurashtra was also the part of the Gupta empire.

Hence, the correct option is (D).

13. The writer of the book 'India's Second Freedom' is Loknayak Jaiprakash Narain.

Jayaprakash Narayan popularly referred to as JP or Lok Nayak was an Indian independence activist, theorist, socialist and political leader. He is remembered for leading the mid-1970s opposition against Prime Minister Indira Gandhi, for whose overthrow he had called for a "total revolution". In 1999, he was posthumously awarded the Bharat Ratna, India's highest civilian award, in recognition of his social service and he was also awarded with the Magsaysay award for Public Service in 1965.

Hence, the correct option is (B).

14. 'Social Harmony' written by Shri Narendra Modi is a collection of essays on Dalits, Tribals, Women & Family relations and elaborates on how Social Harmony can be achieved in our society.

In Hindi, the title of the book is Samajik Samrasta.

Narendra Modi has penned many books. Some of the popular books are Exam warriors, Jyotipunj, Convenient Action: Continuity for Change, etc.

Hence, the correct option is (C).

15. In Arunachal Pradesh Ponung folk dance is practised. It belongs to the Adi tribe. This tribe is known for many of its traditional folk dances. Ponung dance is performed during the religious celebration.

Hence, the correct option is (D).

16. Cell wall is not present in cells of Humans.

Cell walls are present in most prokaryotes (except mollicute bacteria), in algae, fungi, and eukaryotes including plants but are absent in animals.

Hence, the correct option is (D).

17. A child receives a tall beautiful plant as a birthday gift from his father with a quiz. The father asked her how she would verify whether this tall plant was the progeny of both the tall parents or one tall and one short parent plant. She could verify this through self-pollination.

Self-pollination occurs when the pollen is transferred from the anther to the stigma on the same flower, from another flower on the same plant, or from a flower on another plant of the same cultivar.

Self-pollinated plants are said to be self-fruitful.

Hence, the correct option is (B).

18. A student was doing an experiment on increasing the cell division among plants. She asked her supervisor to suggest the specific plant hormone for the same.

Cytokinins (CK) are a class of plant growth substances (phytohormones) that promote cell division, or cytokinesis, in plant roots and shoots.

They are involved primarily in cell growth and differentiation, but also affect apical dominance, axillary bud growth, and leaf senescence.

Hence, the correct option is (C).

19. The correct answer is A virus does not use biochemical pathways which can be blocked by an antibiotic. But a vaccine can boost an immune system to fight the virus.

- Viruses are different from bacteria they have a different structure and a different way of surviving.

- The viruses don't have cell walls that can be attacked by antibiotics instead they are surrounded by a protective protein coat.

- Vaccines can help limit the spread of antibiotic resistance.

- The global increase in disease caused by drug-resistant bacteria, due to overuse and misuse of antibiotics, is a major public health concern.

- It is more difficult and costly to treat antibiotic-resistant infections and people do not always recover.

Hence, the correct option is (D).

20. The sleeping sickness is caused by microscopic parasites of the species Trypanosoma brucei.

It is transmitted by the tsetse fly (Glossina species), which is found only in sub-Saharan Africa.

Trypanosoma, any member of a genus (Trypanosoma) of parasitic zooflagellate protozoans belonging to the order Kinetoplastida.

The adult trypanosomes are mainly blood parasites of vertebrates, especially fishes, birds, and mammals.

Most species require an intermediate host (often an insect or a leech) to complete their life cycle.

The other species of trypanosomes induce economically important diseases of livestock nagana, surra, mal de caderas, and dourine.

Hence, the correct option is (A).

21. There are 0.24 gram calories in a joule.

Joule is a unit of energy and is indicated by 'J'. It is expressed as the work required to produce one watt of power for one second. Mathematically, Joule can be expressed as:

$$1 \text{ Joule} = 1 \, kg \cdot m^2/s^2$$

Hence, the correct option is (A).

22. The correct relationship between Moment of Inertia, Torque, and Angular acceleration is

Angular acceleration = Torque / Moment of inertia.

- The rate of change of angular velocity is termed angular acceleration.

- The measure of the force required to rotate an object about an axis is called Torque.
- The moment of inertia or the 'rotational inertia', is the resistance shown by a rigid body against the alteration in the rotational speed caused by the application of torque.

Hence, the correct option is (B).

23. The image formed by objective lens of compound microscope is real and enlarged and inverted.

The objective lens produces a real, inverted image and the eyepiece acts as a simple magnifier and does not re-invert and produces a virtual image.

Hence, the correct option is (C).

24. The element M in the Dobereiner triad Ca, M and Ba is I.

Dobereiner was a German scientist. He studied as a pharmacist at Munchberg (Germany). In 1829, he found some groups of three-element which showed similar properties. These groups were called triads.

In these triads, the atomic mass of the middle element was approximately the mean of the atomic masses of the other two elements.

- The first three elements were Li, Na, K.
- He arranged the elements as per their atomic masses in increasing order.
- The second triad he found was Ca, Sr, Ba.

Hence, the correct option is (C).

25. Wood grain alcohol is nothing but Methanol.

Methanol (methyl alcohol), is the simplest of the alcohols. It is the natural by-product of wood distillation an older method of producing drinking Alcohol (ethanol). Chemically synthesized methanol is a common industrial solvent found in paint remover, cleansing agents, and antifreezers.

Methanol is a non-drinking type of alcohol (also known as wood alcohol and methyl alcohol) that is mostly used to create fuel, solvents, and antifreezers. It is also used to produce a variety of other chemicals, including acetic acid.

Hence, the correct option is (A).

26. Water is often treated with chlorine to kill germs.

As a halogen, chlorine is a highly efficient disinfectant and is added to public water supplies to kill disease-causing pathogens, such as bacteria, viruses, and protozoans, that commonly grow in water supply reservoirs, on the walls of water mains, and in storage tanks.

In particular, chlorination is used to prevent the spread of waterborne diseases such as cholera, dysentery, and typhoid. As a strong oxidizing agent, chlorine kills via the oxidation of organic molecules.

Hence, the correct option is (B).

27. Corrosion takes place as a result of only chemical reactions.

Corrosion can be defined as the process through which refined metals are converted into more stable compounds such as metal oxides, metal sulfides, or metal hydroxides.

The rusting of iron involves the formation of iron oxides via the action of atmospheric moisture and oxygen. Corrosion is usually an undesirable phenomenon since it negatively affects the desirable properties of the metal.

Hence, the correct option is (B).

28. Snell's law is a formula used to describe the relationship between the angles of incidence and refraction.

The law refers to light or other waves passing through a boundary between two different isotropic media, such as water, glass, or air. In optics, the law is used to calculate the angles of incidence or refraction, and to find the refractive index of a material. The law states that the ratio of the sine of the angle of incidence to the sine of the angle of refraction is a constant.

Hence, the correct option is (D).

29. The amplitude of the sound wave determines its loudness.

A louder sound is represented by a larger amplitude. A softer sound indicates a smaller amplitude. Due to the larger amplitude, there is a more energetic vibration. The sensitivity of the ear also determines the loudness of a sound.

Hence, the correct option is (A).

30. The chemical formula of Sodium Benzoate is C_6H_5COONa. It is widely used as a food preservative. Sodium benzoate is a preservative. As a food additive, sodium benzoate has the E number $E211$. It is bacteriostatic and fungistatic under acidic conditions. The mechanism starts with the absorption of benzoic acid into the cell.

Hence, the correct option is (C).

31. Given:

Amount, A = Rs. 7000

Time, T = 4 years

Rate, R= 10%

Formula used:

$$\text{Simple Interest} = \frac{(Principal \times Rate \times Time)}{100}$$

Amount = Principal + Simple Interest

Let the sum of money be Rs. P.

Amount = Principal + Simple Interest

$$\Rightarrow 7000 = (P) + \left[\frac{(P \times 10 \times 4)}{100}\right]$$

$$\Rightarrow 7000 = \left[P + \left(\frac{2P}{5}\right)\right]$$

$$\Rightarrow 7000 = \frac{7P}{5}$$

$$\Rightarrow 1000 \times 5 = P$$

$\Rightarrow P = 5000$

∴ The sum of money is Rs. 5000.

Hence, the correct option is (B).

32. Given:

Number of points in plane n = 20.

Number of colinear points m = 5.

Number of triangles from by joining n points of which m are colinear = $^nC_3 - {}^mC_3$

Therefore the number of triangles = $^{20}C_3 - {}^5C_3$

$= \dfrac{20!}{(20-3)!.3!} - \dfrac{5!}{(5-3)!.3!}$

= 1140-10

= 1130

Hence, the correct option is (A).

33. Given, Let ΔABC be a triangle whose area is $10\sqrt{3}$ units with side lengths |AB| = 8 units and |AC| = 5 units.

Area of triangle = $\dfrac{1}{2} \times AB \times AC \times \sin A$

$\Rightarrow 10\sqrt{3} = \dfrac{1}{2} \times 8 \times 5 \times \sin A$

$\Rightarrow 10\sqrt{3} = 20 \sin A$

$\Rightarrow \sin A = \dfrac{\sqrt{3}}{2}$

$\Rightarrow A = 60°$ or $120°$

Thus, the possible values of angle A are 60° or 120°.

Hence, the correct option is (A).

34. Given,

$16 - 2 \div 14 + 6 \times 2$

$= 16 - \dfrac{2}{14} + 12$

$= 28 - \dfrac{2}{14}$

$= \dfrac{28 \times 14 - 2}{14}$

$= \dfrac{392 - 2}{14}$

$= \dfrac{390}{14}$

$= 27\dfrac{12}{14}$

Hence, the correct option is (A).

35. Given,

The cash difference between the selling price of an article at a profit of 4% and 8% = Rs. 3

As we know,

Selling price = Cost price + Profit

Profit $\% = \dfrac{\text{Profit}}{\text{Cost price}} \times 100$

Let the cost price be $100x$.

Selling price will be when profit is $4\% = 100x + 4\%$ of $100x$

$= 100x + \dfrac{4}{100} \times 100x$

$= 100x + 4x$

$= 104x$

Similarly,

Selling price when profit is $8\% = 100x + 8\%$ of $100x$

$= 100x + \dfrac{8}{100} \times 100x$

$= 100x + 8x$

$= 108x$

Difference between the selling price of an article at a profit of 4% and 8% = Rs. 3

$\Rightarrow 108x - 104x = 3$

$\Rightarrow 4x = 3$

$\Rightarrow x = \dfrac{3}{4}$

Selling price will be when profit is $4\% = 104x = 104 \times \dfrac{3}{4} = 78$

Selling price will be when profit is $8\% = 108x = 108 \times \dfrac{3}{4} = 81$

∴ Ratio of two selling prices $= 78 : 81 = 26 : 27$

So, the ratio of two selling prices is $26 : 27$.

Hence, the correct option is (B).

36. Suppose he planned to cover x km every 1 hour 15 minutes (i.e., in $\dfrac{5}{4}$ hours).

Planned speed $= \dfrac{x}{\left(\frac{5}{4}\right)} = \dfrac{4x}{5}$ km/hr

Actual speed $= \dfrac{x+1}{1} = (x+1)$ km/hr

The time difference is 2 hour

$\Rightarrow \dfrac{96}{\left(\frac{4x}{5}\right)} - \dfrac{96}{x+1} = 2$

$\Rightarrow \dfrac{120}{x} - \dfrac{96}{x+1} = 2$ ....(i)

$\Rightarrow 120(x + 1) - 96x = 2x(x + 1)$

$\Rightarrow 60(x + 1) - 48x = x(x + 1)$

$\Rightarrow 60x + 60 - 48x = x^2 + x$

$\Rightarrow x^2 - 11x - 60 = 0$

$\Rightarrow (x - 15)(x + 4) = 0$

$\Rightarrow x = 15$

Speed at which he travelled

$\Rightarrow (x + 1) = 16$ km/hr

Hence, the correct option is (A).

37. Given:

A : B = 3 : 6 = 1 : 2   ----(i)

B : C = 7 : 28 = 1 : 4   ----(ii)

We know that:

If P : Q and Q : R are given, then P : Q : R is given by:

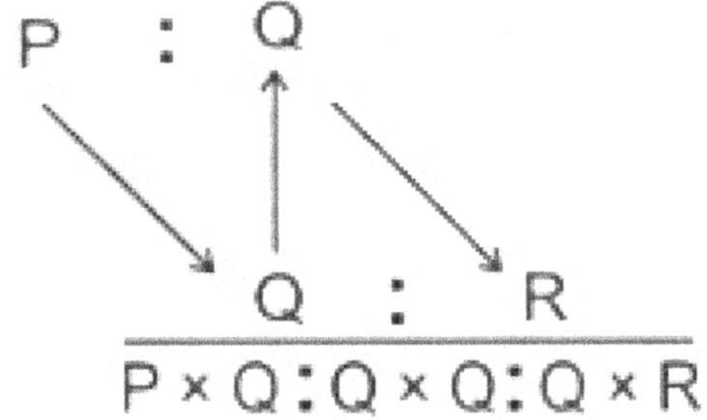

To equate the value of B in both equation we will multiply equation (ii) by 2 so we get,

A : B = 1 : 2

B : C = 2 : 8

A : B : C = 1 × 2 : 2 × 2 : 2 × 8

$\Rightarrow$ A : B : C = 2 : 4 : 16 = 1 : 2 : 8

$\therefore$ A : B : C = 1 : 2 : 8

Hence, the correct option is (B).

38. The logic follows here is;

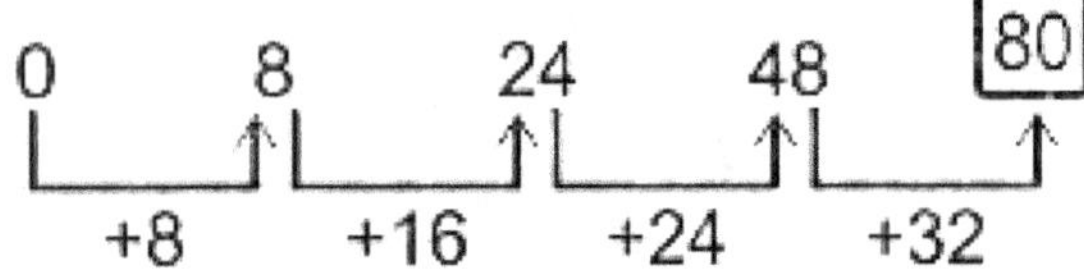

Thus, "80" is the correct answer.

Hence, the correct option is (D).

39. Let the two numbers be $3x$ and $5x$.

HCF of $3x$ and $5x = x$

Given,

HCF $= 20 = x$

$\therefore$ Two numbers $3x = 3 \times 20 = 60$ and $5x = 5 \times 20 = 100$

LCM of 60 and $100 = 300$

Hence, the correct option is (B).

40. Average of given numbers $=$

$$\frac{7+3+9+7+9+5+7+9+9+5}{10} = \frac{70}{10} = 7$$

(There are 3 times 7 in the given numbers)

Therefore Number of outcomes $n(A) = 3$

Number of total outcomes $n(S) = 10$

$\therefore$ Required Probability $= \dfrac{n(A)}{n(S)}$

$\Rightarrow \dfrac{3}{10}$

Hence, the correct option is (C).

41. Given:

Total employees $= 50$

Time is taken by 50 employees to complete work $= 23$ days

After every 5 days, 5 employees more join them.

Total work is always equal to the product of time and number of people.

Total employees $= 50$

Time is taken by 50 employees to complete work $= 23$ days

Then total work $= 50 \times 23 = 1150$ units

So, work that done in the first 5 days by 50 employees $= 5 \times 50 = 250$ units

After every 5 days, 5 employees more join them.

After 5 days total employees $= 50 + 5 = 55$

So, work that done in the next 5 days by 45 employees $= 5 \times 55 = 275$ units

Again after 5 days total employees $= 55 + 5 = 60$

So, work that done in next 5 days by 60 employees $= 5 \times 60 = 300$ units

Again after 5 days total employees $= 60 + 5 = 65$

So, work that done in the next 5 days by 65 employees $= 5 \times 65 = 325$ units

Total work that done $= 250 + 275 + 300 + 325 = 1150$ units

Thus, the total work is done.

Now, time taken by employees to complete work $= 5 + 5 + 5 + 5 = 20$ days

$\therefore$ In 20 days the work will be completed.

Hence, the correct option is (C).

42. $h = 1.45$ m

$r = 30$ cm

Let r be the common radius of the cylinder and hemisphere and h be the height of the hollow cylinder.

Then $r = 30$ cm; $h = 1.45$ m $= 145$ cm)

Total surface area = curved surface area of the cylinder + curved surface area of the hemisphere

$= 2\pi rh + 2\pi r^2$

$= 2\pi(h + r)$

$= 2 \times \dfrac{22}{7} \times 30(145 + 30)$ cm ^{2}

$= 3.3$ m ^{2}

Hence, the correct option is (B).

43. Let 'x' be the first number and 'y' be the second number.

Therefore,

7% of $x = 11\%$ of y

$\dfrac{7}{100}x = \dfrac{11}{100}y$

$7x = 11y$

$\dfrac{x}{y} = \dfrac{11}{7}$

$x = \dfrac{11}{7}y$

Now, the sum of the two numbers $= x + y = 216$

$\dfrac{11}{7}y + y = 216$

$11y + 7y = 1512$

$18y = 1512$

$y = 84$

$x = \dfrac{11}{7}y$

$x = \dfrac{11}{7} \times 84$

$x = 11 \times 12$

$x = 132$

Therefore, the two numbers are 132 and 84.

Hence, the correct option is (B).

44. Given:

Difference between two numbers $= 335$

Quotient $= 13$

Remainder $= 11$

We know that,

Dividend $=$ Quotient $\times$ Divisor $+$ Remainder

Let, the smaller number $= x$

$\therefore$ The larger number $= (x + 335)$

According to the question,

$\Rightarrow x + 335 = x \times 13 + 11$

$\Rightarrow x + 335 = 13x + 11$

$\Rightarrow 12x = 324$

$\Rightarrow x = 27$

Larger number $= (27 + 335)$

$= 362$

Hence, the correct option is (B).

45. Given:

Average of 40 numbers $= 71$

Formula:

$$\text{Average} = \dfrac{\text{Sum of all observations}}{\text{Total number of all observations}}$$

Sum of 40 numbers $= 40 \times 71 = 2840$

New sum of 40 numbers $= 2840 - 100 + 140 = 2880$

New average of 40 numbers $= \dfrac{2880}{40} = 72$

$\therefore$ The average increased $= 72 - 71 = 1$

Hence, the correct option is (D).

46. Except for River, all are synonyms of Storm.

River: A large natural flow of water that goes across land and into the sea.

Tornado: A tornado is a violently rotating column of air, in contact with the ground, either pendant from a cumuliform cloud or underneath a cumuliform cloud, and often visible as a funnel cloud.

Hurricane: A hurricane is a type of storm called a tropical cyclone, which forms over tropical or subtropical waters.

Cyclone: A cyclone is a system of winds rotating counterclockwise in the Northern Hemisphere around a low-pressure center.

Hence, the correct option is (C).

47. Sunil's father's wife is Sunil's mother and Sunil's mother's brother is Sunil's maternal uncle. Thus, Mohit is the son of Sunil's maternal uncle.

Symbol in Diagram	Meaning
◯	Female
▢	Male
══	Married Couple
──	Siblings
│	Difference of A Generation

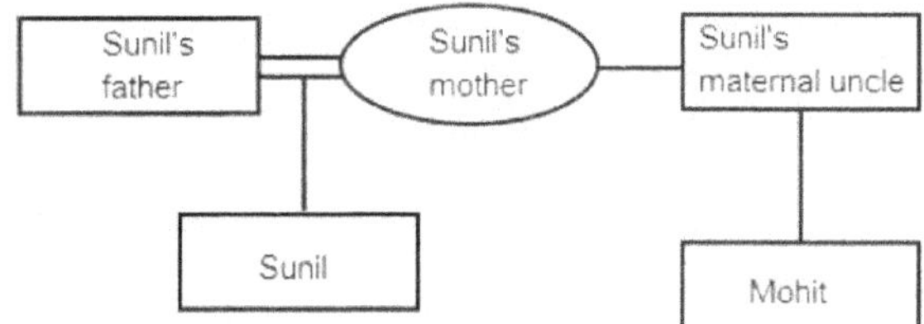

So, Mohit is the cousin of Sunil.

Hence, the correct option is (A).

48. Given statement: Z O M _ Q _ Y O _ S Q _ X _ M S _ N

Option (A)	Z	O	M	S	Q	N	Y	O	M	S	Q	O	X	Q	M	S	O	N
Option (B)	Z	O	M	Q	Q	M	Y	O	S	S	Q	N	X	O	M	S	Q	N
Option (C)	Z	O	M	S	Q	N	Y	O	M	S	Q	N	X	O	M	S	Q	N

Option (D)	Z	O	M	S	Q	M	Y	O	N	S	Q	O	X	Q	M	S	M	N

Hence, the correct option is (C).

49. The pattern here is that the codes are already given in the question. So, we identify the code for each letter based on the given question:

S	E	V	E	N
2	3	1	3	6

And,

E	I	G	H	T
3	4	5	7	9

∴ NINE can be coded as:

N	I	N	E
6	4	6	3

NINE is coded as 6463.

Hence, the correct option is (A).

50. Draw the diagram according to the information given in the question:

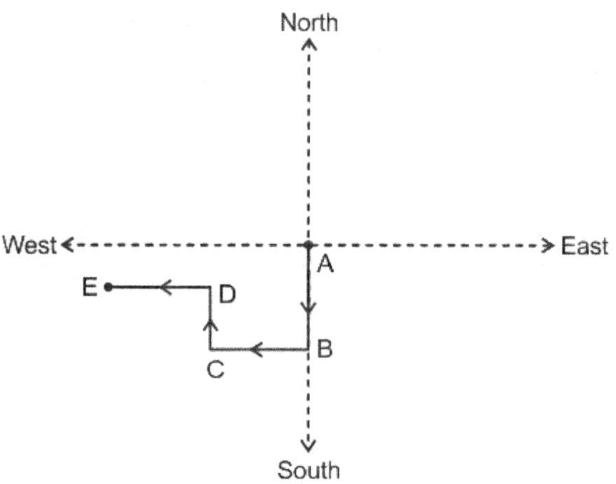

A is the starting point and E is the ending point.

As mention in the figure, he runs in the west direction.

Hence, the correct option is (C).

General Knowledge

Q.1 Which of the following ministers is named in the '100 Most Influential in UK-India Relations: Celebrating Women' list?

[SSC MTS, 2019]

A. Smriti Irani

B. Nirmala Sitharaman

C. Sushma Swaraj

D. Maneka Gandhi

Q.2 Who is the author of the book titled 'Maverick Messiah'?

A. Shashi Tharoor

B. Rohinton Mistry

C. Ramesh Kandula

D. Vikram Chandra

Q.3 Whose autobiography is 'India Wins Freedom'?

A. MK Gandhi

B. Abul Kalam Azad

C. JL Nehru

D. Rajendra Prasad

Q.4 The river basin which is called 'Ruhr of India' is _______.

A. Damodar

B. Hooghly

C. Godavari

D. Swarnarekha

Q.5 Harishankar Parsai, who hailed from Madhya Pradesh, was a famous writer in which branch of Hindi literature?

A. Satire

B. Poetry

C. Translation

D. Novel

Q.6 Gurdwara Patalpuri Sahib is located on the bank of river ____________.

[SSC CGL, 2021]

A. Ganga **B.** Beas **C.** Yamuna **D.** Sutlej

Q.7 The currency of Azerbaijan is:

A. Dollars **B.** Euro **C.** Manat **D.** Ruble

Q.8 When is Navy Day celebrated every year?

A. 1 December

B. 2 December

C. 3 December

D. 4 December

Q.9 Timber vegetation is generally not found in which of the following regions?

[Officers Training Academy (OTA), 2020], [Indian Military Academy (IMA), 2020]

A. Subtropical region

B. Temperate region

C. Alpine region

D. Tundra region

Q.10 Uttarakhand Jal Sansthan is located at_______________.

A. Dehradun

B. Nainital

C. Haldwani

D. Mussoorie

Q.11 Who among the following has been recommended by the Board of Control for Cricket in India (BCCI) for the Rajiv Gandhi Khel Ratna Award 2021?

A. Virat Kohli

B. Shikhar Dhawan

C. R Ashwin

D. Jasprit Bumrah

Q.12 Shri Tarlochan Singh awarded Padma Bhushan 2021 in the field of:

A. Civil Service

B. Medicine

C. Public Affairs

D. Literature

Q.13 Who is the Constitutional head of the state government?

A. Health Minister of the State

B. Governor

C. Chief Minister of the State

D. High court judge

Q.14 Name the freedom fighter who designed and handed over the tricolour (which later became the national flag) to Mohandas Karamchand Gandhi.

A. Pingali Venkayya

B. Ayyadevara Kaleshwara Rao

C. Mutnuri Krishna Rao

D. Gottipati Brahmaiah

Q.15 Where did Mahatma Gandhi start the Salt Satyagraha?

A. Dandi

B. Sabarmati

C. Sevagram

D. Pawanar

General Science

Q.16 Under which of the following conditions is a person most likely to fall sick?

[MP Jail Prahari, 2018]

A. When she has recovered from malaria and is taking care of someone suffering from chicken pox.

B. When she is recovering from malaria.

C. When she is at home having a healthy diet.

D. When she is on a four-day fast after recovering from malaria and is taking care of someone suffering from chicken pox.

Q.17 Viruses are placed as marginal between living and non-living things because they are ___________________.

[MP Jail Prahari, 2018]

A. able to multiply on their own

B. like crystals inside the body of the host

C. living only inside the body of the host

D. primitive organisms

Q.18 An object is executing uniform circular motion. Which of the following quantities remain(s) constant during the object's motion?

A. Velocity and acceleration

B. Speed and velocity

C. Speed and acceleration

D. Speed only

Q.19 The lens used in a simple microscope is:

A. Concave

B. Cylindrical

C. Convex   **D.** None of these

Q.20 How much time will it take to perform 440 J of work at a rate of 11 W?

A. 50 s   **B.** 40 s   **C.** 30 s   **D.** 20 s

Q.21 From the given graph, the value of acceleration is-

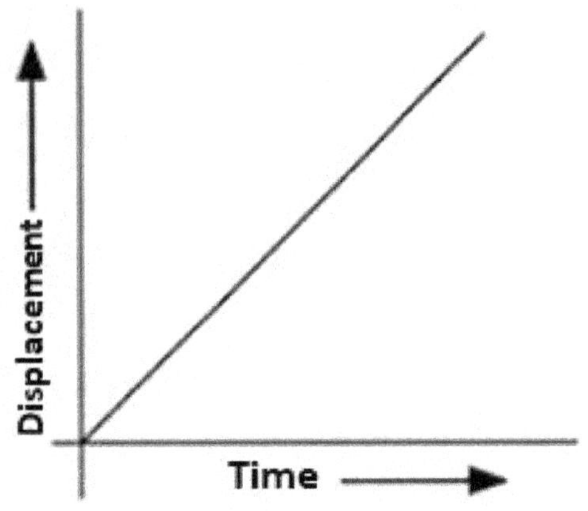

A. + ve   **B.** - ve

C. Zero   **D.** Convertible

Q.22 Why usually do covalent compounds have low melting and boiling points?

A. Strong van der Waal's force

B. Weak van der Waal's force

C. No van der Waals force

D. Strong magnetic force

Q.23 The volume of one mole of a gas at normal temperature and pressure is _____ Litre.

A. 11.2   **B.** 22.4   **C.** 33.3   **D.** 44.4

Q.24 Which of the following is called laughing gas?

A. Carbon dioxide

B. Methane

C. Chlorofluorocarbons

D. Nitrous oxide

Q.25 Atomic radii of fluorine and neon in Angstrom units are respectively given by:

A. 0.72, 1.60   **B.** 1.60, 1.60

C. 0.72, 0.72   **D.** 0.72, 0.78

Q.26 Ringworm is a _________ disease.

A. bacterial   **B.** protozoan

C. viral   **D.** fungal

Q.27 Which one of the following organisms is responsible for sleeping sickness?

[Officers Training Academy (OTA), 2019], [Indian Military Academy (IMA), 2019]

A. Leishmania   **B.** Trypanosoma

C. Ascaris   **D.** Helicobacter

Q.28 What phenomenon is responsible for the twinkling of stars?

A. Diffraction   **B.** Refraction

C. Dispersion   **D.** Scattering of Light

Q.29 Which among the following is a base?

A. H_2SO_4 **B.** $NaOH$ **C.** HNO_3 **D.** HCl

Q.30 Amino acids are the building blocks of:

A. minerals   **B.** vitamins

C. carbohydrates   **D.** proteins

Maths

Q.31 Aamir invested Rs. 5000 in a business that pays 5% interest annually. Then find out the time in which this amount will become Rs. 6250.

A. 10 year   **B.** 8 year   **C.** 5 year   **D.** 4 year

Q.32 A tea party is arranged for 16 people along two sides of a long table with eight chairs on each side. Four particular men wish to sit on one particular side and two particular men on the other side. The number of ways they can be seated is:

A. $\frac{6!8!10!}{4!6!}$ **B.** $\frac{8!8!10!}{4!6!}$

C. $\frac{8!8!6!}{6!4!}$ **D.** None of these

Q.33 In ΔABC, ∠B is 25° more than ∠A and ∠C is 5° more than four time ∠A. The biggest angle is _____.

A. 25°   **B.** 50°   **C.** 95°   **D.** 105°

Q.34 $5\frac{3}{4} + x + 2\frac{1}{2} = 10\frac{1}{8}$ Find the value of x.

A. $2\frac{1}{4}$ **B.** $2\frac{7}{8}$ **C.** $1\frac{7}{8}$ **D.** $1\frac{7}{6}$

Q.35 8 litres are drawn from a cask filled with wine and is then filled with water. This operation is performed three more times. The ratio of the quantity of wine now left in cask to that of the total solution is 16 : 81. How much wine did the cask hold originally?

A. 24 litres   **B.** 45 litres   **C.** 49 litres   **D.** 44 litres

Q.36 Direction : Find the next number in the given series.

$2, 10, 84, ?$

A. 1028   **B.** 1229   **C.** 1124   **D.** 1032

Q.37 Calculate the least number that is exactly divisible by $12, 16, 24$ and 32.

A. 90   **B.** 96

C. 84   **D.** None of the above

Q.38 The average of seven consecutive numbers is 33. The largest of these numbers is:

A. 39   **B.** 34   **C.** 36   **D.** 38

Q.39 A box contains 90 discs which are numbered from 1 to 90. If one disc is drawn at random from the box, find the probability that it bears a perfect square number.

A. 1   **B.** 0.1   **C.** 0.6   **D.** 0.4

Q.40 A person travelled $132km$ by auto, $852km$ by train and $248km$ by bike. It took 21 hours in all. If the speed of train is 6 times the speed of auto and 1.5 times speed of bike, what is the speed of train?

A. $78\ kmh^{-1}$ B. $104\ kmh^{-1}$
C. $96\ kmh^{-1}$ D. $88\ kmh^{-1}$

Q.41 The length and breadth of a rectangle are in the ratio $9:7$. Its area is $252\ cm^2$. Find the perimeter of the rectangle.

A. $16\ cm$ B. $32\ cm$ C. $64\ cm$ D. $48\ cm$

Q.42 If the price of the commodity is increased by 50% by what fraction must its consumption be reduced so as to keep the same expenditure on its consumption?

A. $\frac{1}{4}$ B. $\frac{1}{3}$ C. $\frac{1}{2}$ D. $\frac{2}{3}$

Q.43 4 men can build a small house in 12 days. How long would it take for 6 men to build the same house?

A. 9 days   B. 8 days   C. 8.1 days   D. 8.2 days

Q.44 If selling price of 16 items is same as the cost price of 20 items, then there is a:

A. loss of 20%   B. loss of 25%
C. gain of 20%   D. gain of 25%

Q.45 What will be the remainder if 2^{89} is divided by 9 ?

A. 2   B. 3   C. 4   D. 5

Logical Reasoning

Q.46 A clock is showing 8 A.M. How many degrees the hour hand will move by the time it shows 2 P.M.?

[Uttarakhand Public Service Commission (UKPSC), 2011]

A. 180°   B. 140°   C. 150°   D. 165°

Q.47 Find the next term in the following sequence.
TE, D, RF, C, XB, ?

A. L   B. I   C. K   D. O

Q.48 In a code language, if 'MOON' is coded as '5229', 'FILM' is coded as '6315', 'ARE' is coded as '487', then in the same language How will 'INFORMER' be coded?

A. 39611578   B. 39162258
C. 79627578   D. 39628578

Q.49 Pointing at a lady in a photograph, a man said 'She is niece of my only son'. How is the man related to that lady?

A. Paternal grandfather
B. Brother-in-law
C. Maternal grandfather
D. Uncle

Q.50 Among five friends, Mahesh is taller than Karan but not as tall as Yash. Hrithik is taller than Yash but not as tall as Abhishek. If everyone is standing in a row in ascending order of height, then who will be the first person?

A. Abhishek   B. Yash
C. Karan   D. Hrithik

// Smart Answer Sheet //

Correct   Indicates percentage of students who answered questions correctly.

Skipped   Indicates percentage of students who skipped questions.

Q.	Ans.	Correct / Skipped
1	B	48.77 % / 31.78 %
2	C	87.17 % / 10.94 %
3	B	84.37 % / 10.73 %
4	A	48.24 % / 45.47 %
5	A	67.4 % / 32.28 %
6	D	89.37 % / 10.2 %
7	C	55.94 % / 42.71 %
8	D	76.17 % / 22.65 %
9	D	46.56 % / 30.68 %
10	C	68.98 % / 30.82 %

Q.	Ans.	Correct / Skipped
11	C	57.34 % / 33.21 %
12	C	65.54 % / 34.19 %
13	B	42.92 % / 33.62 %
14	A	66.77 % / 31.73 %
15	B	77.72 % / 13.3 %
16	D	77.34 % / 14.17 %
17	C	87.69 % / 10.44 %
18	D	40.85 % / 42.27 %
19	C	47.03 % / 47.05 %
20	B	65.71 % / 32.41 %

Q.	Ans.	Correct / Skipped
21	C	44.33 % / 42.46 %
22	B	56.57 % / 31.31 %
23	B	50.26 % / 30.97 %
24	D	48.15 % / 30.55 %
25	A	57.0 % / 37.34 %
26	D	82.61 % / 14.98 %
27	B	61.52 % / 31.34 %
28	B	41.22 % / 39.17 %
29	B	57.39 % / 37.9 %
30	D	84.46 % / 11.87 %

Q.	Ans.	Correct / Skipped
31	C	21.99 % / 73.5 %
32	B	85.76 % / 12.27 %
33	D	28.2 % / 71.2 %
34	C	77.86 % / 10.55 %
35	A	26.93 % / 70.1 %
36	A	88.22 % / 11.71 %
37	B	47.17 % / 50.66 %
38	C	77.33 % / 11.26 %
39	B	55.39 % / 35.95 %
40	C	10.52 % / 84.08 %

Q.	Ans.	Correct / Skipped
41	C	54.26 % / 37.17 %
42	B	54.56 % / 31.98 %
43	B	43.56 % / 48.62 %
44	D	49.68 % / 50.25 %
45	D	57.07 % / 42.79 %
46	A	29.72 % / 67.18 %
47	A	57.76 % / 38.14 %
48	D	88.76 % / 10.24 %
49	C	64.0 % / 31.33 %
50	C	61.86 % / 35.15 %

Performance Analysis	
Avg. Score (%)	74.0%
Toppers Score (%)	74.0%
Your Score	

//Hints and Solutions//

1. Finance Minister Nirmala Sitharaman is among the 100 most influential women driving the UK-India relationship forward.

- The '100 Most Influential in UK-India Relations: Celebrating Women' list was launched by UK Home Secretary Sajid Javid to mark India Day in the Houses of Parliament in London.

- Penny Mordaunt, Britain's Secretary of State for Defence, is the other politician in the list.

- Pravasi Bharatiya Divas is a celebratory day observed annually on 9 January by India to mark the contribution of the overseas Indian community towards the development of India.

- The day commemorates the return of Mahatma Gandhi from South Africa to Mumbai on 9 January 1915.

- It was established in 2003 and is sponsored by the Ministry of External Affairs and FICCI, CII, and DoNER.

Hence, the correct option is (B).

2. 'Maverick Messiah' is a political biography of former Andhra Pradesh Chief Minister, late Shri N. T. Rama Rao. The book is authored by senior journalist, Ramesh Kandula.

Shri N. T. Rama Rao was ranked among the top pioneers of 'alternative politics'. His entry into politics and the regional party's 'dramatic' success within about nine months gave a new direction to national politics.

Hence, the correct option is (C).

3. 'India Wins Freedom' is the autobiography of Abul Kalam Azad.

- India Wins Freedom is an enlightening account of the partition from the author, Maulana Azad's perspective.

- It includes his personal experiences when India became independent and his ideas on freedom and liberty.

Hence, the correct option is (B).

4. The river basin which is called 'Ruhr of India' is Damodar.

Damodar River is a river flowing across the Indian states of Jharkhand and West Bengal. Rich in mineral resources, the valley is home to large-scale mining and industrial activity. Earlier known as the Sorrow of Bengal because of its ravaging floods in the plains of West Bengal, the Damodar, and its tributaries have been somewhat tamed with the construction of several dams. It is the most polluted river in India (by 2003). It has a number of tributaries and sub tributaries, such as Barakar, Konar, Bokaro, Haharo, Jamunia, Ghari, Guaia, Khadia and Bhera. The Damodar and the Barakar trifurcate the Chota Nagpur plateau.

Hence, the correct option is (A).

5. Harishankar Parsai, who hailed from Madhya Pradesh, was a famous writer in Satire.

- Nithalle Ki Diary, Apni Apni Bimari, and Do Naak Vale Log are some of his notable writings.

- He won Sahitya Akademi Award in 1982, for his satirical work "Viklaang Shraddha ka daur''.

Hence, the correct option is (A).

6. Gurdwara Patalpuri Sahib is located on the bank of the river Sutlej. It is situated in the Rupnagar district in Punjab. Guru Hargobind in 1644 as well as Guru Har Rai in 1661 were cremated in Gurdwara Patal Puri.

River Sutlej originates from Rakshastal Lake. It is also known as Shatadru (Ancient name). It is one of the major tributaries of the Indus. It enters India through Shipki La pass. The Bhakra-Nangal Dam is constructed across the Sutlej river. The Indira Gandhi canal is situated on the Sutlej river.

Hence, the correct option is (D).

7. The manat is the currency of Azerbaijan. It is subdivided into 100 qəpik. The Azerbaijani manat symbol, ₼, was assigned to Unicode U+20BC in 2013. A lowercase m can be used as a substitute for the manat symbol.
Hence, the correct option is (C).

8. Navy Day is celebrated every year on 4 December.

The day is celebrated in honor of the Indian Navy's role during the war with Pakistan in 1971 when Indian warships attacked Karachi port.

The day is also celebrated to highlight the role the Navy plays in securing the country's marine borders during peacetime and carrying out humanitarian missions.

Hence, the correct option is (D).

9. Timber vegetation is generally not found in Tundra region.

- Timber is a type of wood that has been processed into beams and planks.

- It is also known as 'lumber' in the US and Canada.

- Any wood capable of yielding a minimum dimensional size can be termed timber or lumber. It is a stage in the process of wood production.

- Timbers are used for structural purposes. Those woods which are adapted for building purposes are timbers. Finished timber is supplied in standard sizes for the industry.

- Timber is used for building houses and making furniture.

- The Timber vegetation is generally found in the Subtropical, Temperate, and Alpine regions.

- The tundra is a treeless polar desert found in the high latitudes in the polar regions, primarily in Alaska, Canada, Russia, Greenland, Iceland, and Scandinavia, as well as sub-Antarctic islands. The region's long, dry winters feature months of total darkness and extremely frigid temperatures.

Hence, the correct option is (D).

10. Uttarakhand Jal Sansthan is located at Haldwani.

"Uttarakhand Jal Sansthan" constituted under Section 18 of the Principal Act having jurisdiction throughout the state of Uttarakhand by amalgamation of "Garhwal Jal Sansthan" and

"Kumaun Jal Sansthan" on 26th August 2002. It Extends to the whole of Uttarakhand excluding cantonment areas.

Hence, the correct option is (C).

11. The Board of Control for Cricket in India (BCCI) has decided to nominate R Ashwin for the Rajiv Gandhi Khel Ratna Award.

On the other hand, from the Women Cricket Team ODI skipper, Mithali Raj is nominated for the Rajiv Gandhi Khel Ratna Award.

The board has also decided to recommend the names of KL Rahul, Jasprit Bumrah and Shikhar Dhawan for the Arjuna Award.

Hence, the correct option is (C).

12. Former Member of Parliament Tarlochan Singh has been awarded the Padma Bhushan. He was awarded the Padma Bhushan in the field of 'Public Affairs'.

Padma Awards: The Padma Awards are one of the highest civilian honours of India announced annually on the eve of Republic Day. The Awards are given in three categories:

- Padma Vibhushan (for exceptional and distinguished service),

- Padma Bhushan (distinguished service of higher-order)

- Padma Shri (distinguished service).

Hence, the correct option is (C).

13. The constitutional head of the state government is Governor.

The executive power of the state shall be vested in the governor and shall be exercised by him either directly or through officers' subordinates to him in an accordance with the constitution.

He is the constitutional head of the state, bound by the advice of his council of ministers. He functions as a vital link between the Union Government and the State Government.

Hence, the correct option is (B).

14. Pingali Venkayya is the freedom fighter who designed and handed over the tricolour (which later became the national flag) to Mohandas Karamchand Gandhi.

Venkayya was educated at Cambridge and grew up to become a polymath with interests in geology, agriculture, education and languages. He met Mahatma Gandhi in South Africa during the Second Boer War (1899-1902) when he was posted there as part of the British Indian Army.

In 1916, he also published a booklet on flags of other nations with various samples.

Hence, the correct option is (A).

15. Dandi March or Salt Satyagraha was started by Mahatma Gandhi in Sabarmati launched on March 12 , 1930, and it lasted till April 5, 1930, in Dandi (Navsari).

- It was a part of Non-violent Civil Disobedience.

- It was against the tax collected by the British Raj on salt and Gandhi opposed this by producing salt through evaporation.

- This significantly influenced American activist's Martin Luther King, James Bevel, and others.

- It is also known as the White Flowing River as all people took part in the march by wearing White Khadi.

- Gandhi called it "Poor Man's Struggle".

- Due to this, mass civil disobedience was observed and Indians boycotted British clothes and goods. International Walk for Justice and Freedom - Mahatma Gandhi Foundation re-framed and cast the Salt March in 2005 on the 75th anniversary of Dandi March.

Hence, the correct option is (B).

16. In the conditions of when she is on a four-day fast after recovering from malaria and is taking care of someone suffering from chicken pox is a person most likely to fall sick.

A person is most likely to fall sick in this condition because malarial infection which is caused by protozoa has led to large-scale destruction of red blood cells (RBCs) and has weakened the immune system already. A four-day fast deprives of a proper and sufficient diet which further deteriorates the functioning of the immune system. Lastly taking care of a person suffering from chickenpox which is caused by a virus and is a communicable disease makes it vulnerable to getting infected and falling sick.

Hence, the correct option is (D).

17. Viruses are placed as marginal between living and non-living things because they are living only inside the body of the host.

The viruses are non-cellular organisms that are characterized by having an inert crystalline structure outside the living cell. Once they infect a cell they take over the machinery of the host cell to replicate themselves, killing the host. The name virus that means venom or poisonous fluid was given by Dmitri Ivanowsky in 1892. Viruses did not find a place in Robert Whittaker's five kingdom classification in 1969 since they are not considered truly 'living' if we understand living as those organisms that have a cell structure.

Hence, the correct option is (C).

18. The velocity of an object undergoing uniform circular motion is always changing (because the direction is always changing). Further, since the acceleration is centripetal, it must always point toward the center of the circle; so, as the object moves around the circle, the acceleration vector is also constantly changing direction. Notice that for an object in uniform circular motion, both the velocity and the acceleration are changing because the directions of these vectors are always changing, even though their magnitudes stay the same. In this question, only speed remains unchanged.

Hence, the correct option is (D).

19. A simple microscope is actually a convex lens of small focal length, which is used for seeing the magnified images of small objects. The use of a single convex lens or groups of lenses is found in simple magnification devices such as magnifying glass and eyepieces for telescopes and microscopes.

Hence, the correct option is (C).

20. Power = $\dfrac{Work}{Time}$

$11 = \dfrac{440}{Time}$

Time = 40s
Hence, the correct option is (B).

21. In the given graph displacement is uniform, therefore it has the constant velocity and when velocity is constant the acceleration is zero.

Acceleration is the rate of change of the velocity of an object with respect to time. Accelerations are vector quantities (in that they have magnitude and direction).

Hence, the correct option is (C).

22. Usually, covalent compounds have low melting and boiling points-

- Because they are composed up of electrically neutral molecules and thus very weak van der wall forces, covalent compounds have low melting points.

- As a result, the attraction between the molecules of a covalent compound is negligible.

- It is because of these weaker forces that the compound fails to adhere securely.

- Because the forces are weak, it just takes a small amount of energy to shatter them.

- Because lesser heat (energy) is capable of breaking these weak intermolecular interactions, covalent compounds have low melting and boiling temperatures.

Therefore, due to weak intermolecular forces of attraction and weak van der wall forces, covalent compounds have low melting and boiling point.

Hence, the correct option is (B).

23. At standard temperature and pressure (STP) one mole of any gas occupies a volume of 22.4 L. The standard temperature is 0°C (273.15 K) and the standard pressure is 1 atm.

Avogadro's hypothesis states that equal volumes of any gas at the same temperature and pressure contain the same number of particles. At standard temperature and pressure, 1 mole of any gas occupies 22.4 L. The ideal gas equation is PV = nRT (n=Number of moles, R=The gas constant). The SI value for R is 8.31441 J K^{-1} mol^{-1}.

Hence, the correct option is (B).

24. Nitrous oxide is called laughing gas.

- Nitrous oxide (N_2O) is called laughing gas or happy gas due to its intoxicating effects when inhaled.

- When inhaled, the gas slows down the body's reaction time. This results in a calm, euphoric feeling.

- Its colloquial name "laughing gas", coined by Humphry Davy, is due to the euphoric effects upon inhaling it, a property that has led to its recreational use as a dissociative anesthetic.

- At room temperature, it is a colourless non-flammable gas, with a slight metallic scent and taste.

Hence, the correct option is (B).

25. Atomic radii of fluorine and neon in Angstrom units are respectively given by 0.72, 1.60. Fluorine is a halogen atom and neon is a noble gas. So, the atomic radius of noble gases is greater than halogens of the same period. The radius of fluorine is measured using covalent radius whereas that of neon is measured using Vander Waal's radius. It is known that Vander Waal's radius is greater than the covalent radius. So, fluorine is smaller than neon.

Hence, the correct option is (A).

26. Ringworm is a fungal infection that occurs on the surface of the skin and is characterized by the appearance of round, itchy, scaly, red patches on the skin.

Also known as tinea corporis, ringworm is common in areas with high humidity as fungi thrive in such an environment.

It can be easily contracted through contact with infected skin or by sharing combs, clothing, etc.

Hence, the correct option is (D).

27. Sleeping sickness is also known as African trypanosomiasis.

- It is a disease caused due to the infection by flagellate protozoan Trypanosoma bruclei.

- The disease is transmitted by the tsetse fly (genus Glossina).

- Leishmania is a genus of trypanosomes that are responsible for the disease leishmaniasis.

- Ascaris is a genus of parasitic nematode worms which is also known as the "small intestinal roundworms", a type of parasitic worm.

- Helicobacter is a type of bacteria that can cause an ulcer.

Hence, the correct option is (B).

28. Stars twinkle in the night sky due to atmospheric refraction of stars. When light from a star enters our atmosphere, it is continuously refracted before reaching Earth.

Refraction- When a light ray travels from one transparent medium to another transparent medium then it deviates from its original path and this phenomenon is called Refraction.

- For example- when light travels from the Rarer medium (Air) to the Denser medium (Water) is deviates towards the Normal.

Laws of refraction

- The ratio of the sine of the angle of incidence to the sine of the angle of refraction is constant.

- The Normal, Incident ray, Refracted ray lie on the same plane at the point of Incidence.

Hence, the correct option is (B).

29. $NaOH$ is a base, the other option is an example of an acid.

A Base is a substance which:

- Is bitter in taste.
- Turns red litmus paper into blue.
- Gives hydroxyl ions $(OH-)$ in aqueous solution.
- Can accept a proton.
- Can donate electrons.
- Oxides and hydroxides of metals are bases.
- Water-soluble bases are called alkali.
- All alkalies are bases but all bases are not alkalies because all bases are not soluble in water.
- The pH of a solution is the negative logarithm of the concentration of hydrogen ions on a mole per liter.

Hence, the correct option is (B).

30. The building blocks of proteins are amino acids.

Amino acids:

- Proteins are made up of organic compounds called amino acids. So they are known as the building components of proteins.
- Amino acids are the necessary ingredients for the growth and development of human.
- Basic amino groups (- NH_2) and carboxyl groups $(-COOH)$ are found in amino acids.
- Long chains of amino acids constitute peptides and proteins.
- Proteins are made up of twenty amino acids.

Hence, the correct option is (D).

31. Given:
Principal is Rs. 5000
Rate is 5%
Amount is Rs. 6250
Formula used:

$$A = P + \{\frac{(P \times r \times t)}{100}\}$$

Here, $A =$ Amount
$P =$ Principal
$r =$ Rate
$t =$ Time

Calculation:

$$\text{Rs. } 6250 = \text{Rs. } [5000 + \{\frac{(5000 \times 5 \times t)}{100}\}]$$
$$\Rightarrow \text{Rs. } [5000 + (50 \times 5 \times t)] = \text{Rs. } 6250$$
$$\Rightarrow 5000 + 250t = 6250$$
$$\Rightarrow 250t = 6250 - 5000$$
$$\Rightarrow t = \frac{1250}{250}$$
$$\Rightarrow t = 5$$

$\therefore$ In 5 year amount invested by Aamir will amount to Rs. 6250.

Hence, the correct option is (C).

32. There are 8 chair on each side of the table.

Let the sides be represented by A and B.

Let four persons sit on side A, then number of ways of arranging 4 persons on 8 chairs on side $A = {}^8P_4$

And two persons sit on side B.

The number of ways of arranging 2 persons on 8 chairs on side $B = {}^8P_2$

The remaining 10 persons can be arranged in remaining 10 chairs in $10!$ ways.

Hence, the total number of ways in which the persons can be arranged is ${}^8P_4 \times {}^8P_2 \times 10! = \frac{8!8!10!}{4!6!}$

Hence, the correct option is (B).

33. Given,

$\angle B$ is more than $\angle A$ by 25°.

$\angle C$ is 5° more than four time $\angle A$.

As we know,

Sum of all three angles of a triangle is 180°.

Let $\angle A$ be x.

$\angle B = x + 25°$

$\angle C = 4x + 5°$

$\angle A + \angle B + \angle C = 180°$

$\Rightarrow x + x + 25° + 4x + 5° = 180°$

$\Rightarrow 6x + 30° = 180°$

$\Rightarrow 6x = 180° - 30°$

$\Rightarrow 6x = 150°$

$\Rightarrow x = \frac{150°}{6}$

$\Rightarrow x = 25°$

$\angle A = 25°$

$\angle B = 25° + 25° = 50°$

$\angle C = 4 \times 25° + 5° = 100° + 5° = 105°$

$\therefore$ The biggest angle is 105°.

Hence, the correct option is (D).

34. Given

$$5\frac{3}{4} + x + 2\frac{1}{2} = 10\frac{1}{8}$$
$$\Rightarrow 5\frac{3}{4} + x + 2\frac{1}{2} = 10\frac{1}{8}$$
$$\Rightarrow \frac{23}{4} + x + \frac{5}{2} = \frac{81}{8}$$

$$\Rightarrow \frac{33}{4} + x = \frac{81}{8}$$

$$\Rightarrow x = \frac{15}{8} = 1\frac{7}{8}$$

$\therefore$ The value of x is $1\frac{7}{8}$.

Hence, the correct option is (C).

35. Let the quantity of the wine in the cask originally be x litres.

Using formula:

Final Amount of solute that is not replaced $=$ Initial Amount

$$\times \left(\frac{\text{Vol. after removal}}{\text{Vol. after replacing}}\right)^{N}$$

Where N = No. of operation done.

Then ratio of wine to total solution in cask after 4 operations,

$$1 \times \left(\frac{x-8}{x}\right)^4 = \frac{16}{81}$$

$$\Rightarrow 1 \times \left\{\frac{x-8}{x}\right\}^4 = \left(\frac{2}{3}\right)^4$$

$$\Rightarrow \frac{x-8}{x} = \frac{2}{3}$$

$$\Rightarrow 3x - 24 = 2x$$

$$\Rightarrow x = 24 \text{ litres}$$

Hence, the correct option is (A).

36. The pattern followed is,

$$1^2 + 1 = 2$$

$$2^3 + 2 = 10$$

$$3^4 + 3 = 84$$

$$4^5 + 4 = 1028$$

Therefore, " 1028" is the correct answer.

Hence, the correct option is (A).

37. Given:

Numbers are $12, 16, 24,$ and 32.

The least number that is exactly divisible by $12, 16, 24,$ and 32 will be the LCM.

$$12 = 2^2 \times 3$$

$$16 = 2^4$$

$$24 = 2^3 \times 3$$

$$32 = 2^5$$

$\therefore$ LCM of $(12, 16, 24, 32) = 2^5 \times 3$

$$= 96$$

Hence, the correct option is (B).

38. Given,

Average of seven consecutive numbers $= 33$

Let the seven consecutive numbers be $(x-3), (x-2), (x-1), x, (x+1), (x+2), (x+3)$

Sum of the seven numbers
$$= x - 3 + x - 2 + x - 1 + x + x + 1 + x + 2 + x + 3$$

$$= 7x$$

As we know,

$$\text{Average} = \frac{\text{sum of numbers}}{\text{number of terms}}$$

$$33 = \frac{7x}{7}$$

$$\Rightarrow x = 33$$

So, largest number $= x + 3$

$$= 33 + 3$$

$$= 36$$

$\therefore$ The largest number in the consecutive series is 36.

Hence, the correct option is (C).

Q.39 The total numbers of discs $= 90$

$$P(E) = \frac{\text{(Number of favourable outcomes)}}{\text{(Total number of outcomes}}$$

Total number of perfect square numbers $=$ $9 (1, 4, 9, 16, 25, 36, 49, 64$ and 81)

P (getting a perfect square number) $= \frac{9}{90} = \frac{1}{10} = 0.1$

Hence, the correct option is (B).

40. Let the speed of auto be $x\ kmh^{-1}$.

So, the speed of the train will be $6x$ and that of bike will be

$$= \frac{6x}{1.5} = 4x$$

As per the given information,

Time taken by auto $+$ Time taken by train $+$ Time taken by bike $= 21$ hours

$$\Rightarrow \frac{132}{x} + \frac{852}{6x} + \frac{248}{4x} = 21$$

or, $\frac{132}{x} + \frac{142}{x} + \frac{62}{x} = 21$

or, $21x = 132 + 142 + 62 = 336$

$$\therefore x = \frac{336}{21} = 16$$

$\therefore$ Speed of the train $= 6x = 6 \times 16 = 96\ kmh^{-1}$

Hence, the correct option is (C).

41. Given-

The length and breadth of a rectangle are in the ratio $9:7$.

Let the length of the rectangle $(L) = 9k$

Breadth of the rectangle $(B) = 7k$

Area of rectangle $(A) = 252\ cm^2$

$\Rightarrow 9k \times 7k = 252$

$\Rightarrow 63k^2 = 252$

$\Rightarrow k^2 = 4$

$\Rightarrow k = \pm 2$

Since length and breadth cannot be negative,

$\Rightarrow k = 2$

$\Rightarrow L = 9k = 18\ cm$

$\Rightarrow B = 7k = 14\ cm$

Perimeter of the rectangle $(P) = 2 \times (L + B)$

$\Rightarrow P = 2 \times (18 + 14)$

$\Rightarrow P = 2 \times 32$

$\Rightarrow P = 64\ cm$

Hence, the correct option is (C).

42. Let the initial price of the commodity be 100

After 50% increase in price, It will become, $100 \ldots 50\%$ increase > 150.

Now, we have to reduce the consumption to keep expenditure 100.

Increase in price $= 150 - 100 = 50$

We have to reduce the consumption,

$= \dfrac{50}{150} \times 100$

$= \dfrac{1}{3}$ or 33.33%

Hence, the correct option is (B).

43. Given,

Time taken by 4 men to build a small house $= 12$ days

$\Rightarrow$ Time taken by one man to build a small house $= 12 \times 4 = 48$ days

$\Rightarrow$ Time taken by 6 men to build the same house $= \dfrac{48}{6} = 8$ days

Hence, the correct option is (B).

44. Let, SP of 1 item = Rs 1.

Then SP of 16 items $=$ Rs 16

We are given that CP of 20 items $=$ Rs 16

CP of 1 item $=$ Rs. $\dfrac{16}{20}$

$=$ Rs 0.8

Profit on every item $= SP - CP$

$= 1 - 0.8$

$= 0.2$

Gain Percentage $= \dfrac{\text{Gain}}{CP} \times 100$

$= \dfrac{0.2}{0.8} \times 100$

$= 25\%$

Hence, the correct option is (D).

45. Given,

2^{89} is divided by 9.

If we divide 8 by 9 we will get the remainder as -1

But remainder can not be negative

Therefore we can not use -1 as the remainder

To simplify calculation, we use $9 - 1 = 8$ as a remainder

$\left(\dfrac{2^{89}}{9}\right)$

$\Rightarrow \dfrac{\left\{(2^3)^{29} \times 2^2\right\}}{9}$

$\Rightarrow \dfrac{\left\{(8)^{29} \times 4\right\}}{9}$

$\Rightarrow \dfrac{\left\{(-1)^{29} \times 4\right\}}{9}$

$\Rightarrow \dfrac{(-1 \times 4)}{9}$

$\Rightarrow \dfrac{-4}{9}$

$\Rightarrow$ Remainder $= -4 + 9 = 5$

$\therefore$ The remainder if 2^{89} is divided by 9 is 5.

Hence, the correct option is (D).

46. A clock is showing 8 A.M. The hour hand will move $180°$ by the time it shows 2 P.M.

At 8 o'clock in the morning, the hour hand will be at 8.

At 2 o'clock in the afternoon, the hour hand will be at 2.

In one hour the hour hand rotates $30°$.

8 o'clock morning to 2 o'clock afternoon $= 6$ hrs

Therefore the hour hand rotate $= 6 \times 30° = 180°$

Hence, the correct option is (A).

47. Positional values of T and E are 20 and 5 respectively.

$20 \div 5 = 4$ which is a place value of D.

Positional values of R and F are 18 and 6 respectively.

$18 \div 6 = 3$ which is a place value of C.

Similarly,

Positional values of X and B are 24 and 2 respectively.

$24 \div 2 = 12$ which is a place value of L.

Hence, the correct option is (A).

48. In a certain code language,

M	O	O	N
5	2	2	9
F	I	L	M
6	3	1	5
A		R	E
4		8	7

From above, the code for 'INFORMER' would be:

I	N	F	O	R	M	E	R
3	9	6	2	8	5	7	8

Hence, INFORMER is coded as '39628578'.

Hence, the correct option is (D)

49.

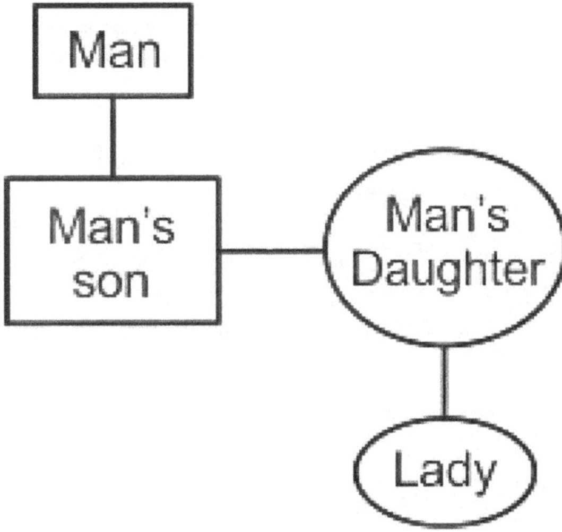

Symbol in Diagram	Meaning
○	Female
□	Male
=	Married Couple
—	Siblings
|	Difference of a generation

Drawing the family tree,

So, the man is the maternal grandfather to that lady.

So, "Maternal grandfather" is the correct answer.

Hence, the correct option is (C).

50. Given,

Among five friends, Mahesh is taller than Karan but not as tall as Yash. Hrithik is taller than Yash but not as tall as Abhishek.

According to the given information,

Yash > Mahesh > Karan ....(i)

Abhishek > Hrithik > Yash ...(ii)

From equations (i) and (ii), we get

Karan < Mahesh < Yash < Hrithik < Abhishek

Hence, the correct option is (C).

General Knowledge

Q.1 Which famous minister launched e-Chhavni portal for residents of Cantonment areas?
A. Nitin Gadkari
B. Piyush Goyal
C. Rajnath Singh
D. Prakash Javadekar

Q.2 Which one of the following Indian places receives minimum rainfall in a year?
[Officers Training Academy (OTA), 2020], [Indian Military Academy (IMA), 2020]
A. Jodhpur
B. Leh
C. New Delhi
D. Bengaluru

Q.3 Who among the following has authored the book- The Epic Battle of Longewala?
A. Air Marshal Parvat Sinha (retd)
B. Air Marshal Balbir Singh (retd)
C. Air Marshal Bharat Kumar (retd)
D. Air Marshal Vivek Chauhan (retd)

Q.4 What is the name of the Arabic book by Al-Biruni?
A. Kitab-ul-Hind
B. Hindustan-nama
C. Tarikh-e-Hindustan
D. Fatawa-e-Hindustani

Q.5 Which among the following is the capital of Colombia?
A. Yerevan
B. Podgorica
C. Nassau
D. Bogota

Q.6 Who has won the Menorca Open Chess tournament 2022 which was held in Spain?
A. Grandmaster B Adhiban
B. Grandmaster D Gukesh
C. Grandmaster Raunak Sadhwani
D. Grandmaster S. P. Sethuraman

Q.7 Where is the headquarters of Garhwal Rifles located in Uttarakhand?
A. Mussoorie
B. Rishikesh
C. Lansdowne
D. None of above

Q.8 Which is India's first digital village?
[RRB/RRC Group D, 2018]
A. Khonoma
B. Chizami
C. Akodara
D. Odanthurai

Q.9 Constitutional government means:
[UPSC Prelims, 2021]
A. A representative government of a nation with federal structure
B. A government whose Head enjoys nominal powers
C. A government whose Head enjoys real powers
D. A government limited by the terms of the Constitution

Q.10 Which day is observed as World Food Day?
A. 10 September
B. 16 August
C. 4 November
D. 16 October

Q.11 The range lying to the south of the greater Himalayas is known as ________.
A. Himachal.
B. Shiwaliks.
C. Himadri.
D. Purvanchal.

Q.12 In which field Rani Laxmibai Award is given by Haryana Government?
A. Sports
B. Defense
C. Dance
D. Literature

Q.13 'Thang ta', a martial art form is associated with which state of India?
A. Mizoram
B. Nagaland
C. Manipur
D. Tripura

Q.14 The British India government set up a committee for the Sergeant Plan, it was related to?
A. Famine policy
B. Education policy
C. Civil services reforms
D. Judicial reform

Q.15 After the failure of the Cripps Mission, Quit India Movement was started in ______.
A. 1940
B. 1935
C. 1922
D. 1942

General Science

Q.16 Small structures inside a cell that works together is called ________.
[MP Police (Constable), 2017]
A. Nucleus
B. Organelles
C. Inclusions
D. Cytoplasm

Q.17 Find out the wrong pair.
[MP Police (Constable), 2017]
A. Intestine - involuntary
B. Hand muscles - voluntary
C. Neck muscles - voluntary
D. Air passage - voluntary

Q.18 Muscle is connected to the bone by __________.
[MP Police (Constable), 2017]
A. Cartilage
B. Ligaments only
C. Both ligaments and tendons
D. Tendons only

Q.19 Hydra reproduces by:

A. Budding
B. Binary fission
C. Cloning
D. In vitro fertilization

Q.20 Name two organelles that have their own genetic material.

[MP Police (Constable), 2017]

A. DNA and RNA
B. Mitochondria and plastids
C. Ribosome and Golgi bodies
D. Dictyosome and endoplasmic reticulum

Q.21 Which of the following is true with respect to diffraction?

A. Diffraction is the bending of light around the corners of a obstacle
B. Diffraction of light is of two types
C. For diffraction, the size of the obstacle should be comparable to wavelength of light
D. All of the above

Q.22 In which unit is capacitance measured for day to day applications?

A. Farad
B. Microfarad
C. Megafarad
D. None of the above

Q.23 Optical fibers are mainly used in:

A. Weaving
B. Communication
C. Musical Instruments
D. Food Industry

Q.24 If two charged bodies having equal potential are connected through a conducting wire, then:

[RRB/RRC Group D, 2018]

A. Magnetic induction flows.
B. Current flows from positive to negative.
C. Current will not flow.
D. Current will flow from negative to positive.

Q.25 'X' and 'Y' are elements which are highly reactive with air, hence stored in Kerosene. What could 'X' and 'Y' be?

[CTET Paper-II (Science & Mathematics), 2022]

A. Phosphorus and Sodium
B. Phosphorus and Sulphur
C. Sodium and Potassium
D. Sulphur and Potassium

Q.26 In which of the following situations, water cannot be used to extinguish fires?

(A) Electrical fire
(B) Burning of wood
(C) Burning of petrol
(D) Burning of paper

[CTET Paper-II (Science & Mathematics), 2022]

A. A and B
B. A and C
C. B and D
D. B and C

Q.27 Metal 'P' displaces metal 'Q' from its salt solution but is not able to displace metal 'R' from its salt solution. Identify the least reactive metal.

[CTET Paper-II (Science & Mathematics), 2022]

A. P
B. Q
C. R
D. Can not be determined.

Q.28 Which of the following sets comprises physical changes?

[CTET Paper-II (Science & Mathematics), 2022]

A. Shredding of paper, baking a cake, bursting of crackers
B. Boiling of water, cooking of food, rusting of iron
C. Burning of paper, setting of milk into curd, breaking a glass
D. Breaking of glass, grinding wheat, boiling of water

Q.29 Which of the following will not be helpful in the process of separating a mixture of chalk and water?

[CTET Paper-II (Science & Mathematics), 2022]

A. Filtration
B. Decantation
C. Sedimentation
D. Sublimation

Q.30 Parsec is the unit of measurement of what?

A. Star density
B. Astronomical distance
C. Brightness of celestial bodies
D. Orbital velocity of a giant star

Maths

Q.31 A sum of Rs. 250000 is deposited for 3 years compounded annually at $4\%, 5\%$ and 6% for the first, second and third year respectively. What will be the amount at the end of the three years?

A. Rs. 301,400
B. Rs. 256,590
C. Rs. 325,680
D. Rs. 289,380

Q.32 A toy is in the form of a cone surmounted on a hemisphere. The radius of the hemisphere and the cone is 3 cm each, the height of the conical part of the toy is 4 cm. What is the total surface area of the toy?

A. 102.25 cm²
B. 103.71 cm²
C. 106 cm²
D. 110 cm²

Q.33 In a school, $\frac{3}{5}$ children are boys and the number of girls is 800. The number of boys is:

[Jawahar Navodaya Entrance Class VI, 2021]

A. 800
B. 1000
C. 1200
D. 2000

Q.34 Simplify the equation $\frac{1}{2} + \frac{1}{4} + \frac{1}{8} + \frac{1}{a} + \frac{1}{6} = \frac{2}{6} + \frac{1}{3} + \frac{2}{3}$ and find the value of a.

[UP Police Sub Inspector, 2017]

A. $\frac{25}{24}$
B. $\frac{24}{7}$
C. 3
D. $\frac{7}{24}$

Q.35 If a television set is sold at Rs. x, a loss of 28% would be incurred. If it is sold at Rs. y, a profit of 12% would be incurred. What is the ratio of y to x ?

[Indian Military Academy (IMA), 2020]

A. $41:9$ **B.** $31:9$ **C.** $23:9$ **D.** $14:9$

Q.36 24 men can complete a piece of work in 18 days while 12 women can complete the same piece of work in 28 days. 27 men start working anc are replaced by 14 women after 8 days. In how many days will 14 women finish the remaining work?

A. 12 days   **B.** 14 days   **C.** 13 days   **D.** $12\frac{1}{2}$

Q.37 In the income statement of Asha and Ravenna, the ratio of their income in the year 2017 was 5 : 4. The ratio of Asha's income in the year 2018 to that in 2017 is 3 : 5 and the ratio of Ravenna's income in the year 2018 to that in 2017 is 3 : 2. If Rs. 10242 is the sum of the income of Asha and Ravenna in the year 2018, then find the income of Ravenna in the year 2017?

A. Rs. 1024   **B.** Rs. 1138   **C.** Rs. 2776   **D.** Rs. 4552

Q.38 Direction: What will come in place of the question mark (?) in the following number series

10, 17, 41, 86, 156, 255, ?

A. 338   **B.** 387   **C.** 376   **D.** 355

Q.39 What is the largest size of square tiles that can be used to cover the floor of a room of size $5.25m \times 4.55m$?

[RRB/RRC Group D, 2018]

A. $25cm$ **B.** $35cm$ **C.** $45cm$ **D.** $55cm$

Q.40 In 4 numbers, 1st number is twice to 4th number, 2nd number is thrice to 3rd number, 3rd number is half of fourth number. If average of all four number is 70. Find the sum of 1st and 4th number.

A. 138   **B.** 88   **C.** 121   **D.** 168

Q.41 Two integers are selected from the first 10 natural numbers. If the sum is even find the probability that both numbers are odd.

A. $\frac{1}{2}$ **B.** $\frac{3}{5}$ **C.** $\frac{2}{5}$ **D.** $\frac{1}{5}$

Q.42 A boat travels 30 km upstream in 10 hours and travels 52 km downstream in 4 hours. What is the time taken to cover 121 km downstream if the speeds of both stream and boat are decreased by 1 km/hr?

A. 12 hrs   **B.** 11 hrs   **C.** 10 hrs   **D.** 9 hrs

Q.43 The radius and height of a right circular cone are in the ratio $3:4$. If its curved surface area (in cm^2) is 240π, then its volume (in cm^3) is:

[SSC CGL, 2020]

A. 1536π **B.** 768π **C.** 384π **D.** 2304π

Q.44 Sohan scored 28% marks and failed by 15 marks in the monthly test. Shruti scored 32% marks and failed by 8 marks. Find the total marks of the monthly test?

A. 140   **B.** 200   **C.** 175   **D.** 150

Q.45 Find the number of different permutations of the letters of the word INDIA.

A. 144   **B.** 36   **C.** 50   **D.** 60

Logical Reasoning

Q.46 Y walked 6 m west, turned right an walked 8m. What is the shortest distance he needs to travel to go back to his starting point?

[UP Police Constable, 2019]

A. 6m   **B.** 8m   **C.** 14m   **D.** 10m

Q.47 Four words have been given, out of which three are alike in some manner and one is different. Select the odd word.

A. Chennai   **B.** Gangtok

C. Hyderabad   **D.** Aurangabad

Q.48 Looking at a portrait of a man, Samir said, "His mother is the wife of my father's son. Brothers and sisters, I have none." At whose portrait was Samir Looking.

A. Uncle   **B.** Nephew   **C.** Son   **D.** Cousin

Q.49 Direction: Find the missing group of alphabets in the following series.

EZ, JU, (...), TK, YF

A. OP   **B.** FH   **C.** IK   **D.** SX

Q.50 In a code language, '$TORCH$' is written as '$UNPSDI$' and '$BEST$' is written as '$CDFTU$'. How will '$MARKS$' be written in that language?

[SSC Sub Inspector (CPO), 2020]

A. $NABSLU$ **B.** $NZCSLT$

C. $OZBSMT$ **D.** $NZBSLT$

// Smart Answer Sheet //

Correct   Indicates percentage of students who answered questions correctly.

Skipped   Indicates percentage of students who skipped questions.

Q.	Ans.	Correct / Skipped
1	C	20.49 % / 74.91 %
2	B	55.72 % / 42.32 %
3	C	89.26 % / 10.31 %
4	A	81.53 % / 12.63 %
5	D	12.33 % / 70.78 %
6	B	19.16 % / 76.31 %
7	C	62.59 % / 30.76 %
8	C	84.36 % / 13.56 %
9	D	22.6 % / 67.01 %
10	D	87.12 % / 10.57 %

Q.	Ans.	Correct / Skipped
11	A	53.26 % / 31.78 %
12	A	17.87 % / 80.92 %
13	C	65.71 % / 33.26 %
14	B	61.28 % / 34.64 %
15	D	52.38 % / 31.61 %
16	B	83.58 % / 10.73 %
17	D	41.23 % / 44.71 %
18	D	47.13 % / 31.31 %
19	A	46.72 % / 31.64 %
20	B	58.47 % / 36.9 %

Q.	Ans.	Correct / Skipped
21	D	86.23 % / 12.51 %
22	B	89.08 % / 10.63 %
23	B	64.92 % / 33.22 %
24	C	51.56 % / 37.15 %
25	C	49.85 % / 40.23 %
26	B	40.82 % / 57.76 %
27	B	85.63 % / 14.16 %
28	D	81.98 % / 14.54 %
29	D	81.98 % / 13.33 %
30	B	56.17 % / 42.51 %

Q.	Ans.	Correct / Skipped
31	D	51.27 % / 30.8 %
32	B	47.91 % / 37.66 %
33	C	48.21 % / 50.74 %
34	B	21.87 % / 78.01 %
35	D	32.06 % / 67.64 %
36	A	58.67 % / 32.35 %
37	D	57.13 % / 35.61 %
38	B	15.21 % / 78.82 %
39	B	86.37 % / 10.23 %
40	D	32.08 % / 67.75 %

Q.	Ans.	Correct / Skipped
41	A	88.59 % / 10.92 %
42	B	19.42 % / 76.52 %
43	B	52.11 % / 37.96 %
44	C	43.95 % / 34.55 %
45	D	77.18 % / 11.06 %
46	D	46.54 % / 30.81 %
47	D	52.2 % / 45.74 %
48	C	63.83 % / 34.54 %
49	A	48.54 % / 38.93 %
50	D	11.69 % / 74.97 %

Performance Analysis

Avg. Score (%)	60.0%
Toppers Score (%)	75.0%
Your Score	

//Hints and Solutions//

1. Defence Minister Rajnath Singh launched e-Chhawani portal on 16 February 2021.

- Residents of Cantonment areas can register their complaints regarding civic issues and resolve them while sitting at home, through this portal.
- It aims to provide online municipal services to more than 20 lakh citizens across 62 Cantonment Boards through a multi-tenancy central platform

Hence, the correct option is (C).

2. The place in India receiving the lowest rainfall is Leh.

- The average annual precipitation in these regions is less than 50 cms. The cities like Jaisalmer in Rajasthan and Leh in Ladakh receive the least rainfall.
- India mainly receives rainfall from the Monsoons which lasts from June-September. Overall, India receives an average of 200-300 mm of rainfall over the country as a whole with the largest values observed during the monsoon season.
- The average annual rainfall in India is about 300–650 millimeters.
- The rainy season in India is affected by the humid southwest summer monsoon.
- The South of India typically receives more rainfall.

Hence, the correct option is (B).

3. Air Marshal Bharat Kumar (retd) has authored the book- The Epic Battle of Longewala.

- The book contends it was actually airpower that decisively won the battle against Pakistan's major armored thrust at the border outpost in Rajasthan on December 5-6, 1971.

Hence, the correct option is (C).

4. The name of the Arabic book of Al-Biruni is Kitab-ul-Hind.

Al-Biruni was an Iranian scholar. He is considered the father of modern geodesy. Alberuni wrote a book named Kitab-ul-Hind (Day of India) in 1030 AD. He died in Ghazni (Afghanistan). Traveling to the major regions of India, he composed his book Kitab-ul-Hind (Tehqeeq-e-Hind) in Arabic language.

Hence, the correct option is (A).

5. Bogota is the capital of Colombia.

Country	Colombia
Capital	Bogota
President	Iván Duque Márquez
Currency	Colombian Peso

Hence, the correct option is (D).

6. Indian Grandmaster D Gukesh has won the Menorca Open chess tournament 2022 which was held in Spain, while Aryan Chopra who finished as runner-up. Indian Grandmaster D Gukesh defeated fellow Indian B Adhiban (placed at tenth) in the seventh and final round to win the title. This is D Gukesh's second title win after the La Roda Open 2022.

Hence, the correct option is (B).

7. Lansdowne is the headquarters of Garhwal Rifles located in Uttarakhand.

Lansdowne is the most notable, albeit small, hill station in the north Indian state of Uttaranchal. It is situated 45 km from Kotdwar en route Kotdwar-Pauri road in the Pauri Garhwal district. The famous Garhwal Rifles of the Indian Army has its command office here.

Hence, the correct option is (C).

8. Akodara village of Gujarat situated in Sabarkantha district became the first digital village of India.

- ICICI Bank in 2015 under its Digital Village Project adopted Akodara village and made cashless by adopting digital technology.
- The village has its own official website, has 100% financial rate and mobile banking facilities in Hindi, English and Gujarati languages.
- Digital India was launched by Prime Minister Narendra Modi on 1 July 2015.

Hence, the correct option is (C).

9. Constitutional government means a government limited by the terms of the Constitution.

Constitutional government:

- The core element of constitutional government is the existence of a Rule-of-Law or set of basic laws that bind both public office-holders and all members of a society within a given territory.
- Presently most states avail of a constitution, which directs the organization of the state, the relations between the public offices within the state, as well the human and civil rights of the individual.
- The Constitution seeks to regulate political power.
- Constitutional government means a limited government.
- A constitutional government is conducted according to rules and principles which are binding on all political actors and which therefore help to constrain the unfettered excise of power by separating it or dividing it.

Hence, the correct option is (D).

10. 16 October is observed as World Food day.

World Food Day was first launched in 1945. The reason World Food Day was created was to celebrate the launch of the United Nation's Food and Agriculture Organisation.

The main principle which World Food Day celebrates is the furtherance of food security all over the world, especially in times of crisis. The launch of the Food and Agriculture Organisation by the UN has played a huge role in taking this worthy goal forward. Its annual celebration serves as a marker of the importance of this organisation and helps to raise awareness of the crucial need for successful agriculture policies to be implemented by governments across the world to ensure there is ample food available for everyone.

Hence, the correct option is (D).

11. The range lying to the south of the greater Himalayas is known as Himachal.

The Lesser Himalaya or Himachal lies towards the south of the Great Himalayas. The altitude of peaks in this range varies from 3,700 m to 4,500 m. The average width of this range is 50 km. This range is mainly composed of highly compressed and altered rocks.

Hence, the correct option is (A).

12. Rani Laxmibai Award is given by the Haryana Government in the field of sports. Rani Laxmi Bai Award is conducted by the Department of Sports and Youth Affairs under the Government of Haryana. The award is to honor the lifetime contribution of sportswomen in Haryana. Sportswomen of National/ International recognition will be awarded a cash prize of INR 2,00,000 and other rewards.

Hence, the correct option is (A).

13. Thang-Ta is a martial art form mainly practiced in the state of Manipur. Here thang refers to a 'sword' and ta refers to a 'spear'. In this martial art form when engaged in unarmed combat or when no weapons are used while performing it, it is known as Sarit Sarak.

Hence, the correct option is (C).

14. The Government of British India formed a committee for the Sargent's Plan which was related to education policy.

It is also known as the Sargent Plan after John Sargent, the then Educational Advisor to the Government of India. This, in a phased program spanning 40 years (1944–1984), established nursery schools on a voluntary basis for children under six, while providing free and compulsory education for both boys and girls between the ages of six and fourteen. offered.

Hence, the correct option is (B).

15. After the failure of the Cripps Mission, the Quit India Movement was started in 1942.

- It was headed by Sir Richard Stafford Cripps, a labour minister in Winston Churchill's coalition government in Britain. Gandhi Ji described Cripps' offer of dominion status as, "a post-dated cheque drawn on a crashing bank". The Cripps Mission was a failure as it failed to give confidence to Congress about Britain's intentions (which were not sincere in any case). Neither did the Indian leadership offer support to Britain's war effort.

- In the same year, Congress started the Quit India Movement in the wake of the mission's failure. Mumbai's Gowalia Tank Maidan also known as August Kranti Maidan is the place where the quit India movement was launched by Mahatma Gandhi. He

along with other leaders gathered here on August 8 and 9, 1942.

Hence, the correct option is (D).

16. Organelles are small, specialized structures present in the cells that have a specific function. Organelles are either separately enclosed within their own lipid bilayers i.e. membrane-bound organelles.

Organelles that have distinct functional units without a surrounding lipid bilayer are non-membrane bound organelles.

Hence, the correct option is (B).

17. The wrong pair is "Air passage- voluntary". Rest all three pairs are matched.

Voluntary muscles are the muscles that can be moved by the free will of the person and are associated with the skeleton system. Voluntary muscles are also known as striated muscles or skeletal muscles. These muscles are attached to bones by means of tendons.

A channel or part through which air passes specifically: an anatomical part (such as the pharynx and bronchial tubes) involved in respiration Pertussis is a bacterial infection of the air passages leading to the lungs.

Hence, the correct option is (D).

18. Tendon is a fibrous connective tissue that attaches muscle to bone.

- It serves to move the bone or structure.

- Tendons are made up of collagen.

- The main cellular component of tendons is called tenocytes which synthesize the extracellular matrix of tendons.

- A ligament is a fibrous connective tissue that attaches bone to bone.

Hence, the correct option is (D).

19. Budding is an asexual method of reproduction. Hydra reproduces by this method. In Hydra, a bud develops as an outgrowth due to repeated cell division at a specific level. These buds develop into small individuals and after full maturity detach from the parent body and become new independent hydra.

Hence, the correct option is (A).

20. Mitochondria and fungi are organisms that have their own genetic material.

- Organelles are small, specialized structures present in the cells that have a specific function.

- They are found in the cytoplasm, a viscous liquid found within the cell membrane.

- Some important cell organelles are the nuclei, which store genetic information, mitochondria, known as the "powerhouse of the cell", and ribosomes, which assemble proteins.

- Two organelles mentioned above that have their own genetic material are Chloroplast also known as Plastids and mitochondria.

Hence, the correct option is (B).

21. Diffraction of light is the phenomenon of bending of light from the sharp corners of a slit or obstacle and spreading into the region of geometrical shadow. Diffraction can occur only when wavelength of light is comparable to the size of the obstacle or width of the slit.

Diffraction is of two types:

- Fresnel Diffraction- It is the type of diffraction which occurs when the light source lies at a finite distance from the slit.

- Fraunhofer Diffraction- It is the type of diffraction which occurs when a plane wavefront is incident on the slit and the wavefront emerging from the slit is also plane.

Hence, the correct option is (D).

22. Microfarad unit is capacitance measured for day to day applications.

- This is because the value of 1 farad is too large to be stored in common capacitors.

- Thus, to avoid decimal calculations, Microfarad is more commonly used.

Hence, the correct option is (B).

23. Optical fibers are mainly used in Communication. Optical fibers are used most often as a means to transmit light between the two ends of the fiber and find wide usage in fiber-optic communications, where they permit transmission over longer distances and at higher bandwidths (data transfer rates) than electrical cables.

Hence, the correct option is (B).

24. If two charged bodies having equal potential are connected through a conducting wire, then current will not flow.

- The flow of current is defined as the rate of flow of electric charge.

- When the electric charge flows in one direction, the current flows in the opposite direction.

- The current only flows when there is a potential difference between two bodies.

Hence, the correct option is (C).

25. Sodium and Potassium are highly reactive metals and react vigorously with the oxygen, carbon dioxide and moisture present in the air such that it may even cause a fire. To prevent this explosive reaction, these elements is kept immersed in kerosene because they doesn't react with kerosene.

Hence, the correct option is (C).

26. Water is a good fire extinguisher. But water can not be used to extinguish electrical fires. This is because water is a good conductor of electricity. It can cause electric shock and can harm the person who is trying to put it off.

We can not use water in case of oil fires. Oil floats over water and thus oil fires cannot be extinguished by using water. So, situation A and C cannot be used to extinguish fires.

Hence, the correct option is (B).

27. Metal P displaces metal Q from its salt solution so P is more reactive than Q. Metal P can not displace metal R from its salt solution so R is more reactive than P.

So reactive order is,

R>P>Q

So, metal Q will be the least reactive metal.

Hence, the correct option is (B).

28. Physical changes are changes affecting the form of a chemical substance, but not its chemical composition.

Example: Breaking of glass, grinding wheat, boiling of water.

In chemical change the chemical composition of substance is changed.

Hence, the correct option is (D).

29. The mixture of chalk and water can be separated by sedimentation, decantation or filtration process.

- **Sublimation**: Sublimation is the transition of a substance directly from the solid to the gas state without passing the liquid state.

- Therefore, sublimation will not be helpful in the process of separating a mixture of chalk and water.

Hence, the correct option is (D).

30. The parsec (sign pc) is an astronomical unit of distance. It is approximately 30 trillion kilometers. Parsec is used in astronomy. Its length is based on trigonometric distance, an ancient method of measuring the distance between stars.

Hence, the correct option is (B).

31. Given:

Principal amount, $P = 250000$

Rate of interest for the 1st year $= 4\%$

Rate of interest for the 2nd year $= 5\%$

Rate of interest for the 3rd year $= 6\%$

For the 1st year,

$$A_1 = 250000 \times [1 + \left(\frac{4}{100}\right)]$$

$$\Rightarrow A_1 = 260000$$

For the 2nd year,

$$P = A_1$$

$A_2 = 260000 \times [1 + \left(\frac{5}{100}\right)]$

$\Rightarrow A_2 = 273000$

For the 3rd year,

$P = A_2$

$A_3 = 273000 \times [1 + \left(\frac{6}{100}\right)]$

$\Rightarrow A_3 = 289380$

$\therefore$ The amount at the end of the three years is Rs.289380.

Hence, the correct option is (D).

32. According to the question,

A toy is in the form of a cone surmounted on a hemisphere. The radius of the hemisphere and the cone is 3 cm each, the height of the conical part of the toy is 4 cm.

The surface area of a cone $= \pi r l$

Where slant height $l = \sqrt{r^2 + h^2} = \sqrt{(4)^2 + (3)^2} = 5$ cm

Surface area of a hemisphere $= 2\pi r^2$

So, total surface area of toy $= \frac{22}{7} \times 3 \times 5 + 2 \times \frac{22}{7} \times 3 \times 3$

$= \frac{22}{7} \times 3 \times 11 = 103.71$ cm^2

Hence, the correct option is (B).

33. Let the total number of students in the school be x.

$\therefore$ Number of boys $= \frac{3}{5}x$

Number of girls $= x - \frac{3}{5}x$

$\Rightarrow 800 = \frac{2}{5}x$

$\Rightarrow x = \frac{800 \times 5}{2}$

$= 2000$

$\therefore$ Number of boys $= \frac{3}{5} \times 2000$

$= 1200$

Hence, the correct option is (C).

34. Given:

$\frac{1}{2} + \frac{1}{4} + \frac{1}{8} + \frac{1}{a} + \frac{1}{6} = \frac{2}{6} + \frac{1}{3} + \frac{2}{3}$

$\Rightarrow \frac{1}{a} = \frac{2}{6} + \frac{1}{3} + \frac{2}{3} - \frac{1}{2} - \frac{1}{4} - \frac{1}{8} - \frac{1}{6}$

$\Rightarrow \frac{1}{a} = \frac{(8 + 8 + 16 - 12 - 6 - 3 - 4)}{24}$

$\Rightarrow \frac{1}{a} = \frac{7}{24}$

$\Rightarrow a = \frac{24}{7}$

$\therefore$ The value of a is $\frac{24}{7}$.

Hence, the correct option is (B).

35. Given:

$SP =$ Rs. x

Loss $= 28\%$

$SP =$ Rs. y

Profit $= 12\%$

Let the cost price be Rs. 100

If television is sold at Rs. x, then

Loss $\% = 28\%$

As we know,

Loss $\% = \left(\frac{\text{Loss}}{CP}\right) \times 100$

$28 = \left(\frac{\text{Loss}}{100}\right) \times 100$

$\Rightarrow$ Loss $= 28$

$SP = CP -$ Loss

$SP = 100 - 28 =$ Rs. 72

$\Rightarrow x =$ Rs. 72

Now,

If television is sold at Rs. y, then Profit $\% = 12\%$

$12 = \left(\frac{\text{Profit}}{100}\right) \times 100$

Profit $=$ Rs. 12

$SP = CP +$ Profit

$SP = 100 + 12 =$ Rs. 112

$\Rightarrow y =$ Rs. 112

We have to find $\frac{y}{x}$

$\frac{y}{x} = \frac{112}{72} = \frac{14}{9}$

$\therefore$ The ratio of y to x is $14 : 9$.

Hence, the correct option is (D).

36. 24 men complete 1 work in 18 days.

We know that,

$$\frac{M_1 D_1}{W_1} = \frac{M_2 D_2}{W_2}$$

$$\Rightarrow \frac{24 \times 18}{1} = \frac{27 \times 8}{W_2}$$

$$W_2 = \frac{27 \times 8}{24 \times 18} = \frac{1}{2}$$

Remaining work $= 1 - \frac{1}{2} = \frac{1}{2}$

$$\therefore \frac{M_1 D_1}{W_1} = \frac{M_2 D_2}{W_2}$$

$$\Rightarrow \frac{12 \times 28}{1} = \frac{14 \times D_2}{\frac{1}{2}}$$

$$\Rightarrow 14 \times D_2 = \frac{1}{2} \times 12 \times 28$$

$$\Rightarrow D_2 = \frac{6 \times 28}{14} = 12 \text{ days}$$

Hence, the correct option is (A).

37. Let the income of Asha in 2018 and 2017 be 5x and 5x respectively.

Let the income of Ravenna in 2018 and 2017 be 3y and 2y respectively

Since, the ratio of their income in the year 2017 was 5 : 4

5x : 2y = 5 : 4

2x = y

The sum of their incomes in 2018 is Rs. 10242

3x + 3y = 10, 242

9x = 10, 242

x = 1,138 and y = 2276

Ravenna's income for the year 2017 = 2y = Rs. 4552

Hence, the correct option is (D).

38. Pattern of the series is:

10 + 7 × 1 = 17

17 + 8 × 3 = 41

41 + 9 × 5 = 86

86 + 10 × 7 = 156

156 + 11 × 9 = 255

255 + 12 × 11 = 387

Hence, the correct option is (B).

39.

3	525
5	175
5	35
7	7
	1

5	455
7	91
13	13
	1

As we know,

$1\ m = 100\ cm$

$5.25m = 525\ cm$

$4.55\ m = 455\ cm$

HCF of 525 and 455

$\Rightarrow 525 = 3 \times 5 \times 5 \times 7$

$\Rightarrow 455 = 5 \times 7 \times 13$

HCF of 455 and $525 = 5 \times 7 = 35$

Hence, the correct option is (B).

40. Given:

1st number = 2 × 4th number

2nd number = 3 × 3rd number

3rd number $= \frac{1}{2} \times$ 4th number

The average of all four number = 70

Sum of all number = Average of number × Total numbers

Let the 4th number be 2x.

According to the given condition

The ratio of all four number is 4x : 3x : x : 2x

The sum of all numbers = 70 × 4 = 280

$\Rightarrow$ 10x = 280

$\Rightarrow$ x = 28

The sum of 1st and 4th number = 4x + 2x

$\Rightarrow$ 6x = 6 × 28 = 168

$\therefore$ The sum of first and 4th number is 168.

Hence, the correct option is (D).

41. Let A be the event that both numbers are odd.

Let B be the event that the sum is even.

Then,

Odd $+$ odd $=$ even

Odd $+$ even $=$ odd

Even $+$ even $=$ even

On using $P\left(\frac{A}{B}\right) = \frac{P(A \cap B)}{P(B)}$

$$P(A \cap B) = \frac{{}^5 C_2}{{}^{10} C_2}$$

$$= \frac{\frac{5!}{2!3!}}{\frac{10!}{2!8!}}$$

$$= \frac{\frac{5 \times 4 \times 3 \times 2 \times 1}{2 \times 1 \times 3 \times 2 \times 1}}{\frac{10 \times 9 \times 8 \times 7 \times 6 \times 5 \times 4 \times 3 \times 2 \times 1}{2 \times 1 \times 8 \times 7 \times 6 \times 5 \times 4 \times 3 \times 2 \times 1}}$$

$$= \frac{2}{9}$$

$$P(B) = \frac{\left({}^5C_2 + {}^5C_2\right)}{{}^{10}C_2}$$

$$= \frac{{}^5C_2}{{}^{10}C_2} + \frac{{}^5C_2}{{}^{10}C_2}$$

$$= \frac{2}{9} + \frac{2}{9}$$

$$= \frac{4}{9}$$

$$\therefore P\left(\frac{A}{B}\right) = \frac{\frac{2}{9}}{\frac{4}{9}}$$

$$= \frac{1}{2}$$

Hence, the correct option is (A).

42. Let the speed of the boat be 'b' and stream be 's'.

$$\frac{30}{(b-s)} = 10$$

$$b - s = 3$$

$$\frac{52}{(b+s)} = 4$$

$$b + s = 13$$

$$b - s = 3$$

$$2b = 16$$

$$b = 8 \text{ km/hr}$$

$$s = 5 \text{ km/hr}$$

Each is decreased by 1 km/hr

So,

$$b = 7 \text{ km/hr}$$

$$s = 4 \text{ km/hr}$$

Time taken for 121 km downstream $= \frac{121}{11}$

$= 11$ hrs

Hence, the correct option is (B).

43. Given:

Ratio of radius and height of the cone $= 3 : 4$

Curved surface area $= 240\pi \ cm^2$

As we know,

Curved surface area of cone $= \pi r l$

Volume of cone $= \left(\frac{1}{3}\right)\pi r^2 h$

Slant height $= \sqrt{(h^2 + r^2)}$

Where,

$r =$ Radius of the cone

$h =$ Height of the cone

$l =$ slant height

Let the radius and height of the cone be $3x$ and $4x$.

Slant height $= \sqrt{[(4x)^2 + (3x)^2]}$

$$= \sqrt{(16x^2 + 9x^2)}$$

$$= \sqrt{25x^2}$$

$$= 5x$$

Curved suface area $= \pi \times 3x \times 5x$

$$\Rightarrow 240\pi = \pi \times 15x^2$$

$$\Rightarrow x^2 = 16$$

$$\Rightarrow x = 4$$

Radius $= 12 \ cm$

Height $= 16 \ cm$

Slant height $= 20 \ cm$

Volume of the cone $= \left(\frac{1}{3}\right) \times \pi \times 144 \times 16$

$$= 48 \times 16 \times \pi$$

$$= 768\pi$$

$\therefore$ The volume of the cone is $768\pi \ cm^3$.

Hence, the correct option is (B).

44. Given:

Pass % - 28% = 15 marks

Pass % - 32% = 8 marks

In this type of question, the gap between the given percentages is equal to the difference between the given marks.

Pass % of total marks – 28% of total marks = 15 marks ------ (1)

Pass % of total marks – 32% of total marks = 8 marks ------(2)

Subtracting (1) and (2);

4% of total marks = 7

$$\Rightarrow \frac{4}{100} \times \text{(total marks)} = 7$$

$\Rightarrow$ Total marks $= \dfrac{(7 \times 100)}{4}$

$\Rightarrow$ Total marks = 175

Hence, the correct option is (C).

45. Let there be n objects, of which m objects are alike of one kind, and the remaining $(n - m)$ objects are distinct. Then, the total number of permutations that can be formed from these objects is $\dfrac{n!}{m!}$.

The given word 'INDIA' contains 5 letters, out of which two are alike of one kind (2 I's), and the other three letters are distinct.

$\therefore$ Total number of their permutations $= \dfrac{5!}{2!}$

$\Rightarrow \dfrac{5\times4\times3\times2\times1}{2\times1}$

$\Rightarrow 60$

Hence, the correct option is (D).

46. According to given conditions,

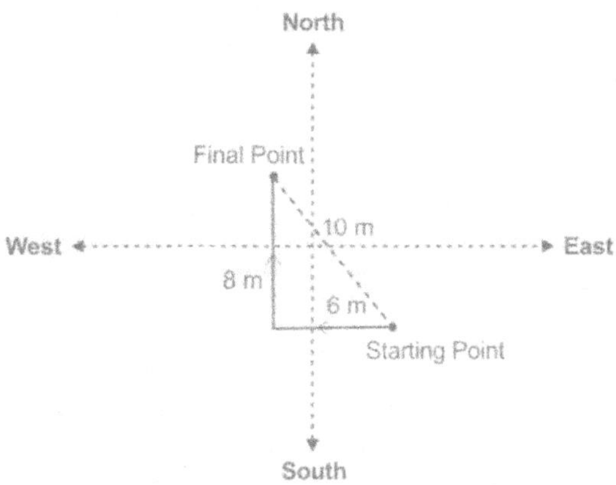

The shortest distance he needs to travel to go back to his starting point $= \sqrt{6^2 + 8^2}\ m$

$= \sqrt{36 + 64}\ m$

$= \sqrt{100}\ m$

$= 10\ m$

Hence, the correct option is (D).

47. Chennai is the capital of Tamil Nadu.

Gangtok is the capital of Sikkim.

Hyderabad is the capital of Telangana.

Whereas,

Aurangabad is a city in Maharashtra.

Hence, the correct option is (D).

48. Since Samir has neither a sister nor a brother,

Therefore, Samir is the only son of his father.

So, the mother of the portrait is the wife of Samir.

Therefore, the portrait was of Samir's son.

Hence, the correct option is (C).

49. The pattern followed is,

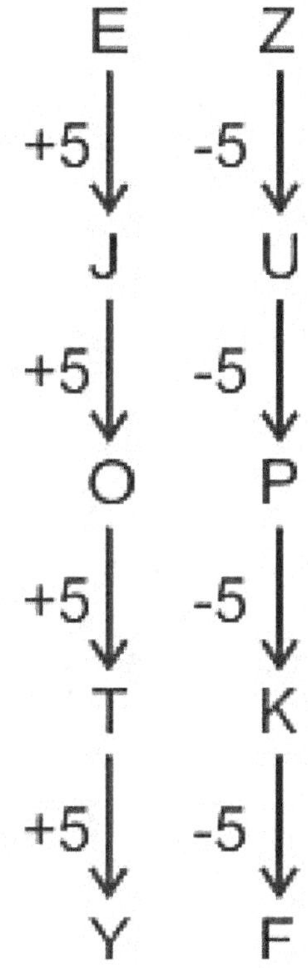

Thus, OP is the correct answer.

Hence, the correct option is (A).

50. Pattern followed:

$TORCH \rightarrow UNPSDI$

$T + 1 = U, O - 1 = N, O + 1 = P, R + 1 = S, C + 1 = D, H + 1 = 1$

$BEST \rightarrow CDFTU$

$B + 1 = C, E - 1 = D, E + 1 = F, S + 1 = T, T + 1 = U$

Similarly,

Code for the word ' $MARKS$ ' will be:

$M + 1 = N, A - 1 = Z, A + 1 = B, R + 1 = S, K + 1 = L, S + 1 = T \Rightarrow NZBSLT$

Hence, the correct option is (D).

General Knowledge

Q.1 Name the Dhrupad artists from Madhya Pradesh to have conferred the 'Padma Shri' in 2012.

[MP Jail Prahari, 2018]

A. Mohan Shukla
B. Sulbha and Manoj Saraf
C. P.V. Kahu
D. Gundecha Brothers

Q.2 Who is the author of "The Exile"?
A. Duleep Singh
B. Eli Amir
C. Navtej Sarna
D. Prajwal Parajuly

Q.3 Which of the following is a river flowing from Central India and join Yamuna/Ganga?
A. Ghagra　　**B.** Gomti　　**C.** Kosi　　**D.** Betwa

Q.4 August 12 is celebrated as:

[Officers Training Academy (OTA), 2020], [Indian Military Academy (IMA), 2020]

A. The World Environment Day
B. The World No-Tobacco Day
C. The International Day against Drug Abuse and Illicit Trafficking
D. The International Youth Day

Q.5 In which city in Rajasthan is the chhatri of eighty-four pillars located?

[Rajasthan Police Constable, 2020]

A. Bundi　　**B.** Alwar　　**C.** Ramgarh　　**D.** Jodhpur

Q.6 Kobe Bryant, who recently died in a helicopter crash, was a legendary personality of which sports?
A. Cricket
B. Basket ball
C. Football
D. Boxing

Q.7 Match the following and select the correct answer from the codes given below:

List - I	List - II
1. Sikkim	a. Kohima
2. Rajasthan	b. Bhubaneshwar
3. Odisha	c. Jaipur
4. Nagaland	d. Gangtok

A. 1-d, 2-c, 3-b, 4-a
B. 1-d, 2-c, 3-a, 4-b
C. 1-c, 2-d, 3-b, 4-a
D. 1-d, 2-b, 3-c, 4-a

Q.8 Which of the following Committee recommended for Panchayati Raj System in India?

[HSSC Canal Patwari, 2021]

A. Singhvi Committee
B. Punchhi committee
C. Balwantrai Mehta Committee
D. None of the above

Q.9 Where is the global headquarter of UNICEF?

[UPPSC Staff Nurse, 2021]

A. Geneva
B. New York
C. New Delhi
D. Islamabad

Q.10 Who is the author of the book 'Crossed Swords: Pakistan, Its Army and the War Within'?

[SSC Sub Inspector (CPO), 2020]

A. Shuja Nawaz
B. JN Dixit
C. Shashi Tharoor
D. SD Muni

Q.11 'Khuang' is a traditional musical instrument of which state?
A. Assam
B. Mizoram
C. Jharkhand
D. West Bengal

Q.12 Who was presented Lifetime Achievement Award at the Indian Film Festival of Melbourne (IFFM) Awards 2022?
A. Mohit Raina
B. Sachin Tendulkar
C. Kapil Dev
D. Dharmendra

Q.13 The 'Swadeshi' and 'Boycott' were adopted as methods of struggle in Bengal at the same time Vande Mataram Movement was in which place?
A. Tamil Nadu
B. Punjab
C. Andhra Pradesh
D. Poona

Q.14 The 1907 Surat session of Indian National Congress is significant in the history of the freedom movement, because:
A. Congress accepted separate electorate for Muslims.
B. Congress split into moderate and extremist groups.
C. Swadeshi movement was launched.
D. "Swaraj" was adopted as the goal of the Indian National Congress.

Q.15 'Saddle Peak' the highest peak of Andaman and Nicobar Islands is located in ________.
A. Great Nicobar
B. Middle Andaman
C. Little Andaman
D. North Andaman

General Science

Q.16 'Mycorrhiza' is a symbiotic association between:
A. Algae and plants
B. Algae and fungi
C. Fungi and plants
D. Blue green algae and fungi

Q.17 Which Vitamin is chemically known as Ascorbic acid?
A. Vitamin D
B. Vitamin C
C. Vitamin K
D. Vitamin E

Q.18 Which of the following is not a multicellular animal?

A. Amoeba   **B.** Cat   **C.** Human   **D.** Horse

Q.19 Which organ of the body is affected by Leucoderma?

A. Heart   **B.** Kidney   **C.** Lungs   **D.** Skin

Q.20 In which of the following plants, chlorophyll is not found?

A. Bryophytes   **B.** Algae

C. Fungi   **D.** Pteridophytes

Q.21 What is the gravitational force between two objects?

A. Attractive at large distances only

B. Attractive at small distances only

C. Attractive at all distances

D. Attractive at large distances but repulsive at small distances

Q.22 The second equation of Motion gives the relationship between _____ and Time.

[RRB/RRC Group D, 2018]

A. Acceleration   **B.** Position

C. Momentum   **D.** Velocity

Q.23 A mixture of sodium chloride (salt) and ammonium chloride can be separated by _______.

[Officers Training Academy (OTA), 2020], [Indian Military Academy (IMA), 2020]

A. sublimation   **B.** filtration

C. chromatography   **D.** distillation

Q.24 Silver articles turn black when kept in the open for longer time due to the formation of _______.

[Officers Training Academy (OTA), 2020], [Indian Military Academy (IMA), 2020]

A. H_2S **B.** AgS   **C.** $AgSO_4$ **D.** Ag_2S

Q.25 The radioactive isotope of hydrogen is _______.

[Officers Training Academy (OTA), 2020], [Indian Military Academy (IMA), 2020]

A. protium   **B.** deuterium

C. tritium   **D.** hydronium

Q.26 Which one of the following does not form an oxide on reaction with oxygen?

[Officers Training Academy (OTA), 2020], [Indian Military Academy (IMA), 2020]

A. Magnesium   **B.** Lead

C. Tin   **D.** Silver

Q.27 The valency of phosphorus is _______.

[Officers Training Academy (OTA), 2020], [Indian Military Academy (IMA), 2020]

A. 2, 3   **B.** 3, 4   **C.** 4, 5   **D.** 3, 5

Q.28 An object moves with a constant speed when the value of _______ is negligible.

A. Pressure   **B.** Velocity   **C.** Force   **D.** Mass

Q.29 The physical quantity that is denoted by area under velocity time graph is _______.

A. Speed   **B.** Displacement

C. Acceleration   **D.** Momentum

Q.30 At a particular temperature, sound propagates in _____ at the fastest speed.

A. water   **B.** vacuum   **C.** iron   **D.** air

Maths

Q.31 The compound interest on a sum of Rs. 15,000 at 15% p.a. for $2\frac{2}{3}$ years, interest compounded annually, is (nearest to Rs.1):

[SSC Selection Post Phase IX, 2020]

A. Rs. 6,795   **B.** Rs. 6,815

C. Rs. 6,781   **D.** Rs. 6,821

Q.32 In a basketball match, all 10 players shake hands with each other once after the match. How many handshakes will be there?

A. 20   **B.** 45   **C.** 55   **D.** 90

Q.33 In a $\triangle PQR, PS$ is the angle bisector of $\angle QPR$ which is equal to $120°$. Find the length of PS, if $PQ = 12\ cm$ and $PR = 8\ cm$.

A. $5.2\ cm$ **B.** $2.4\ cm$ **C.** $4.8\ cm$ **D.** $6.4\ cm$

Q.34 In a school auditorium $\frac{2}{7}$ of the students are girls. If there are 111 more boys than girls, how many boys are there in the school auditorium?

[CTET Paper - I, 2021]

A. 400   **B.** 315   **C.** 259   **D.** 185

Q.35 A person sold an article for Rs. 75 which cost him Rs. x. He finds that he realised $x\%$ profit on his outlay. What is x equal to?

[Indian Military Academy (IMA), 2020]

A. 20%   **B.** 25%   **C.** 50%   **D.** 100%

Q.36 If $A:B:C = 2:3:4$, then the ratio $\frac{A}{B}:\frac{B}{C}:\frac{C}{D}$ is equal to:

A. 8:9:16   **B.** 8:9:12   **C.** 8:9:24   **D.** 4:9:16

Q.37 The LCM of the prime numbers between 1 to 12 is___.

[RRB/RRC Group D, 2018]

A. 1000   **B.** 2020   **C.** 2310   **D.** 1010

Q.38 A batsman in his 20th innings makes a score of 110 and thereby increases his average by 4. What is his average after 20th innings?

[Uttarakhand Public Service Commission (UKPSC), 2016]

A. 30   **B.** 34   **C.** 36   **D.** 43

Q.39 A bag contains 35 balls of three different colors viz. red, orange and pink. The ratio of red balls to orange balls is $3:2$, respectively and probability of choosing a pink ball is $\frac{3}{7}$. If two balls are picked from the bag, then what is the probability that one ball is orange and one ball is pink?

A. $\frac{24}{119}$　　**B.** $\frac{60}{119}$　　**C.** $\frac{96}{595}$　　**D.** $\frac{3}{17}$

Q.40 X can do a piece of work in 30 days. X leaves after working for 3 days and the remaining work is completed by Y in 18 days. How much time is taken by Y to complete the piece of work alone?

A. 5 days　　**B.** 15 days　　**C.** 10 days　　**D.** 20 days

Q.41 A sector is cut from a circle of diameter 42 cm. If the angle of the sector is $150°$ then what is its area in cm^2. (Take $\pi = \frac{22}{7}$)

[SSC Constable (GD), 2019]

A. 584.8　　**B.** 577.5　　**C.** 564.6　　**D.** 580.4

Q.42 If the number when subtracted from 37.5% of itself gives the result as 35, find the original number.

A. 90　　**B.** 49　　**C.** 56　　**D.** 72

Q.43 What will come in place of the question mark '?' in the following question?

$$(0.1 \times 0.004) + (0.02 \times 0.3) - (0.04 \times 0.03) = ?$$

A. 0.0022　　**B.** 0.0034　　**C.** 0.0046　　**D.** 0.0052

Q.44 A boy travels $\frac{2}{3}$rd of the distance of his journey by bus, $\frac{1}{7}$th by Rickshaw and 8 km on foot. The total distance travelled by the man is-

A. 30 km　　**B.** 36 km　　**C.** 42 km　　**D.** 34 km

Q.45 Direction: Select the number from among the given options that can replace the question mark (?) in the following series.

$108, 117, 126, ?$

A. 139　　**B.** 136　　**C.** 135　　**D.** 169

Logical Reasoning

Q.46 A series is given with one term missing. Select the correct alternative from the given ones that will complete the series.

V, R, M, G, ?

A. P　　**B.** Q　　**C.** Z　　**D.** Y

Q.47 Five girls took part in a race. Rajni finished before Mahika but behind Garima. Ashmita finished before Sanchali but behind Mahika. Who came second in the race?

[SSC MTS, 2019]

A. Sanchali　　**B.** Mahika　　**C.** Garima　　**D.** Rajni

Q.48 F is the wife of H. H is son of I. I is son of E. E is the only daughter of her father G. How is G related to I?

A. Father　　**B.** Grand-father
C. Brother　　**D.** Son

Q.49 Arun went for a movie nine days ago. He goes to watch movies only on Thursdays. What day of the week is today?

A. Wednesday　　**B.** Thursday
C. Friday　　**D.** Saturday

Q.50 In a certain coding system, if CHICANERY is written as DNODTHVKS, how will CRANE be written in the same coding system?

[SSC Sub Inspector (CPO), 2020]

A. DKTHV　　**B.** HKSHO　　**C.** CJSGU　　**D.** DOTKV

// Smart Answer Sheet //

Correct — Indicates percentage of students who answered questions correctly.

Skipped — Indicates percentage of students who skipped questions.

Q.	Ans.	Correct / Skipped	Q.	Ans.	Correct / Skipped	Q.	Ans.	Correct / Skipped	Q.	Ans.	Correct / Skipped	Q.	Ans.	Correct / Skipped
1	D	61.38 % / 30.16 %	11	B	31.37 % / 67.83 %	21	C	10.77 % / 84.52 %	31	D	61.71 % / 36.72 %	41	B	58.85 % / 39.16 %
2	C	88.45 % / 10.71 %	12	C	48.14 % / 32.35 %	22	B	86.72 % / 13.28 %	32	B	87.92 % / 10.81 %	42	C	54.45 % / 43.53 %
3	D	87.48 % / 11.0 %	13	C	54.95 % / 41.23 %	23	A	13.82 % / 75.56 %	33	C	18.05 % / 67.39 %	43	D	69.44 % / 30.39 %
4	D	83.24 % / 11.47 %	14	B	17.51 % / 76.92 %	24	D	64.12 % / 31.36 %	34	D	47.1 % / 35.11 %	44	C	50.85 % / 38.32 %
5	A	54.23 % / 39.47 %	15	D	64.02 % / 34.05 %	25	C	68.56 % / 31.08 %	35	C	27.6 % / 67.1 %	45	C	59.87 % / 37.96 %
6	B	83.61 % / 15.76 %	16	C	59.7 % / 35.86 %	26	D	86.64 % / 12.9 %	36	C	67.41 % / 31.38 %	46	C	62.95 % / 33.22 %
7	A	12.75 % / 78.72 %	17	B	43.7 % / 52.5 %	27	D	80.89 % / 18.9 %	37	C	65.0 % / 32.39 %	47	D	28.0 % / 69.44 %
8	C	12.92 % / 79.97 %	18	A	81.92 % / 11.64 %	28	C	87.36 % / 10.11 %	38	B	40.96 % / 54.07 %	48	B	68.01 % / 30.93 %
9	B	82.94 % / 13.79 %	19	D	49.05 % / 31.17 %	29	B	61.24 % / 30.2 %	39	A	31.33 % / 67.69 %	49	D	86.28 % / 12.78 %
10	A	23.03 % / 72.37 %	20	C	42.79 % / 55.35 %	30	C	68.93 % / 30.44 %	40	D	48.12 % / 36.87 %	50	A	59.67 % / 30.98 %

Performance Analysis

Avg. Score (%)	41.0%
Toppers Score (%)	56.0%
Your Score	

//Hints and Solutions//

1. Gundecha Brothers were conferred with the 'Padma Shri' in 2012.

Dhrupad is the oldest classical style of Hindustani vocal music. The word 'Dhrupad' is derived from 'Dhruva,' which means 'fixed' and 'pada', meaning 'word' or 'set-composition'. Dhrupad has traditionally three major parts - alap, jor-jhala, and composition. Dhrupad is a form of Gandharva Veda.

Hence, the correct option is (D).

2. Navtej Sarna is the author of "The Exile". The Exile, published in 2008, is based on the life of Duleep Singh, the last Maharaja of Lahore, and son Raja Ranjit Singh.

Hence, the correct option is (C).

3. Betwa river also known as Vetravati river originates in Vindhyan range and flows Northward to meet Yamuna.

The Betwa is a river in Northern India, and a tributary of the Yamuna. Also known as the Vetravati, the Betwa rises in the Vindhya Range just north of Hoshangabad in Madhya Pradesh and flows northeast through Madhya Pradesh and flow through Orchha to Uttar Pradesh. Nearly one-half of its course, which is not navigable, runs over the Malwa Plateau before it breaks into the upland. A tributary of the Yamuna River, the confluence of the Betwa and the Yamuna Rivers takes place in the Hamirpur town in Uttar Pradesh, in the vicinity of Orchha.

Hence, the correct option is (D).

4. August 12 is celebrated as 'International Youth Day.'

The International Youth Day

- International Youth Day is observed globally on 12th August every year.
- The day is celebrated to recognize the efforts put in by the youth for the betterment of society.
- The Day aims to promote the ways to engage the youth and make them more actively involved in their communities through positive contributions.

Theme

- The theme of International Youth Day 2020, "Youth Engagement for Global Action".
- The theme highlights the ways in which the engagement of young people at the local, national and global levels is enriching national and multilateral institutions and processes, as well as drawing lessons on how their representation and engagement in formal institutional politics can be significantly enhanced.

History of International Youth Day

- In 1999, the General Assembly endorsed the recommendation made by the World Conference of Ministers Responsible for Youth (Lisbon, 8-12 August 1998) that 12 August be declared International Youth Day.
- This day is the first time observed on August 12, 2000, the day marks an awareness day and draws attention to a given set of cultural and legal issues surrounding youth.

Hence, the correct option is (D).

5. Eighty-four pillared chhatri or "84-pillared cenotaph" is located in the Bundi district of Rajasthan. It was built in 1740 by Rao Raja Anirudh, the Maharaja of Bundi, as a memorial to his foster brother Deva. Under whose love and guidance the prince grew up. He loved Dev very much, thus he built an 84-pillared cenotaph in his honor. It is also widely known as the "Umbrella of the Music Queen". It is said that all 84 beams cannot be counted at once.

Hence, the correct option is (A).

6. Kobe Bryant was a 41- year-old American professional basketball player, who recently died in a helicopter crash near Los Angeles. Bryant played in the National Basketball Association (NBA) with the Los Angeles Lakers, throughout his entire career. He entered the NBA directly from high school and had won five NBA championships.

Bryant was on board the helicopter with eight others, including his 13-year-old daughter Gianna Bryant during the crash. The sudden demise of one of the greatest basketball players in history was mourned by basketball enthusiasts all over the world.

Hence, the correct option is (B).

7. The correct answer is 1-d, 2-c, 3-b, 4-a.

States	Capital
Sikkim	Gangtok
Rajasthan	Jaipur
Odisha	Bhubaneswar
Nagaland	Kohima

Gangtok is the capital of Sikkim. It is situated above sea level at the height of 5,500 ft. It is known for learning Buddhist and also connected to commercial, religious, and cultural activities.

The historic city of Jaipur in Rajasthan was founded under the patronage of Sawai Jai Singh II. It was founded in 1727 AD.

Bhubaneswar is the largest city and the capital city in the Indian state Odisha. It is also called as "Temple City of India".

Kohima is the capital city and the second-largest city in Nagaland.

Hence, the correct option is (A).

8. Balwantrai Mehta Committee:

- In January 1957, the Government of India appointed a committee to examine the working of the Community Development Programme (1952) and the National Extension Service (1953) and to suggest measures for their better working.
- The chairman of this committee was Balwant Rai G Mehta.

- The committee submitted its report in November 1957 and recommended the establishment of the scheme of 'democratic decentralisation', which ultimately came to be known as Panchayati Raj.

- The recommendations of the committee were accepted by the National Development Council in January 1958.

- Rajasthan was the first state to establish Panchayati Raj.

Hence, the correct option is (C).

9. The global headquarter of UNICEF is in New York.

- UNICEF stands for United Nations International Children's Emergency Fund.

- It was established post World War II in the General Assembly of the United States on 11 December 1948 to provide supplies and assistance to children after World War II.

- Basically, it provides humanitarian and developmental aid to children worldwide.

- This agency is one of the most recognizable social welfare organizations of the world comprised of 192 countries and territories.

Hence, the correct option is (B).

10. Shuja Nawaz is the author of the book 'Crossed Swords: Pakistan, Its Army and the War Within'.

Shuja Nawaz is a political and strategic analyst from Pakistan. The second edition of the book named 'The Battle for Pakistan – The Bitter US Friendship and a Tough Neighbourhood' published in 2019.

Hence, the correct option is (A).

11. 'Khuang' is a traditional musical instrument of Mizoram state.

Khuang is a Mizo indigenous instrument that has an important value in the Mizo society both socially as well as religiously. Khuang is made up of a Hollow tree wrapped with animal skin on both sides.

Hence, the correct option is (B).

12. Kapil Dev was presented Lifetime Achievement Award. On August 14, 2022, IFFM Awards night was held at the Palais Theatre. '83' was awarded the Best Film.

Shoojit Sircar and Aparna Sen won Best Director for 'Sardar Udham' and 'The Rapist', respectively.

Hence, the correct option is (C).

13. The 'Swadeshi' and 'Boycott' were adopted as methods of struggle in Bengal at the same time the Vande Matram Movement was in Andhra Pradesh.

This was the most important movement in Bengal and was known as Vande Mataram movement in Andhra Pradesh. This movement ended in 1911. The government made the decision of partition of Bengal in December 1903.

Hence, the correct option is (C).

14. At the Surat conference in 1907, congress split. The moderate leaders have captured the machinery of the congress excluded the militant extremist elements from it. The congress split into 2 separate groups of moderates and extremists.

Hence, the correct option is (B).

15. 'Saddle Peak' the highest peak of Andaman and Nicobar Islands is located in Diglipur, a town in North Andaman Island. It is the highest point of the archipelago in the Bay of Bengal with a length of 731 meters (2,418 feet) followed by Mount Thullier at 2,106 feet (642 meters) on Great Nicobar and Mount Harriet at 1,197 feet (365 meters) on South Andaman.

Hence, the correct option is (D).

16. Mycorrhiza is the structure resulting from the symbiosis between Fungi and Plant roots. It is among the most widespread and ancient symbioses on Earth, it is found in about 90% of all land plants.

Through mycorrhization, the fungi colonize the root system of a host plant, providing increased water and nutrient absorption capabilities while the plant provides the fungus with carbohydrates formed from photosynthesis. The symbiotic relationship between algae and fungi is lichen.

Hence, the correct option is (C).

17. Vitamin C is chemically known as Ascorbic acid. The deficiency of Vitamin C causes scurvy. Ascorbic acid (vitamin C) is a water-soluble material that is easily oxidized in aqueous solution.

Hence, the correct option is (B).

18. Amoeba is not a multicellular animal. Amoeba is a unicellular organism that has the ability to alter its shape. Grouped under the Kingdom Protista. The structure of Amoeba consists of cytoplasm, plasma membrane, and nucleus.

Hence, the correct option is (A).

19. Skin is affected by Leucoderma.

Leucoderma is a Latin word where leucos means white and derma means skin. The medical name for leucoderma is vitiligo.

It is a disease caused by destruction of cells called melanocyte in skin, which produce the pigment melanin responsible for our skin colour. Loss of this pigment leads to white patches in different parts of the body; there are no other symptoms associated with it and can occur at any age.

Hence, the correct option is (D).

20. Chlorophyll refers to the green pigments found in the chloroplasts of plants. It is essential for photosynthesis. Fungi have no chlorophyll, hence incapable of producing their own food. So, they get their nourishment from other sources.

Hence, the correct option is (C).

21. The gravitational force is between two objects attractive at all distances because the gravitational force between two objects is proportional to their masses and inversely proportional to the square of the distance between their centers.

Hence, the correct option is (C).

22. The second equation of Motion gives the relationship between Position and Time.

It is given by $S = ut + \frac{1}{2}at^2$

S = Distance

u = Initial Velocity

t = Time

a = Acceleration

Hence, the correct option is (B).

23. A mixture of sodium chloride (salt) and ammonium chloride can be separated by sublimation.

- Under this phenomenon, solid directly changes to gas or conversion of gas to solid without changing into the liquid state.
- It is a process, however, by which compounds can be purified or mixtures separated and as such can be of value as a single step or as an integral part of a more complex analytical method.
- It is applicable to a range of solids of inorganic or organic origin in a variety of different matrices and can be particularly useful when heat-labile materials are involved.
- As a method of the sample, purification sublimation has been used to produce high-purity materials as analytical standards.
- A specific and common example of sublimation used as a means of purification is the removal of water from heat-labile materials in the process known as freeze-drying.

Hence, the correct option is (A).

24. Silver articles turn black when kept in the open for longer time due to the formation of Ag_2S.

When silver articles are kept in open or direct contact with air, then a layer of silver oxide is formed on the surface of the articles.

- Due to the reaction of silver with the oxygen present in the atmosphere Silver oxide turns black in colour.
- After an interval of time, it will form silver sulphide after coming in contact with oxygen and Hydrogen sulphide present in the atmospheric air.
- The phenomenon is known as corrosion.
- It is called silver tarnishing, particularly for silver.
- The black substance obtained is known as the silver sulphide.
- Silver sulphide is also black in colour.
- The reaction that happens is: $4Ag + O_2 + 2H_2S \rightarrow 2Ag_2S + 2H_2O$
- A dense black solid is the only sulfide of silver. It is useful as a photosensitizer in photography. It

constitutes the tarnish that forms over time on silverware and other silver objects.

Hence, the correct option is (D).

25. The radioactive isotope of hydrogen is tritium.

The most stable radioactive isotope is tritium, with a half-life of 12.32 years. Hydrogen is the first element in the periodic table and has the atomic number one.

- Those elements which have the same atomic number but a different mass number are called isotopes.
- The isotopes are different because of the different numbers of neutrons present in them.
- In protium, there is no presence of neutrons, whereas in deuterium we have one neutron and in tritium, we have two neutrons.
- The most prominent form of hydrogen is protium, 0.0156% of hydrogen is present on the earth's surface as deuterium.
- In tritium, the concentration is one atom per 1018 atoms of protium. Out of these three isotopes of hydrogen.

Hence, the correct option is (C)

26. Silver does not form oxide on reaction with oxygen.

The metal which is not from the first row of the d-block of the periodic table will not react with oxygen.

- The metals which have in general low reactivity and do not react with oxygen are called noble metals.
- Here, we are given some metals and we will need to check their reactivity with oxygen to find which one will not react with it.
- Almost all the metals react with oxygen and form their corresponding oxides depending on their valency.
- There is an exception that noble metals do not react with oxygen and so they do not form oxides while reacting with gaseous oxygen.

Hence, the correct option is (D).

27. The valency of phosphorus is 3, 5.

- The atomic number of phosphorus is 15.
- The number of electronic configuration are 2,8,5.
- When the atom gains 3 electrons the orbit is filled. or otherwise the atoms should lose 5 electrons. the valency is the combining capacity of the atom. therefore the valency of phosphorus is 3 and 5.

Hence, the correct option is (D).

28. An object moves with a constant speed when the value of force is negligible. When an object moves with a constant speed there is no change in the value of acceleration hence the force remains constant.

Force is that external cause that when acts on a body, changes or tries to change the initial state of the body.

Hence, the correct option is (C).

29. The physical quantity that is denoted by area under velocity time graph is displacement. The rate of change of position i.e. rate of displacement with time is called velocity. Displacement is velocity multiplied by time.

Hence, the correct option is (B).

30. At a particular temperature, sound propagates in iron at the fastest speed.

The term "speed of sound" refers to the distance sound waves travels per unit of time as it propagates through a medium. So, sound, in order to travel always, needs a medium for its propagation. The speed of sound is thus determined by the properties of the medium in which the dissemination occurs.

Hence, the correct option is (C).

31. Given:

Principal $=$ Rs. 15,000

Rate $\% = 15\%$ p.a compounded annually

Time $= 2\left(\frac{2}{3}\right)$ years

We know that:

Amount $= P \times \left(1 + \frac{r}{100}\right)^2 \left(1 + \frac{2r}{300}\right)$

$\because$ Rate $\%$ for $\frac{2}{3}$ years

$= 15\% \times \left(\frac{2}{3}\right)$

$= 10\%$

$\therefore$ Amount $= P \times \left(1 + \frac{r}{100}\right)^2 \left(1 + \frac{2r}{300}\right)$

$= 15{,}000 \times \left(1 + \frac{15}{100}\right)^2 \left(1 + \frac{10}{100}\right)$

$= 15{,}000 \times \left(1 + \frac{3}{20}\right)^2 \left(\frac{11}{10}\right)$

$= 15{,}000 \times \left(\frac{23}{20}\right)^2 \left(\frac{11}{10}\right)$

$= \frac{(15000 \times 529 \times 11)}{(400 \times 10)}$

$=$ Rs. $21{,}821.2$

$\therefore CI =$ Amount - Principal

$= 21{,}821.2 - 15{,}000$

$=$ Rs. 6821.2

Hence, the correct option is (D).

32. When 10 persons shake hands with one another.

Let the N be a number of people

Use this formula in such types of problems $= \dfrac{N(N-1)}{2}$

$N = 10$ person

$= \dfrac{10(10-1)}{2}$

$= 5 \times 9$

$= 45$

$\therefore$ The total number of Handshakes are $45.$

Hence, the correct option is (B).

33.

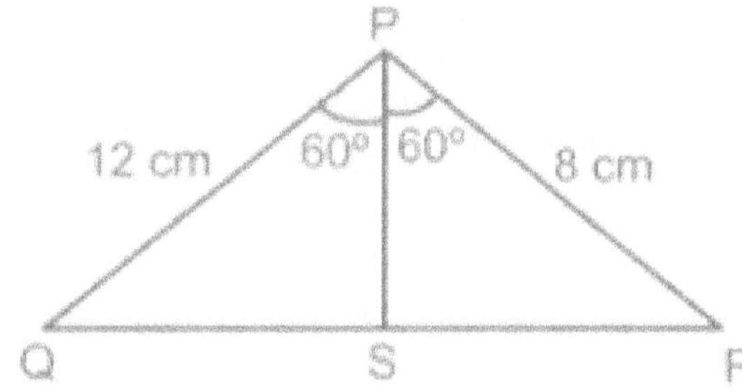

In the figure:

Area of $\Delta PQR =$ Area of $\triangle PQS +$ Area of $\triangle PRS$

$\Rightarrow \frac{1}{2} \times \mathrm{PQ} \times \mathrm{PR} \times \sin 120° = \frac{1}{2} \times \mathrm{PQ} \times \mathrm{PS} \times \sin 60° + \frac{1}{2} \times \mathrm{PR} \times \mathrm{PS} \times \sin 60°$

$\Rightarrow 12 \times 8 \times \frac{\sqrt{3}}{2} = 12 \times PS \times \frac{\sqrt{3}}{2} + 8 \times PS \times \frac{\sqrt{3}}{2}$

$\Rightarrow 96 = 12PS + 8PS$

$\Rightarrow 20PS = 96$

$\Rightarrow PS = 4.8\ cm$

Hence, the correct option is (C).

34. Given,

Total number of girls $= \frac{2}{7}$ of total students

The total number of boys is 111 more than girls.

Suppose, the total number of girls in the school auditorium $= x$

Then, total number of boys in the school auditorium $= (x + 111)$

Total students in the school auditorium $= x + (x + 111) = 2x + 111$

Therefore,

$x = \frac{2}{7} \times (2x + 111)$

$$\Rightarrow x = \frac{(4x+222)}{7}$$

$$\Rightarrow 7x = 4x + 222$$

$$\Rightarrow 7x - 4x = 222$$

$$\Rightarrow 3x = 222$$

$$\Rightarrow x = \frac{222}{3}$$

$$\Rightarrow x = 74$$

Total number of boys $= 74 + 111 = 185$

$\therefore$ Total of 185 boys are there in the school auditorium.

Hence, the correct option is (D).

35. Given:

Cost price of the article $C.P. =$ Rs. x

Selling price of the article $S.P. =$ Rs. 75

Profit $\% = x\%$

As we know,

Profit $\% = \left[\frac{(S.P. - C.P.)}{C.P.}\right] \times 100$

According to the question,

$$x = \left[\frac{(75-x)}{x}\right] \times 100$$

$$\Rightarrow x^2 = 7500 - 100x$$

$$\Rightarrow x(x + 100) = 7500$$

$$\Rightarrow x(x + 100) = 50(50 + 100)$$

On comparing both sides,

$$x = 50$$

$\therefore$ The value of x is 50.

Hence, the correct option is (C).

36. Given that:

$$A:B:C = 2:3:4$$

Let $A = 2x, B = 3x, C = 4x$

$$\therefore \frac{A}{B}:\frac{B}{C}:\frac{C}{A} = \frac{2x}{3x}:\frac{3x}{4x}:\frac{4x}{2x}$$

$$\Rightarrow \frac{2}{3}:\frac{3}{4}:\frac{2}{1}$$

Multiply by the L.C.M of denominator to remove fraction

So, L.C.M of $(3,4,1) = 12$

$$\therefore \frac{A}{B}:\frac{B}{C}:\frac{C}{A}$$

$$\frac{2}{3} \times 12:\frac{3}{4} \times 12:\frac{2}{1} \times 12$$

$$\Rightarrow 8:9:24$$

Hence, the correct option is (C).

37.

2	2,3,5,7,11
3	1,3,5,7,11
5	1,1,5,7,11
7	1,1,1,7,11
11	1,1,1,1,11
	1,1,1,1,1

As we know,

Prime numbers between 1 and 12 are $2,3,5,7,11$.

LCM of $2,3,5,7$ and $11 = 2 \times 3 \times 5 \times 7 \times 11 = 2310$

Hence, the correct option is (C).

38. Given:

A batsman in his 20th innings makes a score $= 110$

His average increases $= 4$

Let his average in 19 innings $= x$

Total score $= 19 \times x = 19x$

Score in next innings $= 110$

Score after 20th inning $= 19x + 110$

Average $= 19x + \frac{110}{20} = x + 4$ [given]

$$\Rightarrow 19x + 110 = 20x + 80$$

$$\Rightarrow x = 30$$

Average after 20 innings $= x + 4$

$$= 30 + 4$$

$$= 34$$

$\therefore$ His average after 20th innings is 34.

Hence, the correct option is (B).

39. Let, the number of pink balls be p.

Probability of choosing a pink ball $= \frac{p}{35}$

$$\Rightarrow \frac{3}{7} = \frac{p}{35}$$

$$\Rightarrow p = 15$$

So, remaining number of balls $= (35 - 15) = 20$

Number of orange balls $= \dfrac{2}{2+3} \times 20$

$= 2 \times 4 = 8$

Therefore, required probability $= \dfrac{{}^{8}C_1 \times {}^{15}C_1}{{}^{35}C_2}$

$\Rightarrow \dfrac{8 \times 15}{35 \times \frac{34}{2}} = \dfrac{24}{119}$

Hence, the correct option is (A).

40. Given:

X can do a piece of work in $= 30$ days,

X leaves after working for $= 3$ days,

Y finished the remaining work in $= 18$ days,

X's 1 day's work $= \dfrac{1}{30}$

X's 3 day's work $= \dfrac{3}{30}$

$= \dfrac{1}{10}$

$\therefore$ remaining work $= 1 - \dfrac{1}{10}$

$= \dfrac{9}{10}$

Now, $\dfrac{9}{10}$ work is done in 18 days

$\therefore 1$ piece of work is done by Y in $= \dfrac{10}{9} \times 18$

$= 10 \times 2$

$= 20$ days

$\therefore Y$ can complete the piece of work alone in 20 days.

Hence, the correct option is (D).

41. Given,

Diameter = 42 cm

Radius $= \dfrac{D}{2}$

Radius = 21 cm

Angle of the sector is $= 150°$

Area of sector $= \dfrac{\theta}{360} \times \pi r^2$

$= \dfrac{22}{7} \times 21 \times 21 \times \dfrac{150}{360}$

$= 577.5 \; cm^2$

Hence, the correct option is (B).

42. Given:

Let the original number be 100x.

The number when subtracted from 37.5%

So, New number $= 100x \times \left(\dfrac{100 - 37.5}{100} \right) = 62.5x$

Resulting number = 35 = 62.5x

$\Rightarrow x = 0.56$

$\Rightarrow 100x = 0.56 \times 100 = 56$

$\therefore$ Original value of number is 56.

Hence, the correct option is (C).

43. Given:

$(0.1 \times 0.004) + (0.02 \times 0.3) - (0.04 \times 0.03) =?$

$\Rightarrow 0.0004 + 0.006 - 0.0012 =?$

$\Rightarrow 0.0064 - 0.0012 =?$

$\therefore ? = 0.0052$

Hence, the correct option is (D).

44. Let the total distance be ' x ' km.

According to the question:

$\dfrac{2x}{3} + \dfrac{x}{7} + 8 = x$

$\Rightarrow \dfrac{17x}{21} + 8 = x$

$\Rightarrow x - \dfrac{17x}{21} = 8$

$\Rightarrow \dfrac{4x}{21} = 8$

$\Rightarrow x = 2 \times 21 = 42$ km

Hence, the correct option is (C).

45. The logic followed here is:

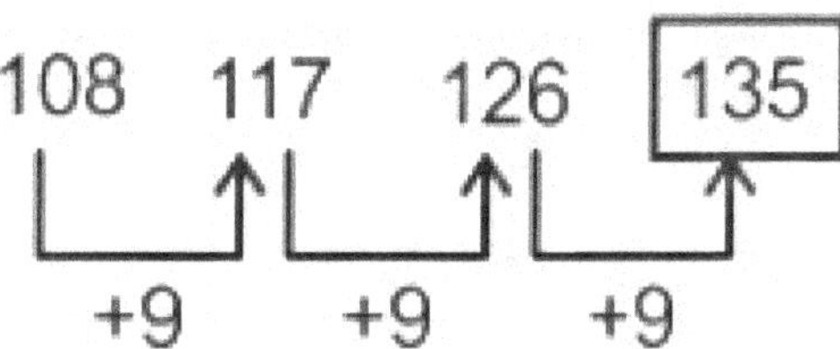

So, 135 will replace the question mark (?).

Hence, the correct option is (C).

46. The pattern followed here is:

V – 4 = R

R – 5 = M

M – 6 = G

G – 7 = Z

Hence, the correct option is (C).

47. 1. Five girls took part in a race.

2. Rajni finished before Mahika but behind Garima.

Garima > Rajni > Mahika

3. Ashmita finished before Sanchali but behind Mahika.

Mahika > Ashmita > Sanchali

Combining (2) and (3), we get:

Garima > Rajni > Mahika > Ashmita > Sanchali

Thus, 'Rajni' came second in the race.

Hence, the correct option is (D).

48. Preparing the family tree using the following symbols:

Symbol in Diagram	Meaning
◯	Female
▢	Male
═══	Married Couple
───	Siblings
│	Difference of A Generation

Drawing the family tree as per the given information:

1) F is the wife of H.

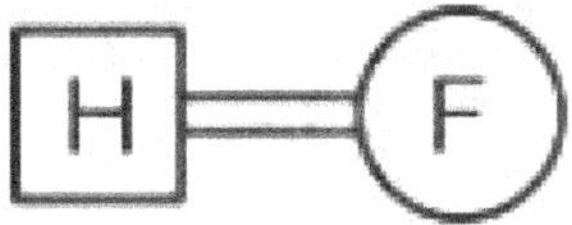

2) H is the son of I.

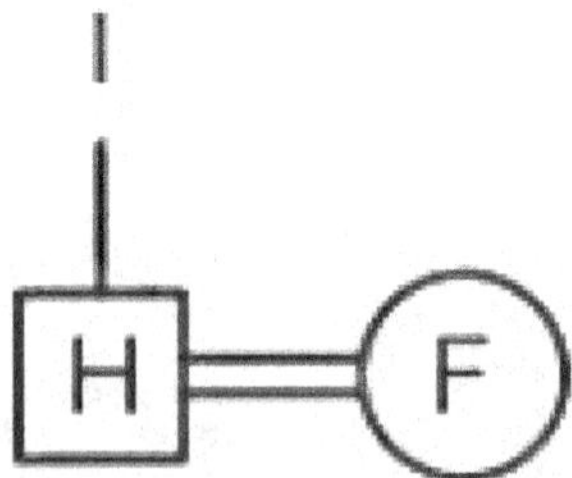

3) I is the son of E.

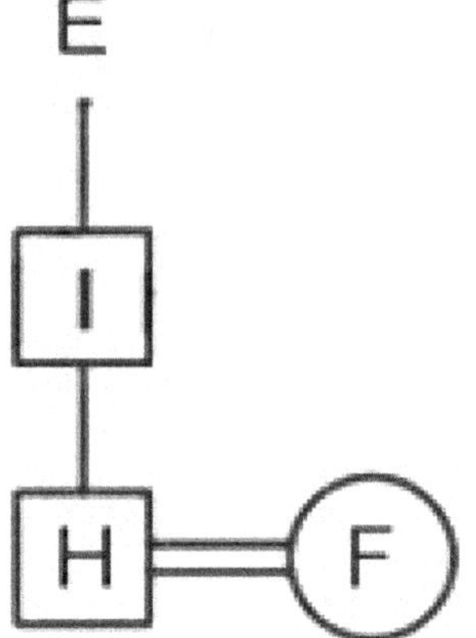

4) E is the daughter of G and we get the final diagram:

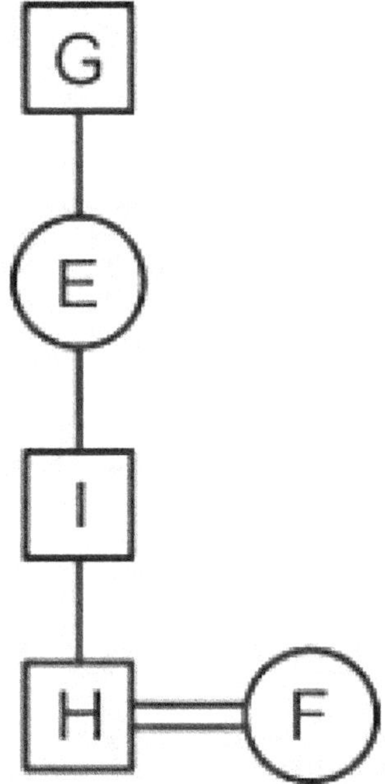

From the family tree, G is related to I as grand-father.

So, the correct answer is "Grandfather".

Hence, the correct option is (B).

49. Clearly ,it can be understood from the question that 9 days ago was a Thursday

Number of odd days in 9 days = 2 (As 9 - 7 = 2, reduced perfect multiple of 7 from total days)

Thus today = (Thursday + 2 odd days) = Saturday

Hence, the correct option is (D).

50. The pattern followed here is:

C	D
H	N
I	O
C	D
A	T

N	H
E	V
R	K
Y	S

Similarly,

C	D
R	K
A	T
N	H
E	V

Hence, the correct option is (A).

Previous Year Paper 01

General Knowledge

Q.1 Who was admired as tempestuous Hindu in 1893 in the world parliament of religions in Chicago?

A. Swami Vivekanand
B. Gautam Buddha
C. Swami Dayananad Saraswati
D. Rabindra Nath Tagore

Q.2 Meenambakkam International Airport is in?

A. Banguluru
B. Hyderabad
C. Chennai
D. Coimbatore

Q.3 Headquarters of which bank are located in Manipal, Karnataka?

A. Vijaya Bank
B. Canara Bank
C. Syndicate Bank
D. Corporation Bank

Q.4 Which of the following kingdoms were associated with the life of the Buddha?

A. Gandhara
B. Kosala
C. Magadha
D. Avanti

Q.5 The air that contains moisture to its full capacity:

A. Absolute humidity
B. Specific humidity
C. Relative humidity
D. Saturated air

Q.6 Which of among following is an important tribe of the Dhauladhar Range?

A. Lepcha
B. Gaddi
C. Tharu
D. Abor

Q.7 Term of Rajya Sabha member is:

A. 6 years
B. 5 years
C. 2 years
D. None of these

Q.8 The largest irrigation canal in India is called the ________.

A. Indira Gandhi Canal
B. Sirhand canal
C. Yamuna canal
D. Upper Bari Doab canal

Q.9 Who was the first muslim woman ruler of Dehli?

A. Begam Hazarat Mahal
B. Sultana Razia
C. Noorjahan
D. Chand Bibi

Q.10 Khasi and Garo tribes mainly live in ______.

A. Meghalaya
B. Mizoram
C. Nagaland
D. Manipur

Q.11 Prime Meridian is located at ______ degree meridian.

A. 0
B. 180
C. 60
D. 90

Q.12 'Kambala race' a traditional buffalo race is being held in ______.

A. Kerala
B. Telangana
C. Tamil Nadu
D. Karnataka

Q.13 The most important uranium mine in India is ________.

A. Vashi
B. Manavalakurichi
C. Gauribidanur
D. Jaduguda

Q.14 Where is Lal Bahadur Shastri National Academy of Administration located______.

A. Shimla
B. Ooty
C. Mussoorie
D. Delhi

Q.15 The first session of the congress was held in:

A. Surat
B. Bombay
C. Calcutta
D. Delhi

General Science

Q.16 Tooth decay starts when pH of mouth is lower than ______.

A. 10
B. 7
C. 8
D. 5.5

Q.17 The melting point of copper is ________.

A. 1038°C
B. 1085°C
C. 100°C
D. None of these

Q.18 The molecular formula of cane sugar is ________.

A. $C_{12}H_{22}O_{11}$
B. H_2CO_3
C. $C_6H_{12}O_6$
D. $H_2C_2O_4$

Q.19 Which among the following helps in circulation of blood?

A. Lymphocytes
B. Monocytes
C. Blood Platelets
D. None of these

Q.20 Which is the correct unit for measuring terrestrial distances?

A. Centimeter
B. Light year
C. Meter
D. Kilometer

Q.21 Botany is the study of ________.

A. Animals life
B. Human life
C. Birds life
D. Plants life

Q.22 At high altitude nose bleeding occurs due to:

A. Low atmospheric pressure
B. High atmospheric pressure
C. Severe cold
D. None of these

Q.23 Which of the following is a primary fuel?

A. Charcoal
B. Petroleum
C. Coal
D. None of these

Q.24 Photosynthesis occurs maximum in:

A. Red light
B. Blue light

C. White light   **D.** Green light

Q.25 What do you understand by Aerodynamics?
A. It is a science that deals with the study of body pain.
B. It is a science of movement in a flow of air and gas.
C. It is a science of generative organs.
D. None of these

Q.26 Coronagraph is used for ______.
A. Study the veins
B. Study blood pressure
C. Observing and photographing the sun's corona
D. Studying the arteries

Q.27 Which of the following was the first calculating device?
A. Calculator   **B.** Turing machine
C. Abacus   **D.** Pascaline

Q.28 Hertz (Hz) is the unit of ______.
A. Frequency   **B.** Pressure
C. Number of cycles   **D.** None of these

Q.29 Who among the following is considered as the 'father of artificial intelligence'?
A. John McCarthy   **B.** Charles Babbage
C. JP Eckert   **D.** Lee De Forest

Q.30 The revolver was invented by ______.
A. Theodor Bergmann   **B.** Henry Deringer
C. John Browning   **D.** Samuel Colt

Mathematics

Q.31 A motor boat takes 2 h to travel a distance of 9 km down the current and it takes 6 h to travel the same against the current. The speed of the boat in still water and the current (in km /h), respectively are:
A. 3 km /h and 1 km /h
B. 3 km /h and 1.5 km /h
C. 3 km /h and 2 km /h
D. 3 km /h and 2.5 km /h

Q.32 Find 30% of $(1500 + 600) =?$
A. 650   **B.** 610   **C.** 600   **D.** 630

Q.33 The perimeter of a triangle is 600 m. If the ratio of sides is $12:13:15:$ then find the longest side.
A. 195   **B.** 180   **C.** 220   **D.** 225

Q.34 A person sells 4000 mangoes at the cost price of 320 mangoes. What is his profit percentage?
A. 10%   **B.** 25%   **C.** 15%   **D.** 20%

Q.35 The product of a rational and an irrational number is ______.
A. always an integer
B. sometimes rational and sometimes irrational number
C. always an irrational number
D. always a rational number

Q.36 In how many different ways can the letters of the word ARISE be arranged?
A. 60   **B.** 90   **C.** 120   **D.** 180

Q.37 Convert 1589 miligram into grams.
A. 15.89 grams   **B.** 1.589 grams
C. 158.9 grams   **D.** 0.1589 grams

Q.38 If an event cannot occur, then its probability is ______.
A. 0   **B.** $\frac{3}{4}$ **C.** $\frac{1}{2}$ **D.** 1

Q.39 A batsman in his 12th innings makes a score of 63 runs and there by increasing his average score by 2, what is his average after the 12th innings?
A. 41   **B.** 39   **C.** 13   **D.** 87

Q.40 Find which is the next number in series?
$$31,7,25,13,19,19,13\_\_\_$$
A. 7   **B.** 31   **C.** 25   **D.** 14

Q.41 A polygon has 44 diagonal's. Find the number of its side?
A. 12   **B.** 13   **C.** 11   **D.** 10

Q.42 The difference of two number is 2 and difference of their squares is 28. The sum of the numbers will be:
A. 15   **B.** 19   **C.** 14   **D.** 21

Q.43 Which is the next number in the series?
$$5,25,125,\_\_\_$$
A. 625   **B.** 650   **C.** 675   **D.** 600

Q.44 'A' and 'B' can do a work in 10 days and 15 days respectively. If 'A' starts on the work and both work alternately days after day, in how many days will be work be completed?
A. 10   **B.** 9   **C.** 8   **D.** 12

Q.45 The average age of 7 boys is 20 years. If the average age of the first six boys is $19\frac{1}{2}$ years, then the 7th boy will be how many years old?
A. 20 years   **B.** 23 years   **C.** 21 years   **D.** 18 years

Logical Reasoning

Q.46 An accurate clock shows 7 a.m. Through how many degrees will the hour hand rotate when clock shows 1 p.m.?
A. 180°   **B.** 170°   **C.** 154°   **D.** 160°

Q.47 Choose the number pair/group which is different from others.
A. 15:5   **B.** 32:2   **C.** 42:4   **D.** 36:6

Q.48 'Man' is coded as 'woman', 'woman' is coded as 'girl', 'girl' is coded as 'boy', 'boy' as coded as 'worker', then 6 year old female is coded as ______.
A. Man   **B.** Girl   **C.** Woman   **D.** Boy

Q.49 Find the odd one out from the series $3,5,7,9,11$.

A. 7   **B.** 11   **C.** 9   **D.** 5

Q.50 Pointing to a gentlemen, Dinesh (male) said, "His only brother is the father of my daughter's father." How is the gentleman related to Dinesh?

A. Uncle   **B.** Grandfather

C. Father   **D.** Brother-in-law

// Smart Answer Sheet //

Correct — Indicates percentage of students who answered questions correctly.

Skipped — Indicates percentage of students who skipped questions.

Q.	Ans.	Correct / Skipped	Q.	Ans.	Correct / Skipped	Q.	Ans.	Correct / Skipped	Q.	Ans.	Correct / Skipped	Q.	Ans.	Correct / Skipped
1	A	44.83 % / 5.6 %	11	A	39.22 % / 10.78 %	21	D	61.64 % / 15.52 %	31	B	25.0 % / 19.83 %	41	C	30.17 % / 19.4 %
2	C	36.21 % / 11.2 %	12	D	31.47 % / 11.63 %	22	A	34.05 % / 15.95 %	32	D	39.22 % / 19.83 %	42	C	37.07 % / 20.26 %
3	C	28.88 % / 10.78 %	13	D	27.16 % / 9.05 %	23	C	42.24 % / 15.52 %	33	D	23.71 % / 19.39 %	43	A	59.48 % / 18.11 %
4	B	30.6 % / 12.07 %	14	C	35.34 % / 12.07 %	24	A	45.69 % / 15.52 %	34	B	18.53 % / 20.26 %	44	D	18.53 % / 20.69 %
5	D	16.38 % / 10.78 %	15	B	36.64 % / 11.2 %	25	B	50.0 % / 15.95 %	35	C	20.69 % / 19.83 %	45	B	28.88 % / 19.83 %
6	B	22.84 % / 11.64 %	16	D	36.21 % / 15.08 %	26	C	41.81 % / 15.09 %	36	C	19.83 % / 19.83 %	46	A	34.05 % / 15.95 %
7	A	60.34 % / 10.78 %	17	B	28.88 % / 15.52 %	27	C	36.21 % / 15.51 %	37	B	23.71 % / 20.26 %	47	C	43.97 % / 16.37 %
8	A	70.69 % / 12.07 %	18	A	35.78 % / 14.65 %	28	A	65.09 % / 14.22 %	38	A	36.21 % / 21.12 %	48	D	26.29 % / 16.38 %
9	B	66.38 % / 11.64 %	19	A	26.72 % / 15.95 %	29	A	33.62 % / 15.95 %	39	A	12.93 % / 20.26 %	49	C	34.48 % / 16.38 %
10	A	31.47 % / 11.2 %	20	B	50.86 % / 15.52 %	30	D	26.72 % / 15.09 %	40	C	33.19 % / 20.26 %	50	A	14.66 % / 16.37 %

Performance Analysis	
Avg. Score (%)	28.0%
Toppers Score (%)	100.0%
Your Score	

//Hints and Solutions//

1. Swami Vivekanand was admired as tempestuous Hindu in 1893 in the world parliament of religions in Chicago.

- The first Parliament of the World's Religions was held in Chicago in 1893.

- It marked the first concerted effort to bring all the different religions to a common platform where leaders and representatives of all faiths were able to communicate and share their views.

- Swami Vivekananda won wide recognition for India's ancient culture, philosophy, and faith through his powerful words.

- The 1893 Parliament of the World's Religions was attended by 400 men and women, representing 41 religious traditions.

- It was there that Catholicism and Judaism were recognized as major American religions, and that Hinduism and Buddhism were first introduced to the west.

Hence, the correct option is (A).

2. Meenambakkam International Airport is in Chennai.

Meenambakkam is a southern neighbourhood of Chennai in the Indian state of Tamil Nadu. It is the part of Chennai International Airport and the DGQA Complex.

Hence, the correct option is (C).

3. Headquarters of Syndicate bank are located in Manipal, Karnataka.

Syndicate Bank was founded in 1925 in Manipal, Udupi, Princely State of Mysore. It was founded by Upendra Ananth Pai, T. M. A. Pai, and Vaman Srinivas Kudva. Syndicate Bank was nationalized in 1969. At the time of its establishment, the bank was known as Canara Industrial and Banking Syndicate Limited. Syndicate bank, along with the other 13 major commercial banks of India, was nationalized on 19 July 1969, by the Government of India. The Bank was headquartered in the university town of Manipal, India. On 1st April 2020, the bank was merged into Canara Bank.

Hence, the correct option is (C).

4. Kosala kingdoms were associated with the life of the Buddha.

- Gandhara is not directly associated with the life of Buddha. It flourished during the ruling of the Mauryan Period, especially during the period of Ashoka.

- Rajgir was the early capital of Magadh Janapada, which was ruled by Bimbisara during Buddha's time. But not directly associated.

- Maha Maya, the mother of Gautama Buddha belongs to the Kosala Dynasty. So Kosala is most appropriate.

Hence, the correct option is (B).

5. The air that contains moisture to its full capacity saturated air.

Saturated air: Saturated air has a relative humidity of 100%. Humidity is the amount of water vapor in the air. If there is a lot of water vapor in the air, the humidity will be high. The higher the humidity, the wetter it feels outside. There are three main measurements of humidity- relative, absolute, and specific.

Hence, the correct option is (D).

6. Gaddi is an important tribe of the Dhauladhar Range.

Gaddi tribes are mainly living in Himachal Pradesh and Jammu and Kashmir region. Gaddi is a generic name and it includes Khatris, Brahmins, and Rajput. At present, the people of Gaddi tribe are settled in Chamba and Kangra districts of Himachal Pradesh in the lower parts of Dhauladhar range. Initially, they settled in the higher mountainous parts, but later gradually they established their settlements in the lower ranges, valleys and flat parts of Dhaulaghar mountain also. After this, gradually this tribe got mixed with the local tribes by making good contacts and relations and established itself completely.

Hence, the correct option is (B).

7. Term of Rajya Sabha member is 6 years.

The Council of States or Rajya Sabha is the upper house of the bicameral Parliament of India. Rajya Sabha is a permanent body and it can never dissolve. There is no tenure of Rajya Sabha whereas the member of Rajya Sahba has a tenure of 6 years. One-third of members of the Rajya Sabha retire every second year in a cyclic manner.

As of 2021, the Rajya Sabha has a maximum membership of 245. Out of 245, 233 are elected by the legislatures of the states and union territories using single transferable votes through Open Ballot and the President can appoint 12 members for their contributions to literature, art, science, and social services. The potential seating capacity of the house (Rajya Sabha) is 250 (238 elected, 12 nominated by the President of India), according to article 80 of the Constitution of India. The Vice President of India is the ex-officio Chairman of the Rajya Sabha.

Hence, the correct option is (A).

8. The largest irrigation canal in India is called the Indira Gandhi Canal. It was originally called the Rajasthan Canal. It is 650 km long.

Indira Gandhi canal starts from the Harike Barrage at Harike, near the confluence of the Satluj and Beas rivers in the state of Punjab and terminates in irrigation facilities in the Thar Desert in the north-west of Rajasthan state. The canal consists of the Rajasthan feeder canal with the first 167 kilometres (104 mi) in Punjab and Haryana state and a further 37 kilometres (23 mi) in Rajasthan. This is followed by the 445 kilometres (277 mi) of the Rajasthan main canal, which is entirely within Rajasthan. The canal enters Haryana from Punjab near Lohgarh and runs through the western part of the Sirsa district before entering Rajasthan near Kharakhera village in the Tibbi tehsil of the Hanumangarh district.

Hence, the correct option is (A).

9. Sultana Razia was the first muslim woman ruler of Dehli.

Sultana Razia was the first female Muslim ruler of the Indian subcontinent. She ruled the Delhi sultanate from 1236 to 1240. She was defeated by her half-brother Muizuddin Bahram in 1240. Mamluk Sultan Iltumish was the father of Sultana Razia Begum.

Hence, the correct option is (B).

10. Khasi and Garo Tribes mainly live in Meghalaya.

The state of Meghalaya comprises Khasi, Garo and Jaintia hills. The scheduled tribe populations (mainly belonging to khasi, Jaintia and Garo tribes) constitute 85.53% of the total population. The Garos inhabit western Meghalaya, the Khasis central Meghalaya and the Jaintias eastern Meghalaya.

Hence, the correct option is (A).

11. Prime Meridian is located at 0 degree meridian.

The prime meridian passes through Greenwich in England which is zero degrees longitude. So It is also called the Greenwich Meridian. For locating places on a map, imaginary lines called latitudes and longitudes are drawn. Longitudes are vertical lines that run from north to south. Prime Meridian is the 0° longitude that divides Earth into the Eastern and Western hemispheres.

Hence, the correct option is (A).

12. 'Kambala race' a traditional buffalo race is being held in Karnataka.

- Traditionally, it is sponsored by local Tuluva landlords and households in the coastal districts of Dakshina Kannada and Udupi of Karnataka and Kasaragod of Kerala and Kannada landlords of Kundapura region.

- Traditional Kambala was non-competitive, and the pair was run one by one.

- In modern Kambala, the contest generally takes place between two pairs of buffaloes.

- In villages such as Vandaro and Choradi, there is also a ritualistic aspect, as farmers race their buffaloes to give thanks for protecting them from diseases.

Hence, the correct option is (D).

13. The most important uranium mine in India is Jaduguda.

The first Uranium mine of India, the Jaduguda mines, is located in Jharkhand. The Jaduguda Mine is a uranium mine situated in Jaduguda village, in Jharkhand Indian state's Purbi Singhbhum district. It started operation in 1967 and became India's first uranium mine. The deposits were found at that mine in 1951. India possesses only two functional uranium mines as of March 2012, including this Jaduguda Mine. The Jaduguda mine provides up to 25 per cent of the raw materials required to power the nuclear reactors in India.

Hence, the correct option is (D).

14. Lal Bahadur Shastri National Academy of Administration is located in Mussoorie.

Foundational courses and refresher courses organized by the National Academy of Administration, Mussoorie is an example of pre-entry training for IAS.

National Academy of Administration It is the premier training institution in our country.

- It was established in 1959 at Mussoorie, a famous hill station in Uttaranchal.

- In 1972, it was renamed the Lal Bahadur Shastri National Academy of Administration.

- Presently, it is under the Ministry of Personnel.

Hence, the correct option is (C).

15. The first session of the congress was held in a hall at the Gokuldas Tejpal Sanskrit College in Bombay.

Indian National Congress was formed in 1885 by A.O Hume a member of the Imperial Civil Service. The first meeting of the Indian National Congress was held on December 28th, 1885. Womesh Chunder Bonnerjee was the first president of the Indian National Congress. He was an Indian barrister. In the first session out of 72, 39 were lawyers and this trend continued i.e. more than one-third of delegates were from the legal background.

Hence, the correct option is (B).

16. Tooth decay starts when pH of mouth is lower than 5.5.

Tooth enamel, made up of calcium phosphate is the hardest substance in the body. It does not dissolve in water but is corroded when the pH in the mouth is below 5.5. Bacteria present in the mouth produce acids by the degradation of sugar and food particles remaining in the mouth after eating. The best way to prevent this is to clean the mouth after eating food. At the pH of 5.5, the teeth risk of cavities and tooth decay begins in the mouth.

Hence, the correct option is (D).

17. The melting point of copper is 1085°C.

Copper is a physical element. Its sign is Cu. Its atomic number is 29 and atomic weight is 63.5. It is a ductile metal which is mainly used as a conductor of electricity. During metallic bond formation the d-electrons of Copper are involved, so large amounts of free electrons are present, thus increasing its melting point.

Hence, the correct option is (B).

18. The molecular formula of cane sugar is $C_{12}H_{22}O_{11}$.

Cane sugar is called Sucrose, as it is obtained from sugarcane. Sucrose is also called Table Sugar. It is basically a nonreducing disaccharide composed of glucose and fructose. The fructose and glucose molecules are connected via a glycosidic bond. It can also undergo a combustion reaction to yield carbon dioxide and water. Commercially, it is obtained from sugarcane, sugar beet, etc. It is extensively used as a sweetener. It also serves as an antioxidant and a food preservative.

Hence, the correct option is (A).

19. Lymphocytes helps in circulation of blood.

Lymphocytes: These are a type of white blood cell that provides an immune response to the body. Lymphocytes, which are part of the lymphatic system collect excess fluid that drains from cells and tissue throughout your body and returns it to your bloodstream, which is then recirculated through your body. So, we can say that Lymphocytes help in the overall circulation of blood by maintaining the concentration of blood. Lymphocytes are mainly of two types: B-lymphocytes and T-lymphocytes.

Hence, the correct option is (A).

20. Light year is the correct unit for measuring terrestrial distances.

Light year: The distance travelled by light in one year is called a light-year. It is a unit of astronomical distance.

1 light-year = 9.461 trillion kilometres which is a very large distance.

Hence, the correct option is (B).

21. Botany is the study of Plants life.

Biology is the science of life. Biology can be divided into several branches like Botany, Zoology, microbiology, virology, genetics, ecology, morphology, biotechnology, etc.

Botany: It is the scientific study of plants. Botany is further divided into many branches: Morphology, histology, anatomy, plant physiology, taxonomy, plant breeding, plant embryology, etc.

Hence, the correct option is (D).

22. At high altitude nose bleeding occurs due to low atmospheric pressure.

We know that atmospheric pressure decreases with high altitude. The blood pressure is counterbalanced with the atmospheric pressure at normal altitude. But, at higher altitudes, atmospheric pressure is lower compared to the pressure at the surface of the earth. So, at higher altitudes, the blood pressure inside our body is more than the atmospheric pressure which forces the blood to ooze out from openings like the nose. So, bleeding starts from body parts having weak skin like the nose and eyes (in severe cases). In some cases, internal bleeding may also occur from capillaries.

Hence, the correct option is (A).

23. Coal is a primary fuel.

Primary fuels are fuels that are found in nature and can be extracted, captured, cleaned, or graded without any sort of energy conversion or transformation process. Coal is a Primary fuel because it can be extracted directly without any sort of energy conversion or transformation process. There are other primary energy sources like wind and solar power. Please note that there is a difference between fuel and energy sources. Fuels are anything that can be burned to release energy. Energy sources on the other hand provide energy that can be transformed into usable forms to meet our needs (burning not required necessarily). All fuels are energy sources but all energy sources are not fuels.

Hence, the correct option is (C).

24. Photosynthesis occurs maximum in red light.

Chlorophyll is a proteinaceous complex chemical compound. It is the main pigment of photosynthesis. There are two types of chlorophyll a and chlorophyll b. It is found in the chloroplasts of all autotrophic green plants. Chlorophyll molecules absorb sunlight and convert it into chemical energy. The chlorophyll molecules get excited by absorbing the light energy of the sun. These active molecules break down water molecules into H^+ and OH^- ions. Thus chlorophyll molecules initiate the biochemical process of photosynthesis.

Sunlight is essential for photosynthesis. The process of photosynthesis also takes place in the bright artificial light of bulbs etc. This action is highest in red light.

Hence, the correct option is (A).

25. Aerodynamics is a science of movement in a flow of air and gas.

Aerodynamics is the way air moves around things. The rules of aerodynamics explain how an airplane is able to fly. Anything that moves through air reacts to aerodynamics. A rocket blasting off the launch pad and a kite in the sky react to aerodynamics. Aerodynamics even acts on cars, since air flows around cars.

Hence, the correct option is (B).

26. Coronagraph is used for observing and photographing the sun's corona.

A coronagraph is a specialized instrument designed to block out the light of the sun so that researchers can glimpse the burning star's hot, thin, outermost layer, called the corona. A French astronomer Bernard Lyot invented the coronagraph in the 1930s, according to the American Museum of Natural History, and the instrument has since found many other uses. The sun's corona is normally visible only during solar eclipses when the moon's shadow covers the bright central layers of our parent star and allows its dimmer corona to appear.

Hence, the correct option is (C).

27. Abacus was the first calculating device.

The abacus was one of the counting devices invented in ancient times to help count large numbers, but it is believed that the abacus was first used by the Babylonians as early as 2,400 B.C. The abacus was used in Europe, China, and Russia, centuries before the adoption of the written Hindu-Arabic numeral system. It is a manual device that takes time and a great deal of learning experience. To reflect numbers, an abacus utilizes many rows of beads; every row stands for a place value and a digit stands for the arrangement of beads in a row.

Hence, the correct option is (C).

28. Hertz (Hz) is the unit of frequency.

Frequency: It tells us how frequently an event occurs. The number of complete waves produced in one second is called the frequency of the waves. Hertz is the SI unit of Frequency. It is named in honor of Rudolf Hertz. 1 Hertz = 1 vibration per second.

Hence, the correct option is (A).

29. John McCarthy is considered as the 'father' of artificial intelligence.

John McCarthy is widely recognized as the father of Artificial Intelligence due to his astounding contribution in the field of Computer Science and AI. It was in the mid-1950s that McCarthy coined the term "Artificial Intelligence" which he defined as "the science and engineering of making intelligent machines".

Hence, the correct option is (A).

30. The revolver was invented by Samuel Colt.

Samuel Colt was an American inventor, industrialist, and businessman who established Colt's Patent Fire-Arms Manufacturing Company (now Colt's Manufacturing Company) and made the mass production of revolvers commercially viable.

Hence, the correct option is (D).

31. Given,

A motor boat takes 2 h to travel a distance of 9 km down the current.

It takes 6 h to travel the same against the current

As we know,

$$\text{Speed} = \frac{\text{Distance}}{\text{Time}}$$

Speed of boat downstream $= (x + y)$ km /h

Speed of boat upstream $= (x - y)$ km /h

Let the speed of boat in still water be x km /h,

Speed of current be y km /h,

Speed of boat downstream,

$$\Rightarrow x + y = \frac{9}{2}$$

$$\Rightarrow x + y = 4.5 \text{ km /h ... (i)}$$

Speed of boat against the current

$$\Rightarrow x - y = \frac{9}{6}$$

$$\Rightarrow x - y = 1.5 \text{ km /h ... (ii)}$$

Add equations (i) and (ii) we get,

$$\Rightarrow x = \frac{(4.5 + 1.5)}{2}$$

$$\Rightarrow x = 3 \text{ km /h}$$

Substracting equations (i) from (ii) we get

$$\Rightarrow y = \frac{(4.5 - 1.5)}{2}$$

$$\Rightarrow y = 1.5 \text{ km /h}$$

Speed of boat in still water $= 3$ km /h

Speed of boat against the current $= 1.5$ km /h

Hence, the correct option is (B).

32. Given,

$$30\% \text{ of } (1500 + 600)$$

$$= 2100 \times \left(\frac{30}{100}\right)$$

$$= 30 \times 21$$

$$= 630$$

$\therefore$ The value of 30% of $(1500 + 600)$ is 630.

Hence, the correct option is (D).

33. Given,

Perimeter of triangle $= 600$ m

Ratio of sides of triangle $= 12 : 13 : 15$

As we know,

Sum of all sides of triangle $=$ Perimeter of triangle

Sum of all sides of triangle,

$$\Rightarrow 12x + 13x + 15x = 40x$$

$$\Rightarrow 40x = 600$$

$$\Rightarrow x = 15$$

Longest side $= 15x$

$$= 15 \times 15$$

$$= 225 \text{ cm}$$

$\therefore$ The longest side is 225 cm.

Hence, the correct option is (D).

34. Given,

A person sells 400 mangoes at the cost price of 320 mangoes.

As we know,

Profit $=$ SP $-$ CP

Profit $\% = \left(\frac{\text{Profit}}{\text{CP}}\right) \times 100$

Let the cost price of one mango be Rs. 1.

Cost Pice of 320 mangoes $=$ Rs. 320

Selling price of 320 mangoes $=$ Cost price of 400 mangoes

Selling price of 320 mangoes $=$ Rs. 400

Selling price $=$ Rs. 400

Gain $= 400 - 320$

Gain $=$ Rs. 80

Profit $\% = \left(\frac{80}{320}\right) \times 100$

Profit $\% = \left(\frac{1}{4}\right) \times 100$

Profit $\% = 25\%$

$\therefore$ The profit percentage is 25%.

Hence, the correct option is (B).

35. As we know,

Any number which can be represented in the form of $\frac{p}{q}$ is rational number.

An irrational number is a real number that cannot be expressed as a ratio of integers, for example $\sqrt{2}$

Product of rational and irrational number is always irrational if rational no is non zero.

Example:

Rational no $= 4$

irrational no $= \sqrt{2}$

Rational $\times$ irrational $= 4\sqrt{2}$

Hence, the correct option is (C).

36. Given,

Word $=$ ARISE

As we know,

Arrangement of n different things $= n!$

$n! = n(n-1)(n-2)\ldots\ldots.2 \times 1$

Here number of letters in word ARISE is 5.

Different ways in which ARISE can be arranged is $5!$.

$5! = 5 \times 4 \times 3 \times 2 \times 1$

$5! = 120$

$\therefore$ The way of arrange of the word ARISE is 120.

Hence, the correct option is (C).

37. As we know,

1000 miligram $= 1$ gram

1000 miligram $= 1$ gram

1 miligram $= \dfrac{1}{1000}$ gram

1589 miligram $= \dfrac{1589}{1000}$ gram

$= 1.589$ grams

Hence, the correct option is (B).

38. If there is no event then its probability is zero.

For probability some event has to happen.

Probability is a branch of mathematics that deals with the occurrence of a random event. For example, when a coin is tossed in the air, the possible outcomes are Head and Tail.

Hence, the correct option is (A).

39. Given,

A batsman in his 12th inning makes a score of 63 runs and there by increasing his average score by 2.

As we know,

$$\text{Average} = \frac{\text{Sum of the observation}}{\text{Total observation}}$$

Let the total number of runs in 11 innings be "x".

the average number of runs in 11 innings is $\dfrac{x}{11}$

Let the total number of runs in 12 innings after scoring 63 runs in 12th innings $b + 63$.

Average number of runs in 12th innings is $= \dfrac{(x+63)}{12}$

$\Rightarrow \dfrac{(x+63)}{12} = \dfrac{x}{11+2}$

$\Rightarrow \dfrac{(x+63)}{12} = \dfrac{(x+22)}{11}$

$\Rightarrow 11(x+63) = 12(x+22)$

$\Rightarrow 11x + 693 = 12x + 264$

$\Rightarrow 693 - 264 = 12x - 11x$

$\Rightarrow 429 = x$

Average of his score after 12 innings,

$= \dfrac{(x+63)}{12}$

$= \dfrac{(429+63)}{12}$

$= 41$

$\therefore$ His average after the 12th innings is 41.

Hence, the correct option is (A).

40.

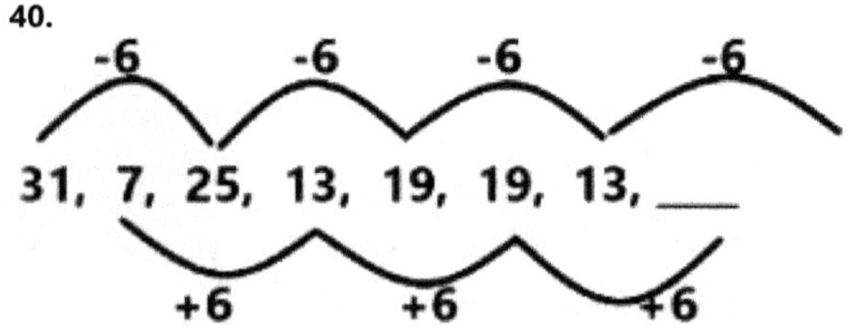

Here we can see the difference of six in first, third, fifth and same in the second, fourth and sixth term.

We will follow the downward pattern of adding 6.

$\Rightarrow 7 + 6 = 13$

$\Rightarrow 13 + 6 = 19$

$\Rightarrow 19 + 6 = 25$

$\therefore$ The next number is 25.

Hence, the correct option is (C).

41. Given,

Number of diagonal $= 44$

As we know,

Number of diagonal $= \dfrac{n(n-3)}{2}$

Where, $n =$ number of sides of polygon

Let assume the number of sides be x,

$\Rightarrow 44 = \dfrac{x(x-3)}{2}$

$\Rightarrow 88 = x^2 - 3x$

$\Rightarrow x^2 - 3x - 88 = 0$

$\Rightarrow x^2 - 11x + 8x - 88 = 0$

$\Rightarrow x(x - 11) + 8(x - 11) = 0$

$\Rightarrow (x - 11)(x + 8) = 0$

$\Rightarrow x - 11 = 0$ or $x + 8 = 0$

$\Rightarrow x = 11$, or -8

Sides can't be negative,

Side of polygon $= 11$

$\therefore$ The number of sides is 11.

Hence, the correct option is (C).

42. Given,

Difference of two numbers is 2.

Difference of their squares is 28.

As we know,

$a^2 - b^2 = (a - b)(a + b)$

Let the two number be x and y

$\Rightarrow x - y = 2 \ldots$ (i)

Difference of their squares

$\Rightarrow x^2 - y^2 = 28 \ldots$ (ii)

Using the formulae,

$\Rightarrow 28 = 2(x + y)$

$\Rightarrow x + y = \dfrac{28}{2}$

$\Rightarrow x + y = 14$

$\therefore$ The sun of the number is 14.

Hence, the correct option is (C).

43. Given,

$\Rightarrow 5 \times 5 = 25$

$\Rightarrow 25 \times 5 = 125$

$\Rightarrow 125 \times 5 = 625$

$\therefore$ The next number is 625.

Hence, the correct option is (A).

44. Given,

'A' and 'B' can do a work in 10 days and 15 days respectively.

'A' starts on the work and both work alternately days after days.

As we know,

Total work $=$ Number of days $\times$ efficiency

Let the total work be: Lcm of 10 and 15

Total work be 30 units.

Efficiency of $A = \dfrac{30}{10}$

$= 3$ unit

Efficiency of $B = \dfrac{30}{15}$

$= 2$ unit

A and B works on the alternate days,

$\Rightarrow 2$ days $= (3 + 2)$ units

$\Rightarrow 2$ days $= 5$ unit

Multiplying 6 on both sides,

30 units work done in,

$= 2 \times 6$

$= 12$ days

$\therefore$ In 12 days will be work be completed.

Hence, the correct option is (D).

45. Given,

The average age of 7 boys is 20 years.

average age of the first six boys is $19\frac{1}{2}$ years.

As we know,

$$\text{Average } = \frac{\text{Sum of observations}}{\text{Number of observations}}$$

Sum of Age of 7 boys,

$$= 20 \times 7$$

$$= 140$$

Sum of Age of six boys,

$$= 6 \times \frac{39}{2}$$

$$= 117$$

Age of 7th boy,

$$= 140 - 117$$

$$= 23 \text{ years}$$

$\therefore 7^{th}$ boy is 23 years old.

Hence, the correct option is (B).

46. As we know,

Total Central Angle of clock $= 360°$

Total hours in a clock $= 12$

Degree per hour $= \frac{360°}{12}$

$$= 30°$$

Now, according to the question,

From 7 a.m. to 1 p.m. covers 6 hours,

Thus, Total degrees $= 6 \times 30°$

$$= 180°$$

Hence, the correct option is (A).

47. By checking options,

Option (C) $42:4 \rightarrow \frac{42}{4} = 10.5$ (42 is not completely divisible by 4)

Option (A) $15:5 \rightarrow \frac{15}{5} = 3$ (15 is completely divisible by 5)

Option (B) $32:2 \rightarrow \frac{32}{2} = 16$ (32 is completely divisible by 2)

Option (D) $36:6 \rightarrow \frac{36}{6} = 6$ (36 is completely divisible by 6)

So, $42:4$ is different from others.

Hence, the correct option is (C).

48. Given,

'Man' is coded as 'woman',

'Woman' is coded as 'girl',

'Girl' is coded as 'boy',

'Boy' as coded as 'worker'.

Now, we know that a 6 year old female is a girl and girl is coded as boy.

Therefore, 6 year old female is coded as boy.

Hence, the correct option is (D).

49. Given series: $3,5,7,9,11$

Logic: $3,5,7$, and 11 are prime numbers whereas 9 is not a prime number as it is divisible by 3.

So, 9 is the odd one out.

Hence, the correct option is (C).

50.

Symbol in Diagram	Meaning
◯	Female
▢	Male
═══	Married Couple
───	Siblings
│	Difference of a Generation

My (Dinesh) daughter's father means Dinesh himself. His (gentleman) only brother is the father of Dinesh means gentleman is the uncle of Dinesh.

The family tree diagram is shown below:

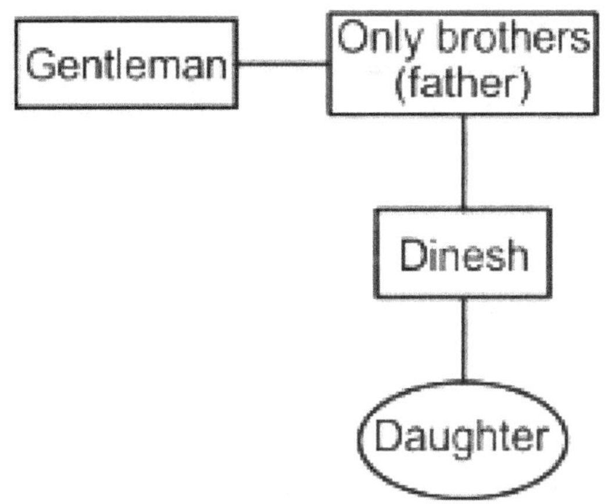

Hence, the correct option is (A).

General Knowledge

Q.1 Who is considered the main supporter of Marxism?

A. M. M. Rai

B. Fourier

C. Karl Marx

D. Lui Block

Q.2 In which state is the famous 'Kamakhya Devi Temple' located?

A. Madhya Pradesh

B. Himachal Pradesh

C. Karnataka

D. Assam

Q.3 Which is the highest military gallantry award/medal?

A. Kirti Chakra

B. Param Vir Chakra

C. Shaurya Chakra

D. Ashoka Chakra

Q.4 Where is the Indian Institute of Science located?

A. Chennai

B. Kolkata

C. Bangalore

D. Mumbai

Q.5 Where is the headquarters of International Cricket Council located?

A. New Delhi

B. London

C. Dubai

D. Melbourne

Q.6 Who wrote the book Ramayana?

A. Surdas

B. Kalidas

C. Veda Vyasa

D. Valmiki

Q.7 What is the capital of Himachal Pradesh?

A. Mandi **B.** Solan **C.** Shimla **D.** Kullu

Q.8 By whom were the Marathas defeated in the third battle of Panipat?

A. Aurangzeb

B. Ahmad Shah Abdali

C. Jahangir

D. Sher Shah Suri

Q.9 Who said 'Swaraj is my birthright'?

A. Bhagat Singh

B. Dadabhai Naroji

C. Bal Gangadhar Tilak

D. Netaji Subhash Chandra Bose

Q.10 Who wrote the holy book 'Gita'?

A. Kalidas

B. Veda Vyasa

C. Valmiki

D. Krishna

Q.11 Apart from India, Pakistan, and Sri Lanka, which Asian country has Rupee as its currency?

A. Bhutan

B. Myanmar

C. Indonesia

D. Nepal

Q.12 Who composed the famous song 'Saare Jahan Se Achcha'?

A. Rabindra Nath Tagore

B. Mohammad Iqbal

C. Jai Dev

D. Bakim Chandra Chatterjee

Q.13 Who founded the Mughal Empire in India?

A. Babur

B. Akbar

C. Humayun

D. Aurangzeb

Q.14 Where is 'Sun Temple' located?

A. Chennai **B.** Madurai **C.** Konark **D.** Goa

Q.15 Who appoints the governors of Indian states?

A. Vice President

B. President

C. Prime Minister

D. Central Cabinet

General Science

Q.16 Which of the following is a major component of biogas?

A. Methane **B.** Oxygen **C.** Nitrogen **D.** Helium

Q.17 Brass contains ______?

A. copper and zinc

B. copper and nickel

C. copper and silver

D. copper and tin

Q.18 The melting point of ice is ______.

A. 50 degrees centigrade

B. 2 degrees centigrade

C. 0 degrees centigrade

D. 10 degrees centigrade

Q.19 Vitamin _____ is found in abundance in oranges.

A. A **B.** B **C.** C **D.** D

Q.20 What was Mendeleev's periodic table based on?

A. Atomic Circle

B. Atomic Numbers

C. Atomic Volume

D. Atomic Mass

Q.21 What is the material used in making lead pencils?

A. Mica **B.** Graphite **C.** Carbon **D.** Coal

Q.22 In which part of the human body is the blood purified?

A. Heart **B.** Kidney **C.** Lungs **D.** Intestine

Q.23 Which instrument is used to observe celestial objects?

A. Bioscope

B. Telescope

C. Microscope

D. Periscope

Q.24 Which of the following metals is used with iron to form stainless steel?

A. Aluminium

B. Chromium

C. Tin

D. Copper

Q.25 In which complex protein is haemoglobin present in the blood-related?

A. Silver **B.** Iron **C.** Copper **D.** Gold

Q.26 Which vitamin strengthens the bones?

A. C **B.** D **C.** A **D.** B

Q.27 The chemical formula of laughing gas is _______.
A. N_2O_2 **B.** NO_2 **C.** N_2O **D.** NO

Q.28 Which of the following gas is not a noble gas?
A. Helium **B.** Oxygen **C.** Argon **D.** Neon

Q.29 BCG vaccine is used for the prevention of _______.
A. Tuberculosis **B.** Dengue
C. Typhoid **D.** Plague

Q.30 Which of the following is the heaviest ray?
A. Beta ray **B.** Gamma ray
C. X ray **D.** Alpha ray

Mathematics

Q.31 The ratio of males and females in a village is $5:3$. If there are 800 males in the village, then find the number of females?
A. 488 **B.** 840 **C.** 240 **D.** 480

Q.32 If the radius of a sphere is 7 cm, then find the surface area?
A. 161 cm ^{2} **B.** 636 cm ^{2} **C.** 116 cm ^{2} **D.** 616 cm ^{2}

Q.33 The sum of any two numbers is 25, and their difference is 13, find the two numbers?
A. 12,13 **B.** 21,4 **C.** 14,11 **D.** 19,6

Q.34 Find the LCM of $8,10,15,16$, and 20?
A. 260 **B.** 250 **C.** 220 **D.** 240

Q.35 Ram can do a piece of work in 10 days and Mohan can do it in 15 days. In how many days will they together complete the same work?
A. 4 days **B.** 6 days **C.** 10 days **D.** 8 days

Q.36 The successive discounts of $10\%, 20\%$, and 30% are equal to which of the following single discounts?
A. 49.6% **B.** 36% **C.** 40.5% **D.** 60%

Q.37 The average age of 12 boys is 10 years, out of which the average age of 11 boys is 9 years. Find the average age of the 12th boy?
A. 33 years **B.** 21 years **C.** 25 years **D.** 24 years

Q.38 If the length of a rectangular field is 30 m and breadth is 20 m, find its perimeter?
A. 90 m **B.** 50 m **C.** 100 m **D.** 80 m

Q.39 Find the cube root of 2197?
A. 19 **B.** 7 **C.** 13 **D.** 11

Q.40 What will be the simple interest on Rs. 18440 at 15% per annum for 4 years?
A. Rs. 11500 **B.** Rs. 11000
C. Rs. 12250 **D.** Rs. 11064

Q.41 Find the HCF of the given numbers:
$12,15,18,21$
A. 6 **B.** 12 **C.** 3 **D.** 8

Q.42 28 dozen bananas are required in a canteen for 1 week then how many bananas will be required for 47 days?
A. 196 **B.** 2256 **C.** 2352 **D.** 322

Q.43 Fill in the blanks from the given options:
$39,41,43,45,$ __
A. 47 **B.** 53 **C.** 49 **D.** 51

Q.44 Find the largest five digit number which is divisible by 17?
A. 0004 **B.** 99994 **C.** 99999 **D.** 10013

Q.45 If one side of an equilateral triangle is 12 cm then find its area?
A. 72 cm ^{2} **B.** 36 cm ^{2}
C. $36\sqrt{3}$ cm ^{2} **D.** $36\sqrt{2}$ cm ^{2}

Logical Reasoning

Q.46 Ram walked 5 km north from place A, then took a left turn and walked 3 km, then took a right turn and walked 2 km and then took a right turn and walked 3 km to reach another place B. Find the distance between A and B?
A. 8 km **B.** 7 km **C.** 13 km **D.** 10 km

Q.47 Fill in the blanks in the given order from the given options:
$64,32,16,8,$ _______?
A. 2 **B.** 4 **C.** 6 **D.** 8

Q.48 Introducing a boy, a girl said 'This is the son of the daughter of my uncle's father'. Then how is the boy related to the girl?
A. Brother **B.** Nephew
C. Uncle **D.** Son-in-law

Q.49 Complete the sequence from the given options:
$DKY, FJW, HIU, JHS,$ ____
A. LGQ **B.** LFQ **C.** KFR **D.** KGR

Q.50 If in a code language the word $BOXER$ is coded as $AQWGQ$ then what will be the code for the word $VISIT$?
A. $UKAKS$ **B.** $WKRKS$
C. $UKRKS$ **D.** $WKSKU$

// Smart Answer Sheet //

Correct Indicates percentage of students who answered questions correctly.

Skipped Indicates percentage of students who skipped questions.

Q.	Ans.	Correct / Skipped	Q.	Ans.	Correct / Skipped	Q.	Ans.	Correct / Skipped	Q.	Ans.	Correct / Skipped	Q.	Ans.	Correct / Skipped
1	C	76.87 % / 20.59 %	11	D	62.76 % / 33.26 %	21	B	81.91 % / 17.91 %	31	D	86.19 % / 12.02 %	41	C	88.26 % / 11.73 %
2	D	82.55 % / 14.09 %	12	B	67.65 % / 30.29 %	22	B	55.13 % / 44.82 %	32	D	86.3 % / 11.9 %	42	B	44.97 % / 43.27 %
3	B	68.44 % / 31.35 %	13	A	79.35 % / 10.33 %	23	B	78.53 % / 16.41 %	33	D	80.17 % / 19.6 %	43	A	88.92 % / 10.73 %
4	C	88.03 % / 10.79 %	14	C	81.39 % / 10.97 %	24	B	42.92 % / 36.25 %	34	D	64.28 % / 33.49 %	44	B	41.26 % / 33.59 %
5	C	56.38 % / 36.48 %	15	B	44.35 % / 47.07 %	25	B	54.88 % / 30.71 %	35	B	68.43 % / 30.49 %	45	C	84.66 % / 10.88 %
6	D	89.95 % / 10.03 %	16	A	76.3 % / 22.03 %	26	B	86.49 % / 11.72 %	36	A	48.24 % / 49.46 %	46	B	86.45 % / 11.49 %
7	C	41.18 % / 43.28 %	17	A	81.66 % / 10.32 %	27	C	82.54 % / 10.75 %	37	B	41.42 % / 42.97 %	47	B	76.97 % / 13.87 %
8	B	66.88 % / 33.0 %	18	C	88.09 % / 11.79 %	28	B	80.93 % / 13.43 %	38	C	89.59 % / 10.05 %	48	A	52.05 % / 43.77 %
9	C	84.05 % / 13.33 %	19	C	80.14 % / 10.95 %	29	B	76.85 % / 15.51 %	39	C	58.03 % / 32.24 %	49	A	66.77 % / 31.09 %
10	B	83.37 % / 12.83 %	20	D	78.4 % / 14.7 %	30	D	83.56 % / 12.15 %	40	D	45.61 % / 48.04 %	50	C	83.55 % / 13.5 %

Performance Analysis	
Avg. Score (%)	63.0%
Toppers Score (%)	68.0%
Your Score	

//Hints and Solutions//

1. Karl Marx is considered the main supporter of Marxism. He was the founder of the theory of 'Marxism'.

On May 5, 1818, Karl Marx was born in the Trier City of Modern-day Germany that time is known as the Kingdom of Prussia. He was a famous Philosopher, Economist, and Political theorist. He was very vocal for the working class and he argued that the industrial society was capitalist and the profit of capitalists was produced by workers. He believed that to overthrow capitalism, workers had to construct a Socialist society where all property was commonly controlled.

Hence, the correct option is (C).

2. The Kamakhya Devi Temple is located at Guwahati, Assam.

The Kamakhya Devi Temple is a Sakta temple dedicated to the mother goddess Kamakhya. It is one of the oldest of the 51 Shakti Pithas. The famous Ambubachi Mela is held here every year. The Temple is Situated in Nilachal Hills in Guwahati. Kamakhya Devi is also known as the Goddess of Fertility. Ambubachi Mela is a four-day festival to mark the annual menstruation of the goddess at Kamakhya temple in Guwahati. Ambubachi Mela is one of the biggest congregations in eastern India. It is the most important festival of the Kamakhya Devi temple and is celebrated in the month of June every year.

Hence, the correct option is (D).

3. Param Vir Chakra is the highest military gallantry award/medal.

The Param Vir Chakra (PVC) is India's highest military decoration, awarded for displaying distinguished acts of valour during wartime. Param Vir Chakra translates as the "Wheel of the Ultimate Brave", and the award is granted for "most conspicuous bravery in the presence of the enemy". As of January 2018, the medal has been awarded 21 times, of which 14 were posthumous and 16 arose from actions in Indo-Pakistani conflicts. Of the 21 awardees, 20 have been from the Indian Army, and one has been from the Indian Air Force. Major Somnath Sharma, was the first recipient. A number of state governments of India as well as ministries of the central government provide allowances and rewards to recipients of the PVC (or their family members in case of the recipient's death).

Hence, the correct option is (B).

4. The Indian Institute of Science is located in Bangalore, Karnataka.

The Indian Institute of Science is a public, deemed, research university for higher education and research in science, engineering, design, and management. The institute was established in 1909 with active support from Jamsedji Tata and thus is also locally known as the "Tata Institute". It was granted the deemed to be university status in 1958 and the Institute of Eminence status in 2018.

Hence, the correct option is (C).

5. The headquarters of International Cricket Council (ICC) is located in Dubai, United Arab Emirates.

The ICC is the global governing body for cricket. Representing 104 members, the ICC governs and administrates the game and works with our members to grow the sport. The ICC is also responsible for the staging of all ICC Events. The ICC presides over the ICC Code of Conduct, playing conditions, the Decision Review System, and other ICC regulations. Through the Anti-Corruption Unit, it coordinates action against corruption and match-fixing. It was established in 1909 by the representatives of England, Australia, and South Africa as Imperial Cricket Conference.

Hence, the correct option is (C).

6. Valmiki wrote the book Ramayana.

Valmiki is celebrated as the harbinger-poet in Sanskrit literature. The epic Ramayana, dated variously from the 5th century BCE to the first century BCE, is attributed to him, based on the attribution in the text itself. He is revered as Adi Kavi, the first poet, and author of Ramayana, the first epic poem.

Hence, the correct option is (D).

7. Shimla is the capital of Himachal Pradesh.

Himachal Pradesh was formed on 25th January 1971. Himachal Pradesh became the 18th state of the Indian Union. The first chief minister of Himachal Pradesh was Dr. Yashwant Singh Parmar. Shimla is the Summer capital of Himachal Pradesh. It is the largest city of Himachal Pradesh. Shimla city gets its name from Shyamala Mata, a fearless incarnation of the goddess Kali. The Kalka–Shimla Railway line built by the British, a UNESCO World Heritage Site, is also a major tourist attraction.

Hence, the correct option is (C).

8. By Ahmad Shah Abdali was the Marathas defeated in the third battle of Panipat.

The third battle of Panipat was fought between Sadashiv Rao Bhau (The Maratha Empire) and Ahmad Shah Durrani (The Afghan army) took place on 14 January 1761 at Panipat. In this battle, three Indian allies were supported by the Afgan army, the Rohilla of (Najib-Ud-Daulah), Afghans of (Doab Region), and Shuja-Ud-Daula (The Nawab of Awadh). The main Maratha army was deployed on the Deccan side with the Peshwa (The Maratha Prime Minister). It is considered one of the largest and most fiercely fought battles in the 18th century. This battle has reported the largest number of fatalities in a single-day formation battle between two armies. The extent of the losses in this battle on both sides is heavily puzzled by many historians, but it is believed that the number of losses is between (60,000–70,000) were killed in the battle. At last, the battle was won by the Afghan army which was led by Ahmad Shah Durrani. This war was the result of declining of the Maratha Empire.

Hence, the correct option is (B).

9. Bal Gangadhar Tilak said 'Swaraj is my birthright'.

Bal Gangadhar Tilak was also known as Lokmanya Tilak. He established a prominent organization Deccan Education Society to promote modern learning. He also established Fergusson College at Pune. He along with Annie Besant played an important role during Home Rule Movement (1916-18). Kesari and Maratha were the two newspapers started by Bal Gangadhar Tilak.

Hence, the correct option is (C).

10. Veda Vyasa wrote the holy book 'Gita'.

The Bhagavad Gita is one of Hinduism's holy books. It was written as part of the Mahabharata around five thousand years ago. Known as "The Song of God", the Bhagavad Gita, is a collection of 700 verses from the great epic Mahabharata. It has teachings that are said to have been given by the Supreme God, Lord Sri Krishna. Krishna is talking to Arjuna, an Archer, in the book (Bhagvat Gita), before the Kurukshetra war begins. It is regarded as the manual on which a human being should follow his life as per the Sanatana Dharma.

Hence, the correct option is (B).

11. Apart from India, Pakistan, Mauritius, Seychelles and Sri Lanka, Nepal has Rupee as its currency.

The rupee is the common name for the currencies of India, Indonesia, the Maldives, Mauritius, Nepal, Pakistan, Seychelles, and Sri Lanka, and of former currencies of Afghanistan, Bahrain, Kuwait, Oman, the UAE (as the Gulf rupee), British East Africa, Burma, German East Africa, and Tibet. In Indonesia and the Maldives, the unit of currency is known as rupiah and rufiyaa respectively.

Hence, the correct option is (D).

12. The 'Sare Jahan Se Achha Hindustan Hamara' song was composed by Mohammad Iqbal. This song is one of the most enduring patriotic poems of the Urdu language. The song is also referred to as 'Tarana-e-Hind'. The poem was published in the weekly journal Ittihad on August 16, 1904. Then the poet Iqbal recited it the upcoming year at Government College in Lahore. Then the song became an anthem for the opposition of the British rule in India.

Hence, the correct option is (B).

13. The Mughal Empire was founded by Babur in the year 1526 AD.

Babur reigned over India from 1526 AD to 1530 AD. He was a Central Asian ruler who was of Turkic-Mongol origin. He was a descendent of Timur on his father's side, and Genghis Khan on his mother's side. The Mughals, Dynasty of Turkic-Mongol origin ruled most of northern India from the early 16th to the mid-18th century.

Hence, the correct option is (A).

14. The Sun Temple is situated at Konark.

Konark Sun Temple was built in 1250 AD. This temple is also called "Black Pagoda". Temple was declared World Heritage Site by UNESCO in 1984. Famous Chandrabhaga Mela took place here every year in the month of February. This temple is attributed to King Narsimhadeva- I of the Eastern Ganga Dynasty. Temple is a classic illustration of Great Kalinga Architecture.

Hence, the correct option is (C).

15. President appoints the governors of Indian states.

The Governor in India is neither directly elected by the people nor indirectly elected by an electoral college as in case of the President of India. He is appointed by the President by warrant under President's hand and seal. Thus Governor is considered a nominee of the Central government. But, in 1979 Supreme Court held that the office of Governor of a state is not an employment under the Central government but an independent constitutional office, so is not under the control of or subordinate to the Central government.

Hence, the correct option is (B).

16. Methane is a major component of biogas.

The byproducts of anaerobic digestion of organic materials are commonly referred to as 'biogas' because of the biological nature of gas production. Biogas is produced by microbial activities and can be used only at the place where it is produced.

The main constituents of biogas are:

- About $55 - 65\%$ Methane (CH_4)
- $30 - 45\%$ Carbon dioxide (CO_2)
- Traces of hydrogen sulfide (H_2S)

Hence, the correct option is (A).

17. Brass contains copper and zinc. In proportions, it can be varied to achieve varying mechanical and electrical properties.

An alloy is an intimately mixed solid mixture of two or more different elements one of which is essentially a metal. An alloy, in which one of the components is mercury, is known as Amalgam.

Hence, the correct option is (A).

18. The temperature at which any solid melts into liquid or liquid freezing into solid is called the melting point of substance. The melting point of ice is 0 degrees centigrade.

Ice is the solid form that liquid water takes when it is cooled below 0 degrees Celsius (32 degrees Fahrenheit). Ice melts due to the chemical properties of water. There are more hydrogen bonds between the molecules of ice than in water. Ice begins to melt when its temperature exceeds 0 degrees Celsius and hydrogen bonds between water molecules break.

Hence, the correct option is (C).

19. Vitamin C is found in abundance in oranges.

Orange contains 53.2 mg of vitamin C per 100 grams. Lemons contain 77 mg of vitamin C per 100 grams. Vitamin C is acidic in nature. The deficiency of Vitamin C leads to Scurvy disease. The chemical name of Vitamin C is Ascorbic acid.

Hence, the correct option is (C).

20. Mendeleev's periodic table was based on atomic mass. In 1869, Dimitri Mendeleev included 63 known elements arranged according to increasing atomic mass.

The Modern Periodic table is based on Atomic numbers. The atomic number is the number of protons found in the nucleus of every atom of that element. The periodic table is managed by the International Union of Pure and Applied Chemistry, or IUPAC. There are 118 elements in a periodic table. There are seven periods and eighteen groups in the modern periodic table.

Hence, the correct option is (D).

21. Natural graphite is used in many ways, from making pencils lead, to forming batteries. The layered structure formed due to rings of carbon atoms present in Graphite makes it slippery and for that reason, it is used in Pencil leads. Graphite was named by Abraham Gottlob Werner in 1789. It is an allotrope of carbon. Graphite is a good conductor of electricity.

Hence, the correct option is (B).

22. The kidney is responsible for the purification of blood.

The kidneys are two bean-shaped organs, each about the size of a fist. Kidneys are located just below the rib cage, one on each side of your spine. Healthy kidneys filter about a half cup of blood every minute. The kidney also removes waste material, extra fluid and removes it from the body in form of Urine. Kidneys also remove acid that is produced by the cells of the body and maintain a healthy balance of water, salts, and minerals such as sodium, calcium, phosphorus, and potassium in the blood. The kidney also helps in developing hormones that control blood pressure, make red blood cells, keeps bones stronger.

Hence, the correct option is (B).

23. Telescope is used to observe celestial objects.

A telescope is an optical instrument designed to make distant objects like stars, planets, appear nearer, containing an arrangement of lenses, or of curved mirrors and lenses, by which rays of light are collected and focused and the resulting image magnified.

Hence, the correct option is (B).

24. Chromium is used with iron to form stainless steel.

All stainless steels have a Chromium content of at least 10.5% and the higher chromium content increases the corrosion resistance. Chromium also increases the resistance to oxidation at high temperatures and promotes a ferritic microstructure. The metal also improves hardenability, strength, response to heat treatment, and wear resistance.

Hence, the correct option is (B).

25. Iron is the complex protein that is haemoglobin present in the blood-related.

Red color of blood is due to the presence of haemoglobin in the blood. Haemoglobin is a protein that is made up of subunit 'hemes' which is red in colour and haemoglobin constitutes the maximum part of human blood. Haemoglobin is a fused protein in which a protein called globin and an iron ion are found. Haemoglobin present in RBC carries or transports oxygen from the lungs to the tissues. It also carries forward carbon dioxide from the tissues to the lungs.

The transportation of carbon dioxide from the tissues to the lungs takes place in a very small amount nearly (10-20 percent) by the protein globin of haemoglobin. The transportation of carbon dioxide in the form of bicarbonate takes place which is formed by the reaction of the carbonic anhydrase enzyme and RBC.

Hence, the correct option is (B).

26. Vitamin D is strengthens the bones.

Vitamin D is necessary for strong bones and muscles. Without Vitamin D, our bodies cannot effectively absorb calcium, which is essential to good bone health. Children who lack Vitamin D develop a condition called rickets, which causes bone weakness, bowed legs, and other skeletal deformities, such as stooped posture.

Hence, the correct option is (B).

27. The chemical formula of laughing gas is N_2O.

Nitrous oxide is a colourless and odourless substance that's also known as "laughing gas." When inhaled, the gas slows down the body's reaction time. This results in a calm, euphoric feeling. Nitrous oxide can be used to treat pain. It also functions as a mild sedative. Because of this, it's sometimes used before dental procedures to promote relaxation and reduce anxiety.

Hence, the correct option is (C).

28. Oxygen is not a noble gas.

Noble gases are those gases that do not react with any other element and are stable to exist on their own. Chlorine is a yellow-green gas at room temperature. It is an extremely reactive element and a strongly oxidising agent. There are a total of 6 noble gases found on the extreme right column of the periodic table. These noble gases are:

- Radon
- Argon
- Xenon
- Krypton
- Helium
- Neon

Hence, the correct option is (B).

29. BCG vaccine is used for the prevention of Dengue.

BCG stands for Bacille Calmette-Guerin. BCG vaccine was first considered by the WHO Expert Committee on Biological Standardization in its thirteenth report. It is one of the most widely used of all current vaccines. It has a documented protective effect against meningitis and disseminated TB in children.

Hence, the correct option is (B).

30. Alpha ray is the heaviest ray. It is produced when the heaviest elements decay. Alpha and beta rays are not waves. They are high-energy particles that are expelled from unstable nuclei. Alpha particles carry a positive charge, beta particles carry a negative charge, and gamma rays are neutral.

- An alpha particle is made up of two protons and two neutrons bound together.
- Beta particles are high energy electrons.
- Gamma rays are waves of electromagnetic energy or photons.

Hence, the correct option is (D).

31. Given,

The ratio of males and females in a village is $5:3$, and there are 800 males in the village.

Let the number of females be x.

According to the question,

$$\frac{800}{x} = \frac{5}{3}$$

$$x = 480$$

Total number of female is 480.

Hence, the correct option is (D).

32. Given,

The radius of the sphere $(r) = 7$ cm

As we know,

The surface area of sphere $= 4\pi r^2$

$$= 4 \times \left(\frac{22}{7}\right) \times 7^2$$

$$= 616 \text{ cm}^2$$

Hence, the correct option is (D).

33. Given,

The sum of any two numbers is 25, and their difference is 13.

Let the number be x and y.

According to the question,

$$x + y = 25 \quad \ldots\ldots(1)$$

$$x - y = 13 \quad \ldots\ldots(2)$$

Now add equations (1) and (2), we get

$$2x = 38$$

$$x = 19$$

Now, put the value of x in equation (1)

$$19 + y = 25$$

$$y = 25 - 19$$

$$y = 6$$

So, the two numbers are 19 and 6.

Hence, the correct option is (D).

34.

2	8,10,15,16,20
2	4,5,15,8,10
2	2,5,15,4,5
2	1,5,15,2,5
3	1,5,15,1,5
5	1,5,5,1,5
	1,1,1,1,1

So, the L.CM of $8,10,15,16$ and 20 is $2 \times 2 \times 2 \times 2 \times 3 \times 5 = 240$.

Hence, the correct option is (D).

35. Given,

Ram can do a piece of work in 10 days and Mohan can do it in 15 days.

As we know,

Per working capacity $\times$ time duration $=$ Total work

Total work $= 30$ units (LCM of 10 and 15)

Ram's per day work $= \frac{30}{10} = 3$ units

Mohan's per day work $= \frac{30}{15} = 2$ units

Both total work per day $= 2 + 3 = 5$ units

Time to complete total work $= \frac{30}{5} = 6$ days

Hence, the correct option is (B).

36. As we know,

If $a\%$ and $b\%$ are successive discounts then,

Total discount $= a + b - \left(\frac{ab}{100}\right)$

Total discounts at 10% and $20\% = 10 + 20 - \frac{(10 \times 20)}{100}$

$$= 30 - 2 = 28$$

$$= 28\%$$

Now, this 28% will be taken as a single discount

Total discount at 28% and $30\% = 28 + 30 - \frac{(28 \times 30)}{100}$

$$= 58 - 8.4 = 49.6$$

$$= 49.6\%$$

Hence, the correct option is (A).

37. Given,

The average age of 12 boys is 10 years, out of which the average age of 11 boys is 9 years.

As we know,

$\text{Average} = \dfrac{\text{sum of all observations}}{\text{Number of observations}}$

$10 = \dfrac{\text{sum of ages of all boys}}{12}$

Sum of ages of all boys $= 120$ years

Average age of 11 boys is 9

So, total sum of ages of 11 boys $= 11 \times 9 = 99$ years

Now,

Age of 12th person $= 120 - 99$

$= 21$ years

Hence, the correct option is (B).

38. Given,

Length and breadth of a rectangular field are 30 and 20 m respectively.

As we know,

Perimeter of rectangle $= 2(\text{Length} + \text{breadth})$

Perimeter of rectangle $= 2(30 + 20)$

$= 2 \times 50$

$= 100$ m

Hence, the correct option is (C).

39. Given:

$2197 = 13 \times 13 \times 13 = 13^3$

So,

$\sqrt[3]{2197} = \sqrt[3]{13^3}$

$\sqrt[3]{2197} = (13^3)^{\frac{1}{3}}$

$\sqrt[3]{2197} = 13^{\left(3 \times \frac{1}{3}\right)}$

$\sqrt[3]{2197} = 13$

Hence, the correct option is (C).

40. Given:

Principle $= 18440$,

Rate of interest $= 15\%$

Time $= 4$ years

$\text{Simple interest} = \dfrac{(Principle \times Rate\ of\ interest \times time)}{100}$

$\text{Simple interest} = \dfrac{(18440 \times 15 \times 4)}{100}$

$\text{Simple interest} = 11064$

Hence, the correct option is (D).

41. HCF is the highest common divisor that can divide all numbers given.

$12 = 2^2 \times 3$

$15 = 3 \times 5$

$18 = 2 \times 3^2$

$21 = 3 \times 7$

HCF $= 3$ (3 is the highest common divisor as 3 is only common among all numbers)

Hence, the correct option is (C).

42. Given,

28 dozen bananas are required in a canteen for 1 week.

Bananas required in 1 week $= 28$ dozens

Bananas required in 1 day $= \dfrac{28}{7} = 4$ dozens

Bananas required in 47 days $= 47 \times 4 = 188$ dozens

$\Rightarrow 188 \times 12$ ($\because 1$ dozen $= 12$ items)

$\Rightarrow 2256$

Hence, the correct option is (B).

43. The logic followed here is:

$\Rightarrow 41 - 39 = 2$

$\Rightarrow 43 - 41 = 2$

$\Rightarrow 45 - 43 = 2$

We can see there is a increment of 2 every time

So,

Next number $= 45 + 2 = 47$

Hence, the correct option is (A).

44. Largest 5 digit number $= 99999$

Now,

$99999 = 17 \times 5882 + 5$

$99994 = 17 \times 5882$

It shows that 99994 is divisible by 17 and the next number divisible by 17 will be 6 digit number.

So, 99994 is the highest 5 digit number divisible by 17.

Hence, the correct option is (B).

45. Given,

Side of equilateral triangle is 12 cm.

As we know,

Area of an equilateral triangle $= \left(\frac{\sqrt{3}}{4}\right)$ side ^{2}

Area of triangle $= \left(\frac{\sqrt{3}}{4}\right)(12)^2$

$= 36\sqrt{3}$ cm ^{2}

Hence, the correct option is (C).

46. According to the given information, we can draw the following diagram:

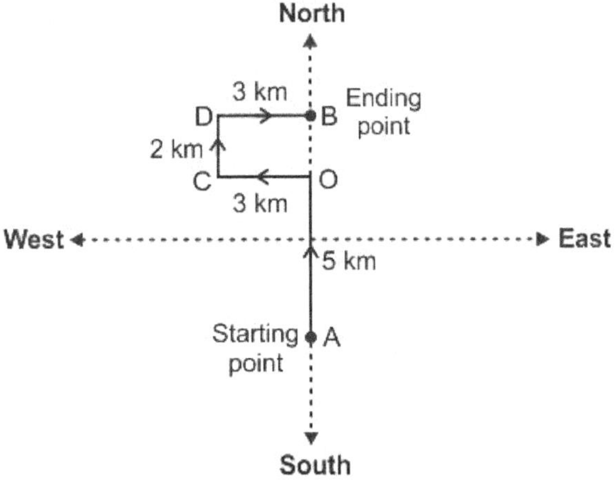

Distance between Starting and end point $= AB$

$AB = AO + OB$

$AO = 5$ km; $OB = CD = 2$ km

$AB = 5 + 2 = 7$ km

Hence, the correct option is (B).

47. The pattern follows here is:

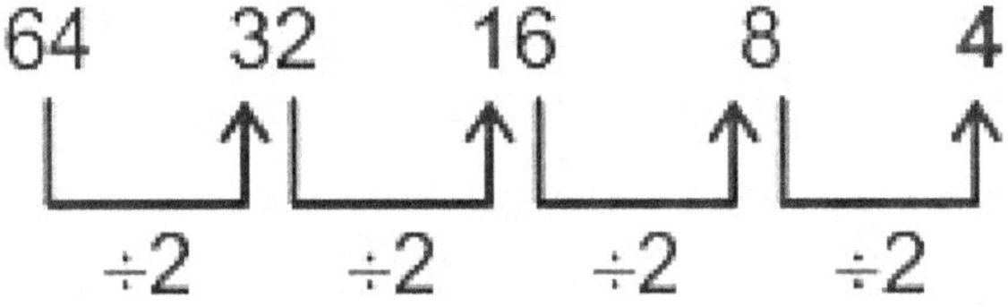

Hence, the correct option is (B).

48. Preparing the family tree using the following symbols:

Symbol in Diagram	Meaning
◯	Female
▢	Male
═	Married couple
─	Siblings
│	Difference of a generation

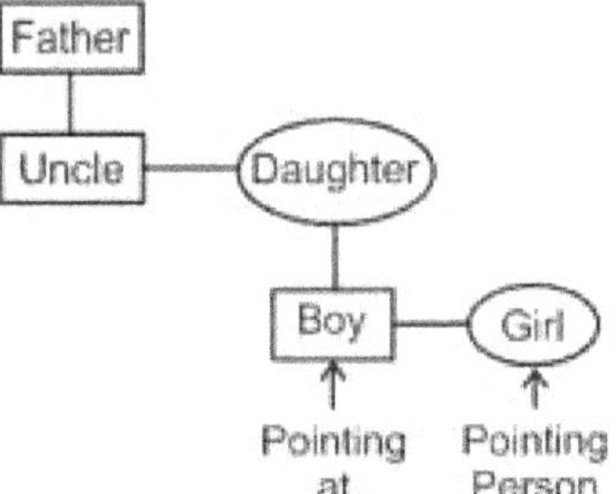

Hence, the correct option is (A).

49. The pattern follows here is:

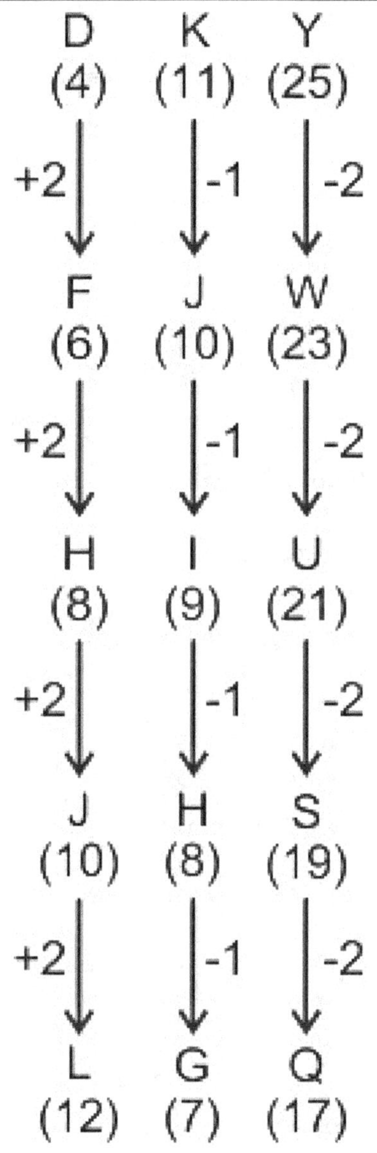

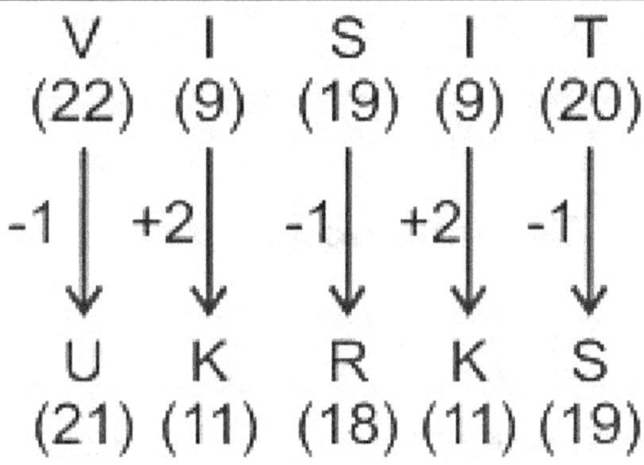

So, the code for the word *VISIT* is *UKRKS*.

Hence, the correct option is (C).

So, the next term will be *LGQ*.

Hence, the correct option is (A).

50. The pattern follows here is:

$$
\begin{array}{ccccc}
B & O & X & E & R \\
(2) & (15) & (24) & (5) & (18) \\
\downarrow_{-1} & \downarrow_{+2} & \downarrow_{-1} & \downarrow_{+2} & \downarrow_{-1} \\
A & Q & W & G & Q \\
(1) & (17) & (23) & (7) & (17)
\end{array}
$$

Similarly,

General Knowledge

Q.1 Who is the developer of 'Social Website-Facebook'?
A. Mark Zuckerberg
B. Sunder Pichai
C. Graham Bell
D. Ratan Tata

Q.2 Where is the largest Petroleum Refinery of India situated?
A. Jamnagar
B. Mumbai
C. Digboi
D. Visakhapatnam

Q.3 The largest island in the world is ______.
A. Greenland
B. Cuba
C. Java
D. Madagascar

Q.4 Which country is known as the 'Land of Thousand Lakes'?
A. New Zealand
B. Ireland
C. Iceland
D. Finland

Q.5 Delhi is located on the banks of which river?
A. Gandak
B. Gomati
C. Yamuna
D. Sarayu

Q.6 Who among the following is also known as the 'Iron man of India'?
A. Lal Bahadur Shastri
B. Mahatma Gandhi
C. Motilal Nehru
D. Sardar Patel

Q.7 ______ is the state capital of Maharashtra.
A. Lucknow
B. Allahabad
C. Mumbai
D. Delhi

Q.8 Who among the following was the father of "King Ashoka"?
A. Chandra Bhan
B. Virbhadra
C. Chandra Gupt
D. Bindusara

Q.9 How are the members of 'Lok Sabha' elected?
A. Directly elected by People
B. Partly elected and partly nominated
C. Indirectly elected
D. Nominated

Q.10 'Sardar Sarover Project' is located on which river?
A. Narmada
B. Godhavari
C. Ganges
D. Kosi

Q.11 'Thar Desert' is located in which country?
A. India
B. Egypt
C. Nepal
D. Mongolia

Q.12 Who was the founder of 'Maurya Dynasty'?
A. Harish Chandra
B. Bindusara
C. Ashoka
D. Chandra Gupta Maurya

Q.13 Which of the following mountain peak is the second highest mountain peak in the world?
A. Kanchanjunga
B. Nanda Devi
C. K2
D. Ganga Parvat

Q.14 'India Gate' is located in which city?
A. Agra
B. Delhi
C. Mumbai
D. Jaipur

Q.15 In which of the following cities is 'Indian Military Academy' located?
A. Dehradun
B. Nagpur
C. Delhi
D. Pune

General Science

Q.16 Rabies is caused by ________.
A. Dog bite
B. Contaminated water
C. Unhygienic food
D. Pollution

Q.17 Natural source of energy is ________.
A. Battery
B. Electricity
C. Sun
D. Friction

Q.18 Largest gland in the human body is ______.
A. Heart
B. Liver
C. Lung
D. Kidney

Q.19 When a moving train stops suddenly, a man tends to fall ______.
A. Downwards
B. Forward
C. Upward
D. Backward

Q.20 Which of the following is 'Universal Recipient' of Blood?
A. O+
B. AB+
C. A+
D. B+

Q.21 Which mirror is used in headlights of car?
A. Concave
B. Convex
C. Plane
D. Black

Q.22 Seismograph is used to measure __________.
A. heart beat
B. earth quake
C. flow of current
D. blood pressure

Q.23 In our body Ligaments connect __________.
A. Muscle to Skin
B. Muscle to Muscle
C. Bone to Bone
D. Muscle to Bone

Q.24 The SI unit of power is ______.
A. Coulomb
B. Ampere
C. Joule
D. Watt

Q.25 What among the following is the reason for Heart-attack?
A. Blood Protein
B. Cholesterol
C. Blood Sugar
D. Blood Urea

Q.26 Which substance is used in Thermometer?
A. Iron
B. Oil
C. Mercury
D. Water

Q.27 The compounds of carbon and hydrogen are called ________.
A. Hydrocarbons

B. Organic Compounds
C. Sugar
D. Carbohydrates

Q.28 Bauxite is an ore of which metal?
A. Gold   **B.** Tin
C. Aluminum   **D.** Copper

Q.29 The chemical symbol of sodium is _____.
A. Nu   **B.** Sd   **C.** So   **D.** Na

Q.30 Sulphuric acid is _____.
A. H_2SO_3 **B.** H_2SO_4 **C.** HCl **D.** HNO_3

Mathematics

Q.31 A vendor loses the selling price of 4 oranges on selling 36 oranges. Find out the loss percentage?
A. 10   **B.** 11.11   **C.** 12.5   **D.** 9.9

Q.32 Find the maximum length of rod that can be placed in a room 10 meters by 10 meters by 5 meters.
A. 16.5 meters   **B.** 17 meters
C. 15 meters   **D.** 18 meters

Q.33 If Simple Interest of two years of an amount is Rs 40 and in two years the amount becomes Rs 1040. Find out the rate of interest?
A. 2%   **B.** 20%   **C.** 0.1%   **D.** 0.05%

Q.34 The L.C.M. of $12,24$ and 30 is _____.
A. 60   **B.** 2   **C.** 30   **D.** 120

Q.35 Find the Simple Interest for 4 months on a principal amount of Rs 600 at 5% rate of interest per annum?
A. Rs 12.5   **B.** Rs 15   **C.** Rs 11   **D.** Rs 10

Q.36 Solve: $(102)^2 =$?
A. 10406   **B.** 10400   **C.** 100404   **D.** 10404

Q.37 Ram had Rs $45,000$. After giving $\frac{2}{5}$ of his money to his eldest son and $\frac{1}{3}$ of the balance money to his youngest son, how much money remained with Ram?
A. Rs 18,000   **B.** Rs 12,000
C. Rs 10,000   **D.** Rs 36,000

Q.38 Find largest number among the following that divides 245 and 1029, leaving remainder 5 in each case?
A. 16   **B.** 18   **C.** 17   **D.** 15

Q.39 By which smallest number 8788 be divided, so that the quotient is a perfect cube?
A. 3   **B.** 4   **C.** 5   **D.** 2

Q.40 If an odd number is divisible by 5, then which of the following will be one of its digit?
A. 5   **B.** 3   **C.** 4   **D.** 2

Q.41 When a dice is thrown, what will be the total number of possible outcomes?
A. 6   **B.** 2   **C.** 9   **D.** 36

Q.42 Change 0.25 into a fraction?
A. $\frac{1}{5}$ **B.** $\frac{1}{2}$ **C.** $\frac{1}{3}$ **D.** $\frac{1}{4}$

Q.43 Find the perimeter of a rectangle whose sides are 5 meter and 4 meter?
A. 12 meter   **B.** 18 meter   **C.** 20 meter   **D.** 16 meter

Q.44 Find out the value of $\left[(64)^{\frac{2}{3}}\right]^{\frac{1}{2}}$?
A. 16   **B.** 08   **C.** 04   **D.** 32

Q.45 A man loses Rs 40 by selling a watch for Rs 660. Find his loss $\%$?
A. 3.45%   **B.** 5.71%   **C.** 5%   **D.** 9.45%

Logical Reasoning

Q.46 From the given options complete the series:-
$6,13,25,51,101,(\_\_\_\_\ )$
A. 205   **B.** 202   **C.** 201   **D.** 203

Q.47 BUILT is written as 5#32@ and TRIBE is written as @935!, then how will RULE be written?
A. @#2!   **B.** 92#5   **C.** !#2@   **D.** 9#2!

Q.48 Pointing towards a man in the photograph, Raju said, "He is my daughter's father's son." How is Raju related to that man?
A. Father   **B.** Son
C. Nephew   **D.** Son-in-law

Q.49 In a certain code language 'CAT' is written as 'DDY'. How will 'BIG' be written in that code?
A. CML **B.** CNL **C.** CLL **D.** CJL

Q.50 In a row of students, Ganesh is 7th from one extreme end and 11th from the other. Find the total number of students in the row?
A. 17   **B.** 20   **C.** 19   **D.** 18

// Smart Answer Sheet //

Correct Indicates percentage of students who answered questions correctly.

Skipped Indicates percentage of students who skipped questions.

Q.	Ans.	Correct / Skipped
1	A	78.33 % / 20.28 %
2	A	87.24 % / 11.21 %
3	A	43.29 % / 38.68 %
4	D	50.52 % / 42.14 %
5	C	80.21 % / 10.75 %
6	D	83.95 % / 12.52 %
7	C	81.96 % / 17.26 %
8	D	24.29 % / 73.58 %
9	A	51.28 % / 39.66 %
10	A	88.96 % / 10.83 %

Q.	Ans.	Correct / Skipped
11	A	82.06 % / 11.27 %
12	D	85.53 % / 10.25 %
13	C	67.88 % / 30.45 %
14	B	46.35 % / 32.76 %
15	A	78.83 % / 17.07 %
16	A	84.76 % / 15.02 %
17	C	60.04 % / 34.64 %
18	B	85.57 % / 13.4 %
19	B	40.85 % / 42.61 %
20	B	56.16 % / 31.61 %

Q.	Ans.	Correct / Skipped
21	A	83.31 % / 10.86 %
22	B	25.02 % / 67.29 %
23	C	76.21 % / 10.99 %
24	D	88.3 % / 11.02 %
25	B	87.65 % / 11.07 %
26	C	59.63 % / 36.29 %
27	A	76.82 % / 20.87 %
28	C	78.21 % / 18.08 %
29	D	80.63 % / 14.76 %
30	B	59.38 % / 30.21 %

Q.	Ans.	Correct / Skipped
31	A	20.9 % / 73.48 %
32	C	65.66 % / 33.01 %
33	A	45.96 % / 45.14 %
34	D	79.83 % / 11.45 %
35	D	77.22 % / 19.03 %
36	D	48.65 % / 32.76 %
37	A	42.67 % / 35.19 %
38	A	45.66 % / 42.36 %
39	B	62.98 % / 36.39 %
40	A	86.72 % / 12.91 %

Q.	Ans.	Correct / Skipped
41	A	88.66 % / 11.08 %
42	D	76.03 % / 10.7 %
43	B	88.84 % / 10.48 %
44	C	63.64 % / 32.5 %
45	B	76.02 % / 16.3 %
46	D	41.89 % / 42.48 %
47	D	62.43 % / 35.55 %
48	A	41.94 % / 44.44 %
49	C	80.57 % / 18.7 %
50	A	58.36 % / 38.09 %

Performance Analysis

Avg. Score (%)	45.0%
Toppers Score (%)	67.0%
Your Score	

//Hints and Solutions//

1. Mark Zuckerberg is the developer of 'Social Website-Facebook'.

Mark Zuckerberg, full name Mark Elliot Zuckerberg is the founder of Facebook. Facebook is a social networking site that makes it easy for you to connect with family and friends online. Originally designed for college students, Facebook was created in 2004 by Mark Zuckerberg while he was enrolled at Harvard University. Facebook is a popular free social networking website that allows registered users to create profiles, upload photos and video, send messages and keep in touch with friends, family, and colleagues. He started Facebook from his college dorm room in 2004 with room-mates Dustin Moskovitz and Chris Hughes and from New York.

Hence, the correct option is (A).

2. The largest Petroleum Refinery of India is situated in Jamnagar.

The Jamnagar Refinery is a private sector crude oil refinery owned by Reliance Industries Limited in Jamnagar, Gujarat, India. The refinery was commissioned on 14 July 1999 with an installed capacity of 668,000 barrels per day (106,200 m³/d). Its current installed capacity is 1,240,000 barrels per day (197,000 m³/d). It is currently the largest refinery in the world.

Hence, the correct option is (A).

3. Greenland, the world's largest island, lying in the North Atlantic Ocean. It covers an area of 2,130,800 km2 (970 sq mi) Greenland is noted for its vast tundra and immense glaciers. Although Greenland remains a part of the Kingdom of Denmark, the island's home-rule government is responsible for most domestic affairs. The Greenlandic people are primarily Inuit (Eskimo). The capital of Greenland is Nuuk (Godthab).

Hence, the correct option is (A).

4. Finland is known as the 'Land of Thousand Lakes'.

There are approximately 168,000 lakes and 179,000 islands in Finland. Saimaa, its biggest lake, is Europe's fourth-largest. The Finnish Lakeland has the most lakes in the world, and many of the country's major cities, including Tampere, Jyvaskyla, and Kuopio, are in close proximity to the large lakes.

Hence, the correct option is (D).

5. Delhi is located on the banks of Yamuna river.

The Yamuna River is the largest tributary of the Ganga River. It originates from the Yamunotri glacier, at the Bandarpoonch peak in Uttarakhand. The main tributaries joining the river include the Sindh, Hindon, Betwa Ken, and Chambal. The Tons is the largest tributary of the Yamuna. The catchment of the river extends to the states of Delhi, Himachal Pradesh, Uttar Pradesh, Haryana, Rajasthan, and Madhya Pradesh.

Hence, the correct option is (C).

6. Sardar Patel is also known as the 'Iron man of India'.

Vallabhbhai Patel popularly known as Sardar Patel was an Indian politician. He served as the First Deputy Prime Minister of India. He was an Indian barrister and a senior leader of the Indian National Congress who played a leading role in the country's struggle for independence and guided its integration into a united, independent nation. He is also remembered as the "patron saint of India's civil servants" for having established the modern all-India services system. He is also called the "Unifier of India". He was the first Home Minister and Deputy Prime Minister of India.

Hence, the correct option is (D).

7. Mumbai is the state capital of Maharashtra.

Maharashtra is the second-most populous state in India. Mumbai is the financial capital of India. Maharashtra state has about 720 km long indented coastline. The Maharashtra coast is popularly known as the Konkan coast. The Arabian Sea lies on the west coast of Maharashtra. Thane, Raigad, Greater Bombay, Ratnagiri, and Sindhudurg are the coastal districts of Maharashtra. The famous pilgrim center Amaravati is in Maharashtra. Gateway of India is located in Maharashtra.

There are five UNESCO world heritage sites in Maharashtra including the Western Ghats. The UNESCO world heritage sites in Maharashtra are:

- Chhatrapathi Shivaji Terminus
- Elephanta Caves
- Ajanta Caves

Hence, the correct option is (C).

8. Bindusara was the father of "King Ashoka".

Ashoka, also known as Ashoka the Great, was the third emperor of the Maurya Dynasty. He ruled the Indian subcontinent from 268 BCE to 232 BCE. He was the son of Bindusara and the grandson of the founder of the Maurya Dynasty, Chandragupta Maurya. Ashoka promoted the spread of Buddhism across ancient Asia.

Hence, the correct option is (D).

9. The members of 'Lok Sabha' are directly elected by People.

The Lok Sabha, or House of the People, is the lower house of India's bicameral Parliament, with the upper house being the Rajya Sabha. The house meets in the Lok Sabha Chambers of the Sansad Bhavan, New Delhi. Members of the Lok Sabha are elected by an adult universal suffrage and a first-past-the-post system to represent their respective constituencies, and they hold their seats for five years or until the body is dissolved by the President on the advice of the council of ministers. The maximum membership of the house allotted by the constitution of India is 550 (Initially, in 1950, it was 500). Currently, the house has 543 seats which are made up by the election of up to 543 elected members and at a maximum. The Lok Sabha has a seating capacity of 550. A total of 131 seats (24.03%) are reserved for representatives of Scheduled Castes (84) and Scheduled Tribes (47). The quorum for the House is 10% of the total membership.

Hence, the correct option is (A).

10. 'Sardar Sarover Project' is located on Narmada river.

The Sardar Sarovar Dam is a concrete gravity dam built on the Narmada river in Navagam near Kevadiya, Narmada District, Gujarat in India. Indian states Gujarat, Madhya Pradesh, Maharashtra and Rajasthan receive water and electricity supply from the dam. The foundation stone of the project was laid out by Prime Minister Jawaharlal Nehru on 5 April 1961. The project took form in 1979 as part of a development scheme funded by the World Bank through their International Bank for Reconstruction and Development, to increase irrigation and produce hydroelectricity, using a loan of US $200 million.

Hence, the correct option is (A).

11. 'Thar Desert' is located in India.

Thar Desert is located partly in Rajasthan state, northwestern India, and partly in Punjab and Sindh (Sind) provinces, eastern Pakistan. The Thar Desert also called the Great Indian Desert covers more than 77,000 square miles (200,000 sq. km), forming a natural border between India and Pakistan. It is a large arid region with a landscape dominated by sand dunes varying in size from 52ft (16m) in the North to 498ft (152m) in the south. The Climate in the Thar desert is like any other desert, Hot in the day and cool at night. The summer days are really hot and the nights are cool but the winter days are warm and the nights are cold. In the summer there is little to no rain.

Hence, the correct option is (A).

12. Chandra Gupta Maurya was the founder of 'Maurya Dynasty'.

Chandragupta Maurya founded the Maurya Empire in 322 BCE when he conquered the kingdom of Magadha and the northwestern Macedonian satrapies. Chandra Gupta Maurya had overthrown the Nanda Dynasty and rapidly expanded his power westward across central and western India in order to take advantage of the disruptions of local powers in the wake of the withdrawal by Alexander the great's armies.

Hence, the correct option is (D).

13. K2 (Godwin Austen) mountain peak is the second highest mountain peak in the world.

Godwin Austen height is 8611 meters. It is known as K2 and is located in the Karakoram ranges of Kashmir. It was named K2 by TG Montgomery in 1852 AD. Climbers climb it between June and August. In terms of Climbing, it is considered more dangerous than climbing Mount Everest. That is why it is also called Killer Peak. It is located in POK i.e., Pakistan Occupied India.

Hence, the correct option is (C).

14. 'India Gate' is located in Delhi.

The India Gate was constructed by the Imperial War Graves Commission. It is also known as the All India War Memorial. It was built as a memorial to the soldiers of World War I. It is the world's largest war memorial which was built in the 20th century. Edward Lutyens was the architect. It was built for the duration of 1921 to 1931 AD. Amar Jawan Jyoti was added to the India Gate in 1972 in the honor of soldiers who sacrificed their lives in the Indo-Pakistan War of 1971.

Hence, the correct option is (B).

15. The 'Indian Military Academy' is located in Dehradun, Uttarakhand.

The Indian Military Academy (IMA) is the oldest Military Academy in India, and trains officers for the Indian Army. Located in Dehradun, Uttarakhand, it was established in 1932 following a recommendation by a military committee set up under the chairmanship of General (later Field Marshal) Sir Philip Chetwode. From a class of 40 male cadets in 1932, IMA now has a sanctioned capacity of 1,650. Cadets undergo a training course varying between 3 and 16 months depending on entry criteria. On completion of the course at IMA cadets are permanently commissioned into the army as Lieutenants.

Hence, the correct option is (A).

16. Rabies is caused by Dog bite.

Rabies is a fatal but preventable viral disease. It can spread to people and pets if they are bitten or scratched by a rabid animal. In the United States, rabies is mostly found in wild animals like bats, raccoons, skunks, and foxes. However, in many other countries dogs still carry rabies, and most rabies deaths in people around the world are caused by dog bites.

Hence, the correct option is (A).

17. Natural source of energy is Sun.

Plants convert light energy from the sun into chemical energy (food) by the process of photosynthesis. So, the food we get from plants and animals also has its primary sunlight source. Every day, the sun radiates (sends out) an enormous amount of energy. It radiates more energy each day than the world uses in one year. Solar energy is a renewable energy source. Like most stars, the sun is made up mostly of hydrogen and helium atoms in a plasma state. The sun generates energy from a process called nuclear fusion.

Hence, the correct option is (C).

18. Largest gland in the human body is Liver.

Liver is an accessory organ of the digestive system. It continuously produces bile. Bile flows out of the liver into the right and left hepatic ducts, into the common hepatic ducts, and toward the small intestine to help with digestion and the absorption of fats. In humans, it is located in the right upper quadrant of the abdomen, below the diaphragm.

Hence, the correct option is (B).

19. When a moving train stops suddenly, a man tends to fall Forward. Because the lower part of the body comes to rest with the bus while the upper part tends to continue its motion due to inertia.

Newton's first law states that, if a body is at rest or moving at a constant speed in a straight line, it will remain at rest or keep moving in a straight line at constant speed unless it is acted upon by a force. This postulate is known as the law of inertia.

Hence, the correct option is (B).

20. AB+ is 'Universal Recipient' of blood because an individual with this blood type can receive blood from any other blood types- A, B, AB and O. In the AB blood type, the red blood cells

comprise both antigen A and B, but the plasma lacks both anti-A or anti-B antibodies. Blood groups are classification as blood, they are classified on the presence and absence of antibodies and other antigens on the surface of Red blood cells.

Hence, the correct option is (B).

21. Concave mirror is used in headlights of car.

Characteristics of Concave Mirrors:

- Light converges at a point when it strikes and reflects back from the reflecting surface of the concave mirror. So, it is also known as a converging mirror.

- When the concave mirror is placed very close to the object, a magnified and virtual image is obtained.

- However, if we increase the distance between the object and the mirror then the size of the image reduces and a real image is formed.

- The image formed by the concave mirror can be small or large or can be real or virtual.

Hence, the correct option is (A).

22. Seismograph is used to measure earth quake.

A seismograph records the waves reaching the surface during an earthquake. The sudden tremors or shaking of the earth's crust is called an earthquake. The earth's crust is made up of different parts of various sizes. They are called plates. Most of the earthquakes in the world are caused by the movements of the plates. 'Richter scale' and 'Mercalli scale' are the instruments to measure and record the magnitude and the intensity of an earthquake respectively.

Hence, the correct option is (B).

23. In our body Ligaments connect bone to bone.

A ligament is the fibrous connective tissue that connects bones to other bones. It is also known as articular ligament, articular lura, fibrous ligament, or true ligament. Other ligaments in the body include:

- Peritoneal ligament: a fold of peritoneum or other membranes.

- Fetal remnant ligament: the remnants of a fetal tubular structure.

- Periodontal ligament: a group of fibers that attach the cementum of teeth to the surrounding alveolar bone.

Hence, the correct option is (C).

24. The SI unit of power is watt. The watt is named after James Watt. Power is the amount of energy transferred per unit of time. Power is a scalar quantity.

1 watt (W) = 1.00 joules per second (J/sec).

Hence, the correct option is (D).

25. The reason for Heart-attack is cholesterol.

A heart attack occurs when an artery supplying your heart with blood and oxygen becomes blocked. Fat deposits build up over time, forming plaques in our heart's arteries. If a plaque ruptures,

a blood clot can form and block your arteries, causing a heart attack.

Cholesterol is a lipid (Sterol). Lipid is a type of blood fat. It is the most abundant steroid in the body. The human body needs cholesterol to build cells and make vitamins and other hormones. Cholesterol production is so important that our liver and intestines make about 80% of the cholesterol we need to stay healthy. Only about 20% comes from the foods we eat.

Hence, the correct option is (B).

26. Mercury is used in thermometer because it remains in liquid form throughout a wide range of temperatures i.e -37.89 degrees Fahrenheit to 674.06 degrees Fahrenheit. The mercury thermometer was invented by physicist Daniel Gabriel Fahrenheit in Amsterdam.

Hence, the correct option is (C).

27. The compounds of carbon and hydrogen are called hydrocarbons. These are also known as 'parent compounds'. Carbon is placed in the second period. The atomic number of carbon is 6 while the weight is 12. Carbon needs 4 electrons to complete the octet state and it is full filled by covalent bonds.

Hence, the correct option is (A).

28. Bauxite is an ore of aluminum.

Bauxite is an aluminium-rich sedimentary rock formed from laterite soil. It is found in tropical or subtropical regions. It is used for the production of aluminium. It is a non-ferrous metallic mineral that is used in the manufacturing of aluminium. It is found mainly in tertiary deposits and is associated with laterite rocks. Odisha is the largest bauxite producing state accounting for more than half of the total production of India.

Hence, the correct option is (C).

29. The chemical symbol of sodium is Na.

Sodium is a chemical element with the atomic number 11. It is a soft, silvery-white, highly reactive metal. Sodium is an alkali metal, being in group 1 of the periodic table. Its only stable isotope is ^{23}Na. Sodium is the sixth most abundant element in the earth's crust and exists in numerous minerals such as sodalite, feldspars, and rock salt (NaCl).

Hence, the correct option is (D).

30. Sulphuric acid is H_2SO_4. It is an inorganic acid. It is also known as "mattling acid" or "oil of vitriol". The "contact method" is used to produce it on a large scale.

Hence, the correct option is (B).

31. Given,

A vendor loses the selling price of 4 oranges on selling 36 oranges.

Let the selling price be S and cost price C.

The cost price of 36 oranges be $36C$

The selling price of 36 oranges be $36S$

According to the question,

Loss $= 36C - 36S$

$4S = 36C - 36S$ (loss is the selling price of 4 oranges)

$40S = 36C$

$\dfrac{S}{C} = \dfrac{36}{40}$

$\dfrac{S}{C} = \dfrac{9}{10}$

Now,

Loss percentage $= \dfrac{\text{(cost price - selling price)}}{\text{(cost price)}} \times 100$

Loss percentage $= \dfrac{(10-9)}{(10)} \times 100$

$= 10\%$

Hence, the correct option is (A).

32. Given,

Dimension of the room is 10 meters 10 meters and 5 meters.

As we know,

Length of longest rod in a room $=$

$\sqrt{(length^2 + breadth^2 + height^2)}$

Length of longest rod $= \sqrt{(10^2 + 10^2 + 5^2)}$

$= \sqrt{(100 + 100 + 25)}$

$= \sqrt{225}$

$= 15$ meters

Hence, the correct option is (C).

33. Given,

Simple Interest of two years of an amount is Rs 40 and in two years the amount becomes Rs 1040.

Time $= 2$ years

Let the interest rate be R.

According to the question,

$1040 = 40$ + Principle   (Amount $=$ Principle $+$ Interest)

Principle $= 1040 - 40 = 1000$ Rs

Now,

Simple interest $= \dfrac{(Principle \times Rate\ of\ interest \times time)}{100}$

$40 = \dfrac{(1000 \times R \times 2)}{100}$

$R = \dfrac{4000}{2000} = 2$

So, rate of interest $= 2\%$

Hence, the correct option is (A).

34.

2	12,24,30
2	6,12,15
2	3,6,15
3	3,3,5
5	1,1,5
	1,1,1

So, L.C.M of $12, 24$ and 30 is $2 \times 2 \times 2 \times 2 \times 3 \times 5 = 120$

Hence, the correct option is (D).

35. Given,

Principal is Rs 600 and rate of interest 5%.

Time $= 4$ months $= \dfrac{4}{12} = \dfrac{1}{3}$ years)

Interest $= \dfrac{(Principle \times Interest\ rate \times Time)}{100}$

According to the question,

Interest $= \dfrac{600 \times 5 \times \frac{1}{3}}{100}$

$= $ Rs 10

Hence, the correct option is (D).

36. As we know,

$(a + b)^2 = a^2 + b^2 + 2ab$

So,

$(102)^2 = (100 + 2)^2$

$(102)^2 = 100^2 + 2^2 + 2 \times 100 \times 2$

$(102)^2 = 10000 + 4 + 400$

$(102)^2 = 10404$

Hence, the correct option is (D).

37. Given,

Ram had Rs $45,000$, he gave $\dfrac{2}{5}$ of his money to his eldest son and $\dfrac{1}{3}$ of the balance money to his youngest son.

Money left after giving $\dfrac{2}{5}$th of $45,000 = 45,000 - \dfrac{2}{5}$ of $45,000$

$45,000 = 45,000 - 45,000 \times \dfrac{2}{5}$

$= 45,000 - 18,000$

$= 27,000$

Now money left after giving $\frac{1}{3}$ of balance money $= 27,000 -$ $\frac{1}{3}$ of $27,000$

$= 27,000 - 27,000 \times \frac{1}{3}$

$= 27,000 - 9,000$

$= 18,000$

Hence, the correct option is (A).

38. Let the number be ' x ' that divides 245 and 1029 leaving the remainder 5.

245 and 1029 leave remainder 5 when divided ' x ',

So, $(245 - 5) = 240$ and $(1029 - 5) = 1024$ must be divisible by x.

Now,

$240 = 2^4 \times 3 \times 5$

$1024 = 2^{10}$

HCF is the highest common number that is common in a set of different numbers.

HCF (x) of 240 and $1024 = 2^4 = 16$ (16 is common between both numbers)

Hence, the correct option is (A).

39. The given number is 8788.

Now, the prime factorization of 8788

$8788 = 2 \times 2 \times 13 \times 13 \times 13$

As we can see that the prime factor 2 doesn't occur 3 times, so the given number is not a perfect cube.

So, we will divide 8788 by $4 = (2 \times 2)$ to get quotient as a perfect cube

$\Rightarrow \dfrac{8788}{4} = \dfrac{2 \times 2 \times 13 \times 13 \times 13}{4}$

$\Rightarrow 2197 = 13 \times 13 \times 13$

2197 is a perfect cube.

Therefore, the smallest number by which 8788 must be divided to get the quotient as a perfect cube is " 4".

Hence, the correct option is (B).

40. As we know,

A odd number can only be divisible by 5 when its unit digit is 5.

Hence, the correct option is (A).

41. Possible outcomes of a dice are $1,2,3,4,5$ and 6.

So, there are total 6 possible outcomes when a dice is thrown.

Hence, the correct option is (A).

42. Given:

$0.25 = \dfrac{25}{100}$

$= \dfrac{25}{100}$

$= \dfrac{1}{4}$

Hence, the correct option is (D).

43. Given,

Sides of rectangle are 5 meter and 4 meter.

As we know,

Perimeter of rectangle $= 2(\text{length } + \text{breadth })$

Perimeter of rectangle $= 2(5 + 4)$

$= 2 \times 9$

$= 18$ meter

Hence, the correct option is (B).

44. Given,

$\left[(64)^{\frac{2}{3}}\right]^{\frac{1}{2}}$

$\Rightarrow \left[(4)^{3 \times \left(\frac{2}{3}\right)}\right]^{\frac{1}{2}}$

$\Rightarrow [(4)^2]^{\frac{1}{2}}$

$\Rightarrow 4$

Hence, the correct option is (C).

45. Given,

A man loses Rs 40 by selling a watch for Rs 660.

According to the question,

Loss $=$ cost price $-$ selling price

$40 =$ Cost price -660

Cost price $= 660 + 40 = 700$

Now,

Loss $\% = \dfrac{(costprice - selling\ price)}{(cost\ price)} \times 100$

Loss $\% = \dfrac{(700 - 660)}{(700)} \times 100$

$= \dfrac{40}{7}$

$= 5.71$

Hence, the correct option is (B).

46. The pattern followed here is:

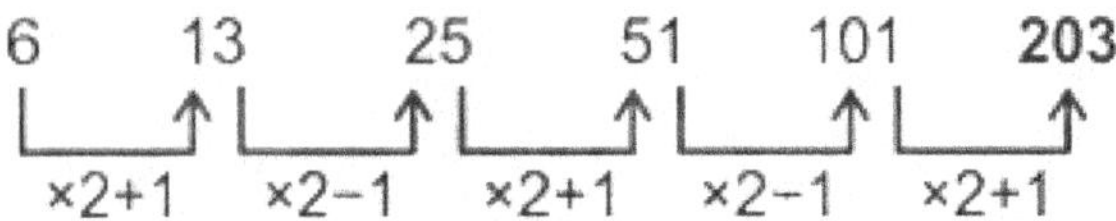

Hence, the correct option is (D).

47. BUILT is coded as B-5, U-#, I-3, L-2, T-@.

TRIBE is coded as T-@, R-9, I-3, B-5, E-!.

Similarly,

By following the coded logic:

RULE is written as R-9, U-#, L-2, E-!.

Hence, the correct option is (D).

48. Preparing the family tree using the following symbols:

Symbol in Diagram	Meaning
◯	Female
☐	Male
═	Married couple
—	Siblings
|	Difference of a generation

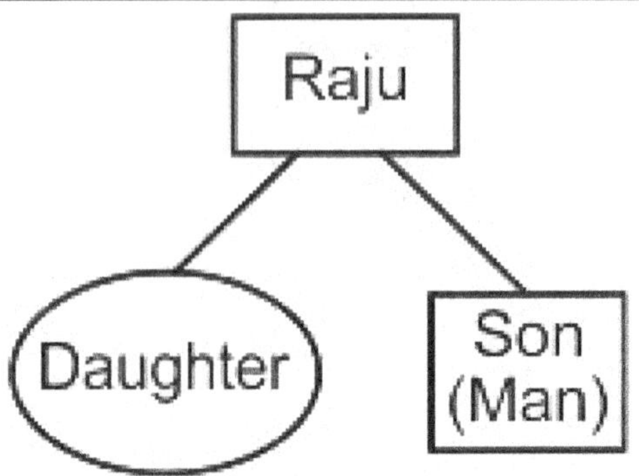

So, Raju is related to that man as father.

Hence, the correct option is (A).

49. The pattern follows here is:

$$
\begin{array}{ccc}
C & A & T \\
+1\downarrow & +3\downarrow & +5\downarrow \\
D & D & Y
\end{array}
$$

Similarly,

$$
\begin{array}{ccc}
B & I & G \\
+1\downarrow & +3\downarrow & +5\downarrow \\
C & L & L
\end{array}
$$

So, BIG will be coded as CLL.

Hence, the correct option is (C).

50. According to the question,

Let the total number of students be T.

Then,

$T = 7 + 11 - 1$ (because Ganesh is added two times)

$T = 18 - 1$

$T = 17$

Hence, the correct option is (A).

General Knowledge

Q.1 On which date International Day of Non-violence is observed?

A. 23 March

B. 30 January

C. 02 October

D. 10 December

Q.2 Where is the Headquarter of UNO located?

A. Switzerland

B. Newyork

C. Geneva

D. Paris

Q.3 'Fatehpur Sikri' was built by which ruler?

A. Akbar

B. Humanyun

C. Babar

D. Shahjahan

Q.4 In which year the third battle of Panipat was fought?

A. 1739   **B.** 1707   **C.** 1761   **D.** 1757

Q.5 Who among the following was known as the 'Lady with the lamp'?

A. Anne Besant

B. Sarojini Naidu

C. Florence Nightingale

D. Indira Gandhi

Q.6 Indian currency notes are printed in which city?

A. Nagpur

B. Mumbai

C. New Delhi

D. Nasik

Q.7 Who appoints Attorney General of India?

A. Governor

B. Chief Justice of Supreme Court

C. Prime Minister

D. President

Q.8 Which of the following rivers originate from 'Amarkantak'?

A. Betwa

B. Narmada

C. Mahanadi

D. Godavari

Q.9 Upper House of the Indian Parliament is known as the ___________?

A. Lok Sabha

B. Vidhan Paridash

C. Rajya Sabha

D. Vidhan Sabha

Q.10 Who was the author of the book 'My Experiment with Truth'?

A. Mahatma Gandhi

B. Tara Ali Beg

C. Maulana Abul Kalam azad

D. Govind Vallabh Pant

Q.11 Who among the following is often referred to as 'Black Pearl'?

A. Pele

B. Venus Williams

C. Maradona

D. Serena Williams

Q.12 Who was the founder of Brahma Samaj?

A. Raja Ram Mohan Roy

B. Swami Vivekananda

C. Dayananda Saraswati

D. Jyotiba Phule

Q.13 Which of the following is known as roof of the world?

A. Pamir Mountains

B. Mount Everest

C. Shivalik Mountain Range

D. Alps

Q.14 The Gateway of India is located in:

A. Kolkata

B. Delhi

C. Mumbai

D. Bengaluru

Q.15 Who conducts the elections of Lok Sabha in India?

A. Election Commission

B. Union Public Service Commission

C. Parliament

D. Delimitation Commission

General Science

Q.16 Which of the following is a non magnetic material?

A. Iron   **B.** Nickel   **C.** Cobalt   **D.** Tin

Q.17 Measure of Frequency is ________.

A. meter

B. second

C. hertz

D. newton meter

Q.18 The process of rusting of iron is called __________.

A. reduction

B. galvanization

C. absorption

D. corrosion

Q.19 The red colour of human blood is due to ______.

A. mayoglobin

B. immunoglobulin

C. heptoglobin

D. haemoglobin

Q.20 Clouds float in the atmosphere because of their __________.

A. low temperature

B. low viscosity

C. low pressure

D. low density

Q.21 Fish breathe through ________.

A. lungs   **B.** gills   **C.** eye   **D.** skin

Q.22 One Horse Power $=$ ______ Watt.

A. 546   **B.** 746   **C.** 846   **D.** 648

Q.23 L.P.G is a hydrocarbon consisting of a minute of ______________.

A. ethane and propane

B. methane and butane

C. ethane and butane

D. propane and butane

Q.24 The quantity of blood in human body is ____.

A. 14%   **B.** 7%   **C.** 1%   **D.** 90%

Q.25 After digestion, protein is converted into __________.
A. glucose   **B.** sucrose
C. fat   **D.** amino acid

Q.26 Main organ of respiratory system in human body is

__________.
A. lung   **B.** kidney   **C.** skin   **D.** heart

Q.27 The basic unit of life is the __________.
A. organ   **B.** organelle
C. tissue   **D.** cell

Q.28 Typhoid is caused by __________.
A. virus   **B.** protozoa   **C.** bacteria   **D.** protein

Q.29 The disease caused by the bite of a mad dog is called

__________.
A. dengue Fever   **B.** cholera
C. malaria   **D.** rabies

Q.30 Photosynthesis takes place in:
A.   Roots of the plants
B.   Green parts of the plants
C.   Stems of the plants
D.   All parts of the plant

Mathematics

Q.31 A and B can do a piece of work in 12 days, C and A in 20 days and B and C in 15 days, then in how many days will they finish it working together?
A. 15 days   **B.** 5 days   **C.** 20 days   **D.** 10 days

Q.32 Find the area of a circle made of 1 meter wire?
A. 796 cm ^{2} **B.** 795.45 cm ^{2}
C. 799 cm ^{2} **D.** 798 cm ^{2}

Q.33 In the radius of a tyre is 7 cm, what distance will it travel in 50 rotations?
A. 7 meter   **B.** 50 meter   **C.** 22 meter   **D.** 44 meter

Q.34 Average salary of 20 workers in an office is Rs. 1900 per month, If manager's salary is added, average becomes Rs. 2000 per month. Find manager's salary?
A. Rs. 4600   **B.** Rs. 2400   **C.** Rs. 4000   **D.** Rs. 2220

Q.35 Find the volume of a circular cylinder whose height is 15 cm and radius of the base is 7 cm?
A. 2510 cm ^{3} **B.** 2310 cm ^{3}
C. 2410 cm ^{3} **D.** 2210 cm ^{3}

Q.36 If the area of a rectangular region is 560 cm ^{2} and one of its side is 20 cm then find its perimeter?
A. 97 cm   **B.** 85 cm   **C.** 96 cm   **D.** 98 cm

Q.37 The radius of a circle is 28 m. Find its area?
A. 2464 cm ^{2} **B.** 2394 cm ^{2}

C. 2828 cm ^{2} **D.** 2586 cm ^{2}

Q.38 Prashant incurred a loss of 75% on selling an article for Rs. 6800. What was the cost price of the article?
A. Rs. 29000   **B.** Rs. 27200
C. Rs. 21250   **D.** Rs. 25600

Q.39 Fill in the blank from given options:-

$39, 41, 43, 45, (\_\_)$
A. 51   **B.** 47   **C.** 53   **D.** 49

Q.40 Find the least number which must be subtracted from 175 to make it a perfect square?
A. 3   **B.** 2   **C.** 6   **D.** 7

Q.41 A number increased by itself and 5 gives 17, the number is ____?
A. 3   **B.** 6   **C.** 5   **D.** 2

Q.42 A motor cycle covers a distance of 140 m in 18 seconds. Find its speed per hour in kms?
A. 32 km /hr   **B.** 24 km /hr
C. 18 km /hr   **D.** 28 km /hr

Q.43 In a music school, 70% students are boys. If the total girls are 255 then find out the number of boys?
A. 595   **B.** 850   **C.** 540   **D.** 575

Q.44 If the product of the numbers is 4725 and their HCF is 15. What will be LCM of these number?
A. 180   **B.** 345   **C.** 315   **D.** 265

Q.45 What is the greatest number that divides $30, 53, 99$ to leave the same remainder?
A. 19   **B.** 13   **C.** 21   **D.** 23

Logical Reasoning

Q.46 The average of three numbers is 27. The second is three times the first and the third number is five times the first. What is the sequence of the numbers?
A. 27,9,45   **B.** 9,27,45   **C.** 24,8,40   **D.** 8,40,24

Q.47 From the given options fill the missing number in the sequence:

$1, 9, 25, 49, (\_\_), 121.$
A. 64   **B.** 100   **C.** 91   **D.** 81

Q.48 A man walks 1 km towards East and then he turns to South and walks 5 kms. Again he turns to East and walks 2 kms and then he turns to North and walks 9 kms. How far is he from his starting point?
A. 7 kms   **B.** 4 kms   **C.** 3 kms   **D.** 5 kms

Q.49 If $PALE$ is coded as 2134, $EARTH$ is coded as 41590, how will $PEARL$ be coded?
A. 23145   **B.** 24153   **C.** 25430   **D.** 29530

Q.50 Arun said, "This girl is the wife of the grandson of my mother". How is Arun related to the girl?

A. Father

B. Husband

C. Father-in-law

D. Grandfather

// Smart Answer Sheet //

Correct   Indicates percentage of students who answered questions correctly.

Skipped   Indicates percentage of students who skipped questions.

Q.	Ans.	Correct / Skipped	Q.	Ans.	Correct / Skipped	Q.	Ans.	Correct / Skipped	Q.	Ans.	Correct / Skipped	Q.	Ans.	Correct / Skipped
1	C	87.77 % / 12.18 %	11	A	68.67 % / 30.14 %	21	B	78.37 % / 20.67 %	31	D	87.09 % / 10.44 %	41	B	82.15 % / 14.16 %
2	B	77.83 % / 17.71 %	12	A	50.89 % / 34.25 %	22	B	82.68 % / 13.83 %	32	B	47.19 % / 51.28 %	42	D	82.1 % / 17.56 %
3	A	42.65 % / 38.44 %	13	A	32.92 % / 67.04 %	23	D	21.43 % / 78.03 %	33	C	40.88 % / 38.27 %	43	A	42.96 % / 55.46 %
4	C	63.03 % / 36.43 %	14	C	76.16 % / 22.59 %	24	B	42.34 % / 31.5 %	34	C	42.7 % / 34.58 %	44	C	61.57 % / 34.16 %
5	C	11.43 % / 67.97 %	15	A	86.49 % / 12.87 %	25	D	64.48 % / 30.27 %	35	B	78.51 % / 15.32 %	45	D	40.62 % / 57.0 %
6	D	76.55 % / 10.81 %	16	D	83.7 % / 10.72 %	26	A	41.31 % / 42.85 %	36	C	66.95 % / 31.69 %	46	B	81.24 % / 10.38 %
7	D	63.52 % / 32.91 %	17	C	87.93 % / 10.28 %	27	D	84.95 % / 14.19 %	37	A	89.58 % / 10.27 %	47	D	83.16 % / 13.52 %
8	B	55.95 % / 36.7 %	18	D	87.85 % / 10.61 %	28	C	45.78 % / 37.61 %	38	B	81.51 % / 16.74 %	48	D	11.03 % / 83.03 %
9	C	65.94 % / 32.86 %	19	D	64.13 % / 33.28 %	29	D	81.23 % / 12.27 %	39	B	88.41 % / 11.56 %	49	B	60.18 % / 37.15 %
10	A	65.66 % / 34.04 %	20	D	23.72 % / 75.14 %	30	B	23.8 % / 72.32 %	40	C	57.82 % / 40.98 %	50	C	19.97 % / 69.04 %

Performance Analysis	
Avg. Score (%)	35.0%
Toppers Score (%)	65.0%
Your Score	

//Hints and Solutions//

1. International Day of Non-violence is observed on 02 October, pioneer of philosophy & strategy of non-violence. It is an occasion to disseminate messages of non-violence, including through education and public awareness. International Day of Non-violence was established by UNGA by passing the resolution in 2007 in an effort to spread the message of non-violence.

Hence, the correct option is (C).

2. The Headquarter of UNO is located in Newyork, United States.

The United Nations is an International organization founded in 1945. It is currently made up of 193 member states. The mission and work of the United Nations are guided by the purposes and principles contained in its founding charter. Antonio Guterres serves as the Ninth Secretary-General of the United Nations. A member of the Portuguese Socialist Party, he served as Prime Minister of Portugal from 1995 to 2002. The main organs of the UNO are the General Assembly, the Security Council, the Economic and Social Council, the Trusteeship Council, the International Court of Justice, and the UN Secretariat.

Hence, the correct option is (B).

3. 'Fatehpur Sikri' was built by Akbar.

Fatehpur Sikri is a city situated in Uttar Pradesh. This town was built by the Mughal Emperor, Akbar. He had planned this city as his capital but the shortage of water compelled him to abandon the city. After this within 20 years, the capital of Mughals was shifted to Lahore. Fatehpur Sikri was built during 1571 and 1585.

Hence, the correct option is (A).

4. The third battle of Panipat was fought in 1761.

The Battle was fought between Sadashiv Rao Bhau (The Maratha Empire) and Ahmad Shah Durrani (The Afghan Army). In this battle, three Indian allies were supported by the Afgan Army, the Rohilla of (Najib-Ud-Daulah), Afghans of (the Doab Region), and Shuja-Ud-Daula (The Nawab of Awadh). The main Maratha Army was deployed on the Deccan side with the Peshwa (The Maratha Prime Minister). It is considered one of the largest and most fiercely fought battles in the 18th century. At last, the battle was won by the Afghan Army which was led by Ahmad Shah Durrani. This war was the result of declining of the Maratha Empire.

Hence, the correct option is (C).

5. Florence Nightingale was known as the 'Lady with the lamp'.

The most famous nurse in history, Florence Nightingale is the founder of modern nursing. She played a significant role during the Crimean War between 1853 and 1856. She nursed wounded soldiers at night while carrying a lamp along with her, which led to the famous epithet. In 1860, Florence Nightingale established her nursing school at St Thomas Hospital, London. It is the world's first nursing school that was in a hospital. Now it is a part of King's College, London.

Hence, the correct option is (C).

6. Indian currency notes are printed in Nasik, Maharastra.

Currency Note Press is situated at Nashik Road, Maharashtra, India 188 Km from Mumbai. The production facility was initially established here in India in 1928 and since then this organization has printed high-quality banknotes with special security features. Currency Note Press, Nashik Road is a Unit of Security Printing and Minting Corporation of India Limited (SPMCIL), a Miniratna Category-I CPSE Wholly owned by Govt, of India. Currency Note Press Nashik Road has also printed banknotes for other countries like Nepal, Burma, Bangladesh, Bhutan, East Africa and Iraq.

Hence, the correct option is (D).

7. Attorney General of India is appointed by the President under Article 76 of the Constitution.

The President of India appoints a person who is qualified for the post of Supreme Court Judge. Attorney General is appointed by the President on the advice of the government. There are the following qualifications:

- He should be an Indian Citizen.
- He must have either completed 5 years in the High Court of any Indian state as a judge or 10 years in High Court as an advocate.
- He may be an eminent jurist too, in the eye of the President.

Hence, the correct option is (D).

8. Narmada rivers originate from 'Amarkantak'.

The historical importance of Amarkantak has emerged as the place of origin of two rivers the Narmada river and the Son river. Johila river (Tributary of Son) also emerges from Amarkantak. The Amarkantak region is a unique natural heritage area and is the meeting point of the Vindhya and the Satpura ranges, with the Maikal Hills being the fulcrum. The Achanakmar-Amarkantak biosphere reserve is the most dramatic and ecologically diverse landscape in the Chhattisgarh and Madhya Pradesh states of India. It was declared a biosphere reserve in 2005.

Hence, the correct option is (B).

9. Upper House of the Indian Parliament is known as the Rajya Sabha.

Article 80 of the Indian Constitution lays down the maximum strength of Rajya Sabha as 250, out of which 12 members are nominated by the President and 238 are representatives of the States and of the two Union Territories. Vice President of India will act as Ex-Officio Chairman of Rajya Sabha. Money Bills can be introduced only in Lok Sabha. Money bills passed by the Lok Sabha are sent to the Rajya Sabha. The amendment suggested by the Rajya Sabha can either be accepted by the Lok Sabha or may be rejected.

Hence, the correct option is (C).

10. Mahatma Gandhi was the author of the book 'My Experiment with Truth'.

My Experiments with Truth is the autobiography of Mahatma Gandhi, covering his life from early childhood through to 1921. It was written in weekly instalments and published in his journal Navjivan from 1925 to 1929. Its English translation also appeared in instalments in his other journal Young India. It was initiated at the insistence of Swami Anand and other close co-workers of Gandhi, who encouraged him to explain the background of his public campaigns. In 1998, the book was designated as one of the "100 Best Spiritual Books of the 20th Century" by a committee of global spiritual and religious authorities.

Hence, the correct option is (A).

11. Pele is often referred to as 'Black Pearl'.

Pele was a Brazilian football (soccer) player who was a member of three World Cup-winning Brazilian national teams (1958, 1962, and 1970). Pele made his debut for the Brazilian national football (soccer) team in 1957 when he was 16 years old. In the 1958 World Cup semifinal against France, he scored a hat trick and two goals in the championship game against Sweden. After that, he was proclaimed a national treasure by the Brazilian government.

Hence, the correct option is (A).

12. Raja Ram Mohan Roy was the founder of Brahma Samaj.

Raja Ram Mohan Roy was an Indian reformer who was one of the founders of the Brahmo Sabha in 1828, the precursor of the Brahmo Samaj, a social-religious reform movement in the Indian subcontinent. He was given the title of Raja by Akbar II, the Mughal emperor. His influence was apparent in the fields of politics, public administration, education and religion. He was known for his efforts to abolish the practices of sati and child marriage. Roy is considered to be the "Father of the Bengal Renaissance" by many historians.

Hence, the correct option is (A).

13. Pamir Mountains is known as roof of the world.

The Pamir Mountains are a mountain range between Central Asia, South Asia, and East Asia, at the junction of the Himalayas with the Tian Shan, Karakoram, Kunlun, and the Hindu Kush. The Pamir Mountains lie mostly in the Gorno-Badakhshan province of Tajikistan. To the north, they join the Tian Shan mountains along the Alay Valley of Kyrgyzstan. To the south, they border the Hindu Kush mountains along Afghanistan's Wakhan Corridor.

Hence, the correct option is (A).

14. The Gateway of India is located in Mumbai.

It was constructed in 1924. The main objective behind the construction of the Gateway of India was to commemorate the visit of King George V and Queen Mary to Bombay (Mumbai). In March 1911, Sir George Sydenham Clarke, who was then the Governor of Bombay, laid down the monument's foundation. The architectural design of the Gateway of India was done by the architect George Wittet.

Hence, the correct option is (C).

15. Election Commission is conducts the elections of Lok Sabha in India.

The First Lok Sabha was constituted on 13 April 1952 after India's first general election. First Session of this Lok Sabha commenced on 13 May 1952. The 1st Lok Sabha lasted its full tenure of five years and was dissolved on 4 April 1957.

- First Lok Sabha period- 13 April 1952- 4 April 1957
- First Lok Sabha Speaker- Shri G.V. Mavalankar
- Present Lok Sabha Speaker- OM Birla.

Election Commission of India was formed on 25 January 1950. The headquarters of the Election Commission is in New Delhi. The First Chief Election Commissioner of India was Sukumar Sen. The President of India appoints the Chief Election Commissioner of the Election Commission. There are three members in the Election Commission which include a Chief Election Commissioner and two election commissioners. They are appointed for 6 years or can work only till the age of 65, whichever comes first.

Hence, the correct option is (A).

16. Tin is a non-magnetic material.

Tin is a chemical element with the symbol Sn and atomic number 50. Tin is a silvery-coloured metal. Tin is soft enough to be cut with little force and a bar of tin can be bent by hand with little effort. When bent, the so-called "tin cry" can be heard as a result of twinning in tin crystals; this trait is shared by indium, cadmium, zinc, and mercury in the solid state.

Hence, the correct option is (D).

17. Measure of Frequency is hertz.

Frequency refers to the number of occurrences of a periodic event per unit of time. The frequency is mainly classified into two categories:

- Angular Frequency: the number of revolutions at a fixed interval of time.
- Spatial Frequency: It depends on the spatial coordinate. It is inversely proportional to the wavelength. It measures the characteristic of the structure that is periodic in space.

Hence, the correct option is (C).

18. The process of rusting of iron is called corrosion.

Corrosion is when a refined metal is converted to a more stable form such as its oxide, hydroxide, or sulfide state this leads to deterioration of the material. It may be a result of some chemical process or it may occur naturally also.

Rust is a form of corrosion, but it specifically refers to the oxidation of iron or its alloys. Only metals with iron or its alloys can get rusted. Rust refers to the iron oxide that is produced in the process. For rusting to take place, there are certain necessary conditions. In the presence of oxygen and moisture or water, iron undergoes this reaction and form a series of iron oxide. The reddish-brown color compound, known as rust is formed. If rusting starts at one place, it will eventually spread, and the whole metal will eventually disintegrate.

Hence, the correct option is (D).

19. The red colour of human blood is due to haemoglobin.

Haemoglobin is a protein that is made up of subunit 'hemes' which is red in colour and haemoglobin constitutes the maximum part of human blood. It is a fused protein in which a protein

called globin and an iron ion are found. Its present in RBC carries or transports oxygen from the lungs to the tissues. It also carries forward carbon dioxide from the tissues to the lungs. The transportation of CO_2 from the tissues to the lungs takes place in a very small amount nearly (10-20 per cent) by the protein globin of haemoglobin. The transportation of CO_2 in the form of bicarbonate takes place which is formed by the reaction of the carbonic anhydrase enzyme and RBC.

Hence, the correct option is (D).

20. Clouds float in the atmosphere because of their low density.

Cloud is a mass of minute water droplets or tiny crystals of ice formed by the condensation of the water vapour in free air at considerable elevations. As the clouds are formed at some height over the surface of the earth, they take various shapes. Clouds have very low density and high volume compared to the air, so they experience high buoyancy force from the surrounding air, to balance their weight.

$F_{buoyancy}$ = Volume × ρ_{air} × g

So, they stay afloat due to buoyancy force from the surrounding air.

Hence, the correct option is (D).

21. Fish breathe through gills.

Fish take water into their mouth, passing the gills just behind its head on each side. Dissolved oxygen is absorbed from-and carbon dioxide released to-the water, which is then dispelled. The gills are fairly large, with thousands of small blood vessels, which maximizes the amount of oxygen extracted.

Hence, the correct option is (B).

22. One Horse Power $= 746$ Watt.

The power of a machine is the rate of doing work or the rate at which it can perform work.

$$Power = \frac{Work\ Done}{Time\ (sec)}$$

The absolute unit of power is Watt (W). The practical unit of power is the Horse Power (H.P). One Horsepower is the amount of work a standard horse can do in one second.

- 1 Metric H.P $= 735.5$ Watts
- 1 British H.P $= 746$ Watts

Hence, the correct option is (B).

23. Liquefied petroleum gas (L.P.G) is a hydrocarbon consisting of a minute of propane and butane.

It is odourless that's why Methyl Mercaptan is added to it so there may be a smell if L.P.G leaks from its storage container. L.P.G is used for cooking. An alternative to electric heating, heating oil, or kerosene.

Hence, the correct option is (D).

24. The quantity of blood in human body is 7% of body weight.

The total volume of blood in the human body in litres normally ranges from 4.5 to 5.7 liters. The average blood percentage in the human body is approximately 7 percent of the body weight. In this article, we'll discuss the quantity and normal blood percentage in the human body, along with shocks and blood loss.

Hence, the correct option is (B).

25. After digestion, protein is converted into amino acid.

In the development and replenishment of body cells and tissues, proteins play a crucial role. In the stomach, protein digestion occurs with the aid of protease enzymes and pepsin enzymes, that break down proteins into amino acids. The hydrochloric acid present in the stomach facilitates the process. Amino acids are tiny components that are absorbed by the wall of the small intestine in the bloodstream.

Hence, the correct option is (D).

26. Main organ of respiratory system in human body is lung because it performs the main function of exchange of oxygen and carbon dioxide to/from our blood.

The respiratory system is the network of organs and tissues that help you breathe. It includes your airways, lungs and blood vessels. The muscles that power your lungs are also part of the respiratory system. These parts work together to move oxygen throughout the body and clean out waste gases like carbon dioxide.

Hence, the correct option is (A).

27. The basic unit of life is the cell.

Cells are considered the basic units of life in part because they come in discrete and easily recognizable packages. That's because all cells are surrounded by a structure called the cell membrane-which, much like the walls of a house, serves as a clear boundary between the cell's internal and external environments.

Hence, the correct option is (D).

28. Typhoid is caused by bacteria.

Typhoid fever is a bacterial infection that can spread throughout the body, affecting many organs. Without prompt treatment, it can cause serious complications and can be fatal. It's caused by a bacterium called Salmonella typhi, which is related to the bacteria that cause salmonella food poisoning. Typhoid fever is highly contagious. An infected person can pass the bacteria out of their body in their poo or, less commonly, in their pee.

Hence, the correct option is (C).

29. The disease caused by the bite of a mad dog is called rabies.

Rabies is an infectious viral disease, caused 99% by domestic dogs. The disease is almost always fatal following the onset of clinical symptoms. Rabies can affect both domestic and wild animals. It is spread to people through bites or scratches, usually via saliva. It is a vaccine-preventable disease. Vaccinating dogs is the most cost-effective strategy for preventing rabies in people.

Initial symptoms of rabies include a fever with pain and unusual or unexplained tingling, pricking, or burning sensation at the wound site. As the virus spreads to the central nervous system, progressive and fatal inflammation of the brain and spinal cord develops.

Hence, the correct option is (D).

30. Photosynthesis takes place in green parts of the plants.

Photosynthesis is the process by which green plants and some other organisms use sunlight to synthesize nutrients from carbon dioxide and water. In this process, plants use chlorophyll, carbon dioxide, water, sunlight and release oxygen. Plants prepare their food by the process called photosynthesis.

During photosynthesis, plants trap solar energy or light energy with the help of chloroplast present in the green leaves and convert it into Chemical energy. A pigment called chlorophyll is present in the chloroplasts which are required in trapping sunlight Plants utilize Carbon dioxide and Water for the synthesis of carbohydrates during photosynthesis, oxygen is liberated as a side product. This gaseous exchange occurs through the stomata present on the leaf surface.

Hence, the correct option is (B).

31. Given,

Time taken by A and $B = 12$ days

Time taken by C and $A = 20$ days

Time taken by B and $C = 15$ days

Ae we know,

Total work $=$ Efficiency $\times$ Number of days

L.C.M of $12, 20$ and $15 = 60 =$ Total work

Efficiency of A and $B = \dfrac{60}{12} = 5$ units/day

Efficiency of C and $A = \dfrac{60}{20} = 3$ units/day

Efficiency of B and $C = \dfrac{60}{15} = 4$ units/day

Total efficiency of $2A + 2B + 2C = (5 + 3 + 4)$ units/day

Total efficiency of $2 \times (A + B + C) = 12$ units/day

Total efficiency of $(A + B + C) = \dfrac{12}{2} = 6$ units/day

Time taken to finish the work together $= \dfrac{60}{6}$ days

$= 10$ days

$\therefore$ The number of days taken to finish the work together is 10 days.

Hence, the correct option is (D).

32. Given:

Circumference of circle $= 1$ meter $= 100\ cm$

According to question,

Circumference of circle $= 2\pi r$

$2\pi r = 100$ cm

$2 \times \left(\dfrac{22}{7}\right) \times r = 100$ cm

$r = \dfrac{700}{44}$ cm

$r = \dfrac{175}{11}$ cm

Now,

Area of circle $= \pi r^2$

$= \pi \times \left(\dfrac{175}{11}\right) \times \left(\dfrac{175}{11}\right)$ cm ^{2}

$= \left(\dfrac{22}{7}\right) \times \left(\dfrac{175}{11}\right) \times \left(\dfrac{175}{11}\right)$ cm ^{2}

$= 795.45$ cm ^{2}

Hence, the correct option is (B).

33. Given,

Radius of a tyre $= 7$ cm

Total number of rotations $= 50$

As we know,

Distance covered in 1 rotation $=$ circumference of circle

Circumference of circle $= 2\pi r$

Total distance covered in 50 rotations $= 2\pi r \times 50$

$= 2 \times \left(\dfrac{22}{7}\right) \times 7 \times 50$ cm

$= 2200$ cm $= 22$ meter

$\therefore$ The distance travelled in 50 rotations is 22 meter.

Hence, the correct option is (C).

34. Given,

Average salary of 20 workers $=$ Rs. 1900

Average salary of 20 workers and 1 manager $=$ Rs. 2000

As we know,

Total salary $=$ Average salary $\times$ Number of persons

Total salary of 20 workers $= 20 \times$ Rs. 1900

$=$ Rs. $38,000$

Total salary of 20 workers and 1 manager $=$ Rs. 21×2000

$=$ Rs. $42,000$

Salary of manager $=$ Rs. $42,000 - 38,000$

$= $ Rs. 4000

Hence, the correct option is (C).

35. Given,

Height of cylinder $= 15$ cm

Radius of base $= 7$ cm

Volume of cylinder $= \pi r^2$ h

Volume of cylinder $= \left(\dfrac{22}{7}\right) \times 7^2 \times 15$ cm^3

$= 22 \times 7 \times 15$ cm^3

$= 2310$ cm^3

Hence, the correct option is (B).

36. Given,

Area of a rectangular region $= 560$ cm^2

One side $= 20$ cm

Area of rectangle $=$ Length $\times$ Breadth

560 cm$^2 =$ Length $\times 20$

Length $= \dfrac{560}{20}$ cm

$= 28$ cm

Perimeter of rectangle $= 2 \times ($ Length $+$ Breadth $)$

Perimeter of rectangle $= 2 \times (28 + 20)$ cm

$= 2 \times 48$ cm

$= 96$ cm

Hence, the correct option is (C).

37. Given,

Radius of a circle $= 28$ m

Area of circle $= \pi r^2$

Area of circle $= \left(\dfrac{22}{7}\right) \times 28 \times 28$ cm^2

$= 22 \times 112$ cm^2

$= 2464$ cm^2

Hence, the correct option is (A).

38. Given,

S.P $=$ Rs. 6800

Loss $\% = 75\%$

As we know,

C.P $=$ S.P. $\times \left[\dfrac{100}{(100 - \text{Los}\%)}\right]$

C.P $=$ Rs. $6800 \times \left(\dfrac{100}{25}\right)$

$=$ Rs. $27{,}200$

Hence, the correct option is (B).

39. The series follows following pattern:

$\Rightarrow 39 + 2 = 41$

$\Rightarrow 41 + 2 = 43$

$\Rightarrow 43 + 2 = 45$

$\Rightarrow 45 + 2 = 47$

Hence, the correct option is (B).

40. The nearest perfect square around 175 is 169.

Least number to be subtracted $= 175 - 169$

$= 6$

$\therefore$ The least number which must be subtracted from 175 to make It a perfect square is 6.

Hence, the correct option is (C).

41. Let the number be x.

According to question,

$\Rightarrow x + x + 5 = 17$

$\Rightarrow 2x = 12$

$\Rightarrow x = 6$

Hence, the correct option is (B).

42. Given,

Distance covered $= 140$ m

Time $= 18$ seconds

Speed $= \dfrac{\text{Distance}}{\text{Time taken}}$

Speed $= \dfrac{140}{18}$ m $/$s

$= \dfrac{70}{9}$ m $/$s

$= \left(\dfrac{70}{9}\right) \times \left(\dfrac{18}{5}\right)$ km $/$hr

$= 28$ km $/$hr

Hence, the correct option is (D).

43. Given,

Percentage of boys $= 70\%$

Total number of girls $= 255$

Percentage of girls $= (100 - 70)\%$

$= 30\%$

According to the question,

$\Rightarrow 30\% = 255$

$\Rightarrow 70\% = \left(\dfrac{255}{30\%}\right) \times 70\%$

$= 595$

The number of boys is 595.

Hence, the correct option is (A).

44. Given,

Product of two numbers $= 4725$

HCF $= 15$

LCM $\times$ HCF $=$ Product of two numbers

LCM $\times 15 = 4725$

LCM $= \dfrac{4725}{15}$

LCM $= 315$

Hence, the correct option is (C).

45. As we know,

Greatest divisor $=$ HCF $[(a-b),(b-c),(a-c)]$; where $a > b > c$

Greatest number $=$ HCF $[(99-53),(99-30),(53-30)]$

Greatest number $=$ HCF $[46,69,23] = 23$

23 is the greatest number that divides $30,53,99$ to leave the same remainder.

Hence, the correct option is (D).

46. Average of three numbers is 27

So, the sum of the three numbers $= (27 \times 3) = 81$

Let the first number be ' a '.

The second is three times the first.

So, 2nd number $= 3a$

The third number is five times the first.

So, 3rd number $= 5a$

According to question,

$\dfrac{(a+3a+5a)}{3} = 27$

$9a = 27 \times 3$

$a = 81 \div 9$

$a = 9$

First number $= a = 9$

Second number $= 3a = 3 \times 9 = 27$

Third number $= 5a = 5 \times 9 = 45$

Hence, the correct option is (B).

47. The logic followed here is:

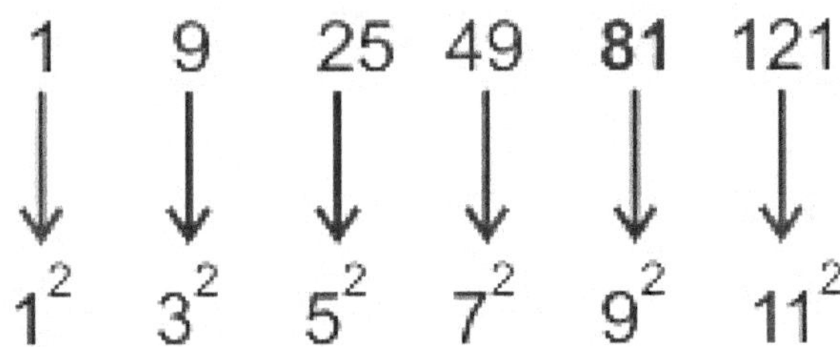

Hence, the correct option is (D).

48. According to the given information, we can draw the following diagram:

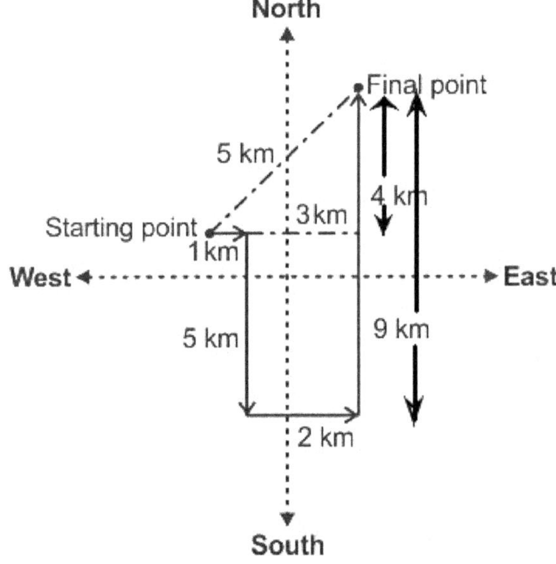

Distance of the man from his starting point $= \sqrt{3^2 + 4^2}$ kms

$= \sqrt{9 + 16}$ kms

$= \sqrt{25}$ kms

$= 5$ kms

So, the man is 5 km far from his starting point.

Hence, the correct option is (D).

49. Given,

$PALE$ is coded as $P - 2, A - 1, L - 3, E - 4$.

$EARTH$ is coded as $E - 4, A - 1, R - 5, T - 9, H - 0$.

Similarly,

$PEARL$ will be coded as $P - 2, E - 4, A - 1, R - 5, L - 3$.

Hence, the correct option is (B).

50. Preparing the family tree using the following symbols:

Symbol in Diagram	Meaning
○	Female
□	Male
=	Married couple
—	Siblings
|	Difference of a generation

Case I:

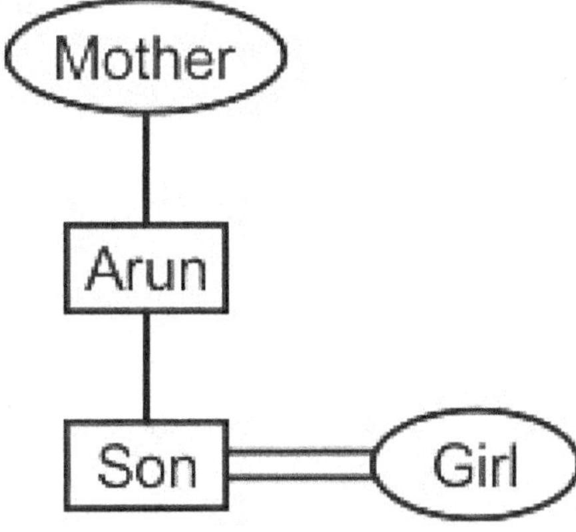

Case II:

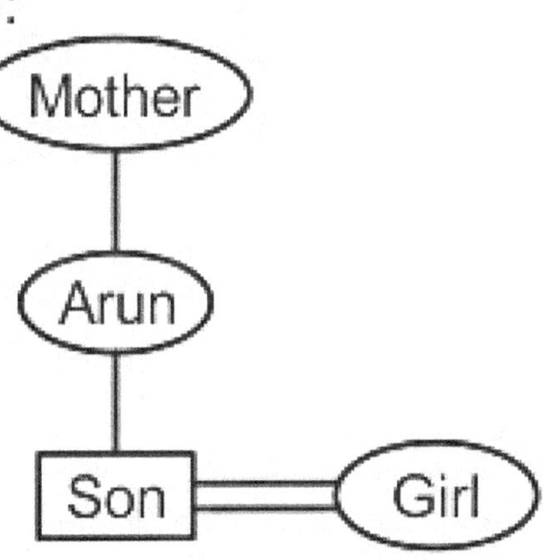

From Case I: Arun is father-in-law of the girl.

From Case II: Arun is mother-in-law of the girl.

So, Arun is father-in-law of the girl.

Hence, the correct option is (C).

// Notes //

// Notes //

www.ingramcontent.com/pod-product-compliance
Lightning Source LLC
LaVergne TN
LVHW080618200726
843509LV00007B/342